Sailorspeak

The Complete Insider's Guide to Yacht Racing Terms, Jargon & Slang

Bob Roitblat

Manifest Destiny Press
Antioch, IL

© 2009 Bob Roitblat

Published in the United States of America by
Manifest Destiny Press
Antioch, IL

ISBN 978-0-9819519-0-4
Library of Congress Control Number 2009900057

A Cataloging-in-Publication record
for this book
is available from the
Library of Congress.

Acknowledgements

The material for this book comes from numerous sources and authorities. I have not attempted to cite each one, as doing so would require more space than is available. The list includes friends, associates, fellow sailors, innumerable books and magazine articles, Web sources, and my own experiences during many years and thousands of miles racing and cruising on lakes and oceans.

I would be remiss if I did not at least offer my sincere thanks to Dr. Dean Raffaelli, Ted Jones, Gary Jobson, John Rousmaniere, Dave Perry, and my brothers Herb and Barry, who generously offered their suggestions, insights, and encouragement throughout this book's development. Thank you to Seth Morrell for expanding my yacht racing vocabulary and for constantly challenging me to be a better sailor. I am also indebted to the Sentence Sleuth and her alto ego, Bonnie Trenga, who sifted through this book in minute detail. Her editing and comments were invaluable in helping me refine and clarify the information presented.

Thanks to Steve Pelke, Gib Black, and all the other skippers and boat owners I have had the privilege to sail with and for, and to all the boats and crews I have had the honor to compete with and against. You have all taught me so much.

Formal, organized, and safe yacht racing exists only because of the countless people involved with yacht clubs, race organizers, and race committees. Their hard work and dedication make it all possible. Thank you. And no discussion about yacht racing can be complete without also acknowledging the efforts of the Royal Yachting Association, International Sailing Federation, US Sailing, and all the other countless national, regional, and local yacht racing associations and venues. My thanks to all of you, too.

Cover photo - Fleet racing in the Pacific Ocean offshore of Honolulu, Hawaii.

Illustrations by author unless otherwise noted.

Disclaimer

This publication is intended to provide accurate and authoritative information, along with the author's opinion concerning the subject matter covered. This publication does not intend to reproduce all the information that is otherwise available; rather, it aims to complement, amplify, and supplement other texts and sources of information. The publisher and author have used their best efforts to ensure the information contained herein is accurate and current. However, there may be mistakes both in content and typography. Similarly, every effort has been made to contact any copyright holders. We apologize for any unintentional errors or omissions.

This publication aims to educate and entertain you. Therefore, the publisher and author make no representations or warranties with respect to this book's accuracy or the completeness of its contents, and specifically disclaim any implied warranties of merchantability or fitness for a particular purpose. No warranty may be created or extended by sales representatives or written sales materials. The advice, strategies, and procedures contained herein may not be suitable for your situation. You should consult with a professional where appropriate. Neither the publisher nor the author shall be liable for any loss of profit or any other damages, including without limitation special, incidental, consequential, commercial, or other damages.

Readers should be aware that Internet Web sites offered as citations or sources for further information may have changed or disappeared between the time this was written and when it is read.

Introduction

"Order and simplification are the first steps
toward the mastery of a subject."

Thomas Mann, *The Magic Mountain*[1]

Yacht racing vocabulary is colorful and crisp. Single words are charged with emotion, packed with meaning, and teeming with direction. Experts use this technical jargon and slang to quickly convey complex information, based on the potentially fatal assumption that everyone understands the words being used. This is a phenomenon known as the "curse of knowledge."[2]

Neophytes can sometimes decipher the jargon or slang's meaning from its context—but not always. At the same time, inexperienced crew members want to avoid appearing brainless, so they are reluctant to ask for clarification. The result is a communications breakdown that is detrimental to any team.

I faced this exact challenge as I began coaching a new team. The solution was to create a sailing glossary. Its purpose was to alleviate each crew member's struggle to understand all of the necessary terms and slang so they could participate and contribute sooner and to a greater degree.

After I added many more terms and invested a considerable amount of time, that original project grew into *Sailorspeak*: the first-of-its-kind compilation of yacht racing terms, jargon and slang, their meanings, common usage, and application.

Knowing what all the terms mean puts every crew member a step closer to correctly knowing what to do with the items referred to, how to properly perform the action requested, and how to intelligently respond to any question posed. Everyone can concentrate on learning and improving their skills and avoid wasting valuable time decoding the words being used. In short, everyone can talk like a racing sailor—minus the cuss words—and be understood.

This book is not intended to be either a scholarly work on nautical language or a polemic. Instead, it aims to help develop more effective communication among the racing crew, to reduce the crew's anxiety, and to build crew skill and confidence. This book can serve as a primer for new racers, a refresher for Old Salts, or a translator for competitors racing in new locations. This book can also help teams discuss, clarify, and refine the terms and techniques they use. But mostly, this book aims to make yacht racing more enjoyable.

Inside, we cover a wide range of subjects, including procedures, tactics, and navigation, as well as parts, knots, sails, and sailcloth. Weather-related terms are included, as sailing depends so much on the weather. And we discuss the racing rules at length, since racing depends so much on the proper application of the rules.

Some entries are traditional technical terms. Others are non-traditional jargon, colloquialisms, or slang terms. Some are more applicable to buoy racing, while others apply more to offshore racing. Some terms or phrases are broadly used, some are used only on a regional level, and a few are so esoteric that only one club, class, or fleet uses them. For every item listed, we go beyond mere definition and include in-depth instructions on use, plus cross-references to related and contrasting terms and other variants.

Many terms and their resultant functions are ancient traditions still in use today, while others seem like they were first spoken this morning. Of course, it remains to be seen whether the more recently invented terms will still be used next season or even next week.

Most of the included terms, jargon, and slang come from three primary sources:
1. From my personal experience as an active big-boat racer—sometimes as a crew member, sometimes as a coach.
2. From live discussions with scores of other racing sailors—often during intense karate yachting sessions (see page 97).
3. From racing-oriented online forums.

Additional terms are from sailing publications such as Nathaniel Bowditch's *The New American Practical Navigator,* first published in 1802; from more recently published books[3] and training manuals; and from contemporary sailing magazines. I have also called upon the expertise of top people in their respective specialties for their ideas on terms, definitions, and applicability.

I have crosschecked every word, term, and phrase with numerous sources and reference works. By language's very nature, though, this collection will never be complete. New terms get invented, old terms get re-purposed or fall into disuse, and the language of yacht racing continues to expand and transform. There may also be contradictions between the terms, and among sailors' use of them.

Although I have taken great care to ensure that all significant modern yacht racing terms are included, and to ensure the information provided is accurate, I may have overlooked something. I may also have discovered new terms or have had second thoughts about some of the entries after this book was printed. You are invited to challenge any information offered and to contribute new terms or slang. We will research and verify all submissions before adding them to later editions of this book or to its related Web site. Please send your comments and suggestions to newterms@sailorspeak.com.

And, lastly, I must warn you that yacht racing is an addiction for which there is no cure, only a lifetime of enjoyment. Or as that great American philosopher Dave Barry said, "There is a very fine line between 'hobby' and 'mental illness.'"[4]

---

1. Paul Thomas Mann (1875–1955), German novelist, social critic, and 1929 Nobel laureate. *The Magic Mountain (Der Zauberberg)*, first published in November 1924. Based on Helen T. Lowe-Porter's 1955 translation, Chapter 5.

2. This term was coined in the article by Camerer, Colin; Loewenstein, George; and Weber, Martin; *The Curse of Knowledge in Economic Settings: An Experimental Analysis*, Journal of Political Economy, University of Chicago Press, Volume 97, Issue 5.

3. General sailing definitions can be found in any of the dozen or more sailing dictionaries listed with the United States Library of Congress. One of the best is John Rousmaniere's *The Illustrated Dictionary of Boating Terms*, W. W. Norton & Company, first published in 1976.

4. Dave Barry (1947-): American journalist and humorist, *Dave Barry Turns 50* (Crown; 1st edition, September 29, 1998), Chapters 8-25, Things I have learned in 50 years.

How to use this book

Words and phrases are arranged in alphabetical order, with regular nouns and verbs in lower case, and proper nouns listed with initial capital letters. For those words that have multiple meanings or different meaning within the yacht racing realm and outside it, we have included only those meanings within the yacht racing context. Several items, maneuvers, and concepts are referred to by multiple terms. Lesser-used, alternative terms are included after each primary description or explanation.

Most terms used within an entry are further defined under their own alphabetical listing. Cross-references are intended to point the reader to other entries that relate to or contrast with the referring entry.

This book is designed to be used in many ways: as an encyclopedia, by looking up a single word or phrase whose meaning is unfamiliar; as a textbook, by starting at the first page and reading every entry; or as a journey of enlightenment and discovery (and occasional bewilderment), by letting each entry lead where it may.

- A

007 — a flat, illuminated data and compass display that displays information such as wind speed by using a needle that indicates apparent wind direction. Also known generally as an instrument repeater, it is often located on the aft face of the cabin.

360 — slang for a One-Turn Penalty, based on earlier versions of the *Racing Rules of Sailing* that required rotating through a full 360 degrees for a penalty turn. Now, to be exonerated for violating *RRS-2009* rule 31—Touching a Mark, a boat takes a One-Turn Penalty by promptly making one turn in the same direction, including one tack and one jibe. See *RRS-2009* rule 44.2.

720 — slang for a Two-Turns Penalty, based on earlier versions of the *Racing Rules of Sailing*, which required rotating through a full 720 degrees for a Two-Turns Penalty. Now, to be exonerated for violating any rule from *RRS-2009* Part 2—When Boats Meet, a boat takes a Two-Turns Penalty by promptly making two turns in the same direction, including two tacks and two jibes. See *RRS-2009* rule 44.2.

abandon ship bag — an emergency survival kit. See also: ditch bag.

abeam — at right angles to the boat's centerline, but not on the boat. Directly to the side.

ABYA — Anchor Bay Yachting Association. For more information, browse to http://www.abya.org.

acceleration mode — trimming and steering the boat for increased speed, usually by bearing off. Pointing ability is traded for speed. Also known as foot mode.

accidental jibe — what happens when a boat is steered or the winds shift such that the boat's stern accidentally passes through the eye of the wind. This causes the main boom to swing violently to the opposite side of the boat. Without proper jibe preparation and execution, the force of the boom's motion can be destructive: injuring or killing crew, damaging equipment, and even dismasting the boat. Sometimes a preventer is used to control the boom's movement, but only proper helmsmanship can prevent an accidental jibe.

advection fog — develops when warm, moist air moves over a colder surface, cooling the air below its dew point; i.e., the point where the air becomes completely saturated with moisture.

adverse current — a current flowing in a direction other than that being sailed.

advertising code — refers to *ISAF Regulations, section 20*, which pertains to any advertising displayed on boats or on competitors' uniforms. Rules covering advertising are exclusionary—anything not specifically permitted is prohibited. The applicable *Notice of Race* or *Sailing Instructions* may modify any requirements.

afterguard — the crew members who collectively determine a race boat's course of action—the decision makers. This can include the tactician, helm, and navigator, or crew who have these additional duties. Many different names—most of which are unprintable—are used to refer to this group. Some of the kinder names include back-of-the-bus and brain trust.

afterguy — a control line used to adjust a spinnaker's angle of attack to the wind and, therefore, its effectiveness, by rotating the spinnaker pole's outboard end fore or aft as needed. An afterguy is adjusted in unison with the downhaul, spinnaker sheet and topping lift to form the spinnaker into the most efficient shape and to position the spinnaker at the most effective angle to the wind. The afterguy, often referred to simply as the guy, is run from a symmetrical spinnaker's windward clew or the tack of an asymmetrical spinnaker flown from a spinnaker pole, through the spinnaker pole's jaw, then aft, optionally through one or more blocks, to a cockpit winch. Also referred to as a spin guy, spinnaker guy, or working guy. An afterguy is part of the running rigging. British and Commonwealth sailors use the term brace. See also: spin gear.

afterguy puck — a specialty snap shackle connected to a ring, surrounded by a donut and eye-spliced to an afterguy's end. An afterguy puck prevents the shackle from jamming in a spinnaker pole's jaw.

afterguy trimmer — a crew member whose core responsibilities are to control the afterguy and to keep the spinnaker pole in a position that maximizes performance.

aids-to-navigation — any devices external to a boat specifically intended to assist in determining a position or safe course, or to warn of danger or obstructions. These include buoys, day beacons, lighthouses, markers, radio beacons, and range lights. Aids-to-navigation are typically shown on nautical charts. Electronic devices used for navigation are also called aids-to-navigation. Alternative terms include ATON and navaid.

air mass — an extensive body of air with uniform horizontal temperature and moisture characteristics.

alee — away from the direction from which the wind blows. The opposite of windward. See also: leeward.

aloft — above deck level, usually in the rigging, but not on the deck.

alto — a prefix added to cloud-type names for medium-altitude clouds, between 6,500 and 23,000 feet (2-7 km) above the ground in the middle latitudes or temperate zone; e.g., altostratus. From the Latin word meaning middle.

altocumulus — mid-level clouds composed mainly of water droplets, but may also contain some ice crystals at higher altitudes or lower temperatures. Altocumulus clouds appear as a wavy or billowy layer, which is why they are nicknamed "sheep" or "woolpack" clouds. Sometimes confused with cirrocumulus clouds, their individual cloud elements have a larger mass and cast a shadow on other elements. Altocumulus may form several sub-types, such as altocumulus castellanus or altocumulus lenticularis. Virga may also fall from these clouds.

altostratus — mid-level clouds composed of water droplets and sometimes ice crystals. White to bluish-gray to gray in color, altostratus clouds can create a fibrous veil or sheet that sometimes obscures the sun or moon. Virga often falls from these clouds. Altostratus clouds cover the entire sky over an area that usually extends hundreds of square miles. These clouds do not allow enough sunlight to break through to form any shadows on the ground. Altostratus usually form ahead of a storm that produces widespread and mostly continuous rain, snow, or ice pellets.

America's Cup — a series of match races between the current cup holder and a challenger qualified under the cup's Deed of Gift. It is the oldest active trophy in international sporting. The America's Cup is as much a design competition as it is a sailing competition. Also known as the Auld Mug.

AMS – Australian Measurement System. A time-on-time class rating system used to handicap boats racing in Australia. For more information, browse to http://www.yachtingvictoria.com.au.

anchor — a device used to prevent the current or wind from moving a boat from her intended stopping place or anchorage. See also: drogue and sea anchor.

angle of attack — the angle between the apparent wind and a sail's chord line, or between the water flow and a keel or rudder's chord line. Also sometimes incorrectly referred to as the angle of incidence. See also: sheeting angle.

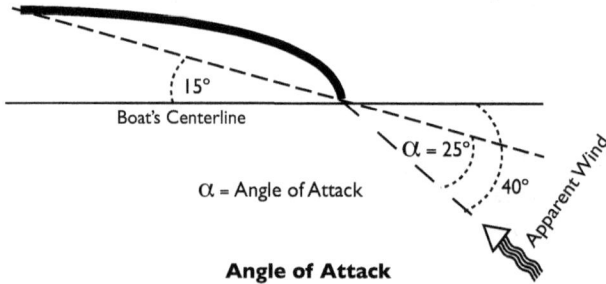

Angle of Attack

angle of vanishing stability — the angle that a boat can heel to and still right herself, even after being knocked down by high winds with her sails in the water. Also referred to as the limit of positive stability. See also: inclining.

anemometer — an instrument for measuring wind speed.

antifouling paint — a coating applied to a boat's underwater surfaces to repel undesirable marine growth. Also known as bottom paint. See also: VC-17.

Antigua Race Week — six days of racing for racing yachts, cruising yachts, and yachts obtained under a bareboat charter. Takes place near the island of Antigua in the Caribbean. The Antigua Sailing Association combines both inshore races and distance races during this event. For more information, browse to http://www.sailingweek.com.

anti-hunting rule — slang for *RRS-2009* rule 16.2, which forbids a boat on starboard tack from putting her bow down in an attempt to prevent a boat on port tack from passing astern.

anti-seize — thread lubricant that prevents binding, galling, and corrosion on turnbuckles, screw shackles, and other threaded devices. Used on anything with threads that you intend to take apart again.

anvil — a cumulonimbus cloud's upper portion that has flattened and spread out, sometimes for hundreds of miles downstream from its parent cloud. It may look smooth or fibrous but resembles a blacksmith's anvil in shape. An anvil's presence indicates a thunderstorm's mature or decaying stage.

AOCYC — Association of Orange Coast Yacht Clubs. For more information, browse to http://aocyc.scyaweb.org.

AP flag — a pennant with three red and two white vertical stripes. An AP flag is used to signal a postponement. Known formally as the Answering Pennant. And, because of its color scheme, an AP flag is called a cat-in-the-hat.

apparent wind angle (AWA) — the vector of the sum of the true wind angle (TWA) and a boat's speed and direction through the water. This is the wind angle you feel on the deck of a moving boat. A wind gust hitting the sail plan moves the apparent wind aft. Except on a dead run, apparent wind is always forward or ahead of the true wind. Any small change in true wind direction will result in a big difference in apparent wind direction. See also: velocity header and velocity lift.

apparent wind direction (AWD) — the compass direction of the wind you feel on deck as a boat moves through the water.

apparent wind speed (AWS) — the vector of the sum of the true wind speed (TWS) and a boat's motion through the water. This is the wind speed you feel on the deck of a moving boat. Apparent wind speed decreases when the true wind angle moves farther behind. Also known as sailing wind.

ARO — an initialism for "area race officer." A US Sailing designated position for the person who administers the club race officer programs within each US Sailing geographic region. Also an initialism for "assistant race officer."

around the cans — inshore racing around the marks of a multi-leg racecourse. See also: buoy racing.

ASA — 1) Alberta Sailing Association. For more information, browse to http://www.albertasailing.com. 2) American Sailing Association. For more information, browse to http://www.american-sailing.com.

a-sail — shorthand for an asymmetrical sail. A-spin is another shorthand term.

ASBA — Australian Sports Boat Association. For more information, browse to http://www.asba.org.au.

ASMBYC — Association of Santa Monica Bay Yacht Clubs. For more information, browse to http://www.asmbyc.org.

ASPBYC — Association of San Pedro Bay Yacht Clubs. For more information, browse to http://www.scya.org/aspbyc.

aspect ratio — the relationship between a sail's height (i.e., its luff length) and its foot length. High aspect ratio describes a sail that is tall and narrow; low aspect ratio describes a short, squat sail. The elliptical shape of a high-aspect-ratio sail has less induced drag and is very efficient when sailing close to the wind. Effective aspect ratio is the longest luff length squared and then divided by the total area.

asshole — 1) Slang for a kink or knot that prevents a sheet or halyard from running freely through a fairlead or block. A kinder term is bug. 2) A term of endearment for another crew member or competitor.

astern — behind the boat, or moving backward or stern first.

asymmetrical spinnaker — a special sail type specifically designed for sailing off the wind from a reaching course to a downwind course; i.e. with the wind 60-180 degrees off the bow. Asymmetrical spinnakers have a distinct luff and leech that differ in length by more than four percent. Lines called sheets—one working and one lazy— control the sail's shape and are led from the clew back to the stern. The tack is controlled by a tack line run through either the end of a bowsprit or a spinnaker pole. The head is attached to a spinnaker halyard that is used to hoist the sail up the mast. Spinnakers are constructed of very lightweight fabric, usually nylon, and are often brightly colored or display intricate logos. Spinnakers may be optimized for particular wind-angle ranges, as either a reaching or running spinnaker, by their panel and seam shapes. A spinnaker is often called a kite or chute because it resembles a parachute in both construction and appearance. Also known as a multi-purpose sail (MPS) and by the slang terms a-kite, a-sail, and a-sym. See also: inside jibe and outside jibe. Compare to: symmetrical spinnaker.

athwartships — at right angles to a boat's centerline.

atmospheric pressure — indicates the force per unit-area exerted by the atmosphere's weight. Expressed in several units such as millibars, inches of mercury or pounds per square inch. Measured with a barometer.

ATON — an acronym for "aids-to-navigation." Charted objects available to assist in determining position, a safe course, or to warn of danger.

attached flow — describes particle movement along a surface, such as air particle flow that bends to follow a sail's surface contour—the Coanda Effect. See also: laminar flow, lift, and separation.

attention flag — a flag hoisted on a committee boat to indicate the beginning of the ten-minute start sequence for a match race. The attention flag is taken down when six minutes remain in the start sequence. The F flag is used as the attention flag. The applicable *Sailing Instructions* may modify the start sequence timing or the flags used.

autopilot — an electro-mechanical instrument designed to automatically control a boat's steering gear so that she follows a pre-determined course or track through the water. Often referred to by a human name, such as Otto or Herman.

auxiliary — an engine that provides occasional driving power or operates a generator.

Azores High — a large subtropical semi-permanent center of high atmospheric pressure found near the Azores in the Atlantic Ocean, at the Horse latitudes (i.e., sub-tropic latitudes between 30 and 35 degrees North). When this weather system moves farther west it is referred to as the Bermuda High or, generally, as the North Atlantic High.

B

B&G — an advanced racing instrumentation system brand name. Formerly known as Brookes and Gatehouse. A division of Navico. For more information, browse to http://www.bandg.com.

babystay — a device used to induce and control mast bend, but mostly to prevent mast bend inversion. Made from composite fiber, or stainless steel wire or rod, a babystay runs forward from mid mast to mid foredeck. It is part of the standing rigging.

back — wind is said to back when it shifts in a counterclockwise direction, as from southeast to northeast—the true wind compass direction numbers decrease. The opposite is to veer. A sail is backed by purposely holding its clew to windward in order to turn the boat or move it astern; i.e., backward. See also: lefty.

back & fill — to use an inboard engine's forward and reverse gears, as well as prop walk and rudder angles, to turn a boat in close quarters.

back down — to move backward or stern first. It is a common practice to back down by holding a boom to weather and backwinding the mainsail in order to clear the keel and rudder of any weeds or debris that either may have picked up.

backsail — a jocular term for a mainsail, a large sail set aft of the mast and above the boom.

backstay — the standing rigging that runs from the masthead to a boat's transom, counteracting headstay/forestay forces. On traditional masthead rigs without running backstays, and on larger fractional rigs, the backstay controls both mast bend and headstay sag. Mast bend is what primarily adjusts draft depth in a mainsail's upper two-thirds. The backstay also has a direct effect on headsail shape through its effect on headstay sag. Also known as the permanent backstay.

backwind — 1) Wind that pushes against what would typically be considered a sail's leeward side. For example, when a boat is tacking, the jib is allowed to backwind momentarily before the working sheet is released, to help the sail move through the foretriangle. Backwinding is also the name for what happens when a bubble forms near a mainsail's luff caused by wind that deflects off the leech of an overlapping genoa's windward side when the slot is too closed. See also: speed bubble. 2) The turbulent air exiting the leech of a boat's sails and extending to leeward. See also: wind shadow.

bag — as in "bag the sail" means to ease the control lines to allow deeper draft in the sail. Usually done in light air. The opposite of blade.

bail — 1) A closed metal loop that a line, block, shackle, or webbing is attached to. These include the loop opposite the opening loop on a snap shackle and the loops found on booms and masts used as anchor points for blocks, sheets, or other control lines. 2) To remove water flooding a boat by using a bucket or other container. 3) The money or other pledge given to a court as surety that a crew member released from custody will return at the appointed time. Also spelled bale.

bald headed — describes having no headsail up while underway. Also referred to as bare headed.

banding — short for rubber banding, which is binding a spinnaker's cloth in such a way that enables fully hoisting it and pre-feeding its tack to the pole end in strong winds without the spinnaker filling prematurely. See also: spinnaker bands / spinnaker stops.

bang the corner — to sail all the way to one side of a racecourse in search of a (usually mythical) strategic advantage. Also called "going to Cornersville," where the population is usually 1. British and Commonwealth sailors call it "ringing the bell."

barber hauler — a mechanism for moving a jib or genoa's sheeting angle farther outboard when reaching or running. This is done to give the sail a more efficient shape and to open the slot between the genoa and main. It is also used to de-power a headsail in heavy air. A barber hauler often consists of a line run through a snatch block positioned at the rail. The line is looped around a jib sheet, just aft of the clew, and is used to pull the sheet outboard. You can obtain the same result by connecting an outboard line directly to a headsail's clew, although in this instance, the line is more correctly called a reaching sheet. Also known as a cross-hauler. Compare to: inhauler, jib lead car, outgrabber, and twinger.

Sheeting Angle

Outboard ◀── ── ── ── ── ── ──▶ Inboard

Outboard	Inboard
•In very light or very heavy air	•When close-hauled
•Decreases pointing	•Increases pointing—in smooth
•Decreases power & drag	water & moderate air
•Decreases backwind in main	•Increases power & drag
•In heavy seas or chop	•Increases backwind in main
•Opens slot	•Closes slot
•Reduces heel	•Increases angle of attack
•Decreases angle of attack	•Lead too far in robs speed
•On a reach, lead goes out &	without adding pointing ability
forward, chasing the clew	

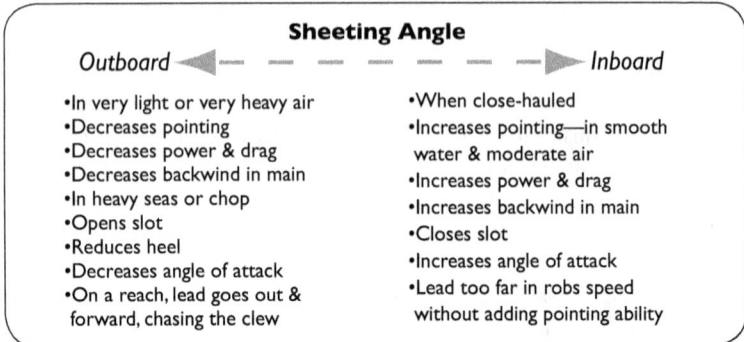

barber pole — 1) Slang for a thunderstorm updraft with a visual appearance including cloud striations that are curved in a manner similar to barber pole stripes. The structure typically is most pronounced on an updraft's leading edge, while drier air from the rear flank downdraft often erodes the clouds on the updraft's trailing side. 2) Slang for some lighthouses, due to their conical shape and colored bands.

bare headed — having no headsail up while underway. In heavy weather, when it may be too dangerous to peel a jib or spinnaker, you douse the sail in use before hoisting a new one. This is known as doing a bare headed change or a bald headed change. Also referred to as bald headed. Compare to: chicken jibe.

bare poles — without having any sails up and without an engine providing driving force while underway. In heavy weather, the windage of the mast and other spars can still be enough to move a boat. When a boat has no sails set and no motor running, she is said to be "under bare poles."

barge / barging — the risky maneuver of approaching the start line from windward of the committee-boat-end layline, and squeezing into the space between a boat to leeward (i.e., one that has right-of-way) and the committee boat. If this is done successfully, the barging boat sails into clear air at the start line's starboard or windward end. It is a risky maneuver because any boat overlapped to leeward (i.e., almost every other boat) has the right-of-way and can sail as high as head-to-wind to squeeze the barging boat out, forcing her to sail to windward of the windward end of the start line and miss the start. There is also the risk that the barging boat will get shut out at the last minute and will be forced into the committee boat. See also: guard mark and *RRS-2009* rule 11.

Barient — a discontinued winch brand. The Australian Yacht Winch Company has acquired much of the tooling and parts inventory. For more information, browse to http://www.huttonwinches.com.

barn door — the trophy for shortest elapsed time by a monohull competing in the Transpac.

barometer — an instrument that measures air pressure, and an aid to forecasting weather.

barometric pressure — the atmospheric pressure as measured by a barometer. Changes in barometric pressure are used to forecast changes in weather. Some rules of thumb include the 1-2-3 rule. If pressure drops 1-2 millibars an hour over a 3-hour period, be alert. The weather is worsening. There is also the 4-5-6 rule. A drop of 4-5 millibars in 6 hours suggests that significantly worsening weather, such as a gale—or worse—is approaching. Barometric pressure is measured in force per unit; e.g., pounds per square inch, millibars, or inches of mercury.

bar sailing — a colloquialism for describing sailing maneuvers by using your hands to represent boats, courses, heel angles, and tactics, usually as part of a postmortem conducted in a drinking establishment. Also known as dry sailing, hand sailing, and karate yachting.

base layer — a clothing layer, worn next to the skin, that moves moisture away and allows it to pass through the fabric, so it will evaporate. Also known as a wicking layer. And referred to as a rash guard because it provides chafe protection.

batten — a flexible wood, fiberglass, or plastic strip that supports the aft portion, or roach of a sail so that it remains straight. Most commonly used in mainsails and non-overlapping jibs. A batten is usually inserted into a batten pocket that is sewn horizontally onto a sail. Some modern cruising sails that roll into a mast or around a headstay furler use battens positioned vertically or use inflatable battens. Battens that extend a sail's full width are referred to as full-length battens.

batten tool — a short handle made from batten material. Used for inserting and removing battens from a sail. Also called a batten poker.

battle flag — a large flag or banner showing a particular boat's colors or insignia, or that of her corporate sponsor. Usually flown from high up on the headstay.

Bayview Mac — Bayview Yacht Club's Race to Mackinac Island, an annual race from Port Huron, Michigan, to Mackinac Island, Michigan. The race is conducted over either the 252-mile Thunder Bay Course or the 298-mile Cove Island Course. Billed as the world's longest consecutively run offshore freshwater yacht race. For more information, browse to http://www.byc.com/mack.

BBYRA — 1) Barnegat Bay Yacht Racing Association. For more information, browse to http://www.bbyra.org. 2) Biscayne Bay Yacht Racing Association. For more information, browse to http://www.bbyra.net.

BCSA — British Columbia Sailing Association. For more information, browse to http://www.bcsailing.bc.ca.

beam — 1) A boat's maximum width. 2) In or from a direction perpendicular to a boat's longitudinal axis, extending right (i.e., to starboard) or left (i.e., to port) toward the horizon. Directly to the side. Also known as abeam.

beam reach — a point of sail where a boat is sailing at a right angle to the apparent wind. The wind is coming from abeam. A beam reach is the point of sail between a broad reach and a close reach. If a boat is heading towards the 12:00 position and the wind is coming from approximately 3:00 or 9:00, the boat is on a beam reach. She is flying an asymmetrical or symmetrical spinnaker, or her jib is eased considerably and her boom is set about half way to leeward. See also: barber hauler and reaching sheet.

beam seas — a wave direction at right angles to a boat's centerline.

bear away — to turn away from the wind; fall off. The opposite of heading up. See also: foot and foot mode.

bear away set — to round a weather mark, bear away (i.e., to steer a lower course), and then set a spinnaker. Compare to: jibe set.

bearing — the direction to or from an object expressed relative to a compass or boat.

beat / beating — 1) To sail towards the direction the wind blows from (i.e., windward) by making a series of tacks. A point of sail also known as close-hauled. Apparent wind speed is higher than true wind speed, because the boat is sailing into the wind. Boat speed and wind speed are cumulative. Also referred to as work. 2) A windward-leeward or Olympic course's upwind leg.

Beaufort wind scale — a way to describe wind velocity and severity based on observed sea conditions. The scale goes from force 0 to force 12, with 0 indicating less than one knot of wind (1 mile per hour) and a smooth, mirror-like sea surface. Force 12 indicates a wind speed of 64 knots (74 miles per hour) or greater, the air filled with foam, waves over 45 ft., seas completely white with driving spray, and visibility greatly reduced. The scale was developed in 1805 by England's Admiral Sir Francis Beaufort, Also known as the Beaufort wind force scale.

becalmed — unable to make forward progress due to a lack of wind. The opposite of what the crew feels when there is no wind. See also: drifter, parked up, and zephyr.

becket — an eye used for securing the end of a line to the end of a block; i.e., a line that is dead-ended. See also: standing part.

beer can racing — semi-organized, informal boat racing. The idea is to "drop some beer cans" in the water and then race around them instead of buoys that require lots of powerboats—and people—to set, move, and recover. Also known as twilight racing.

before the wind — sailing with the wind from astern. Sailing in the same direction in which the wind blows.

belly — slang for a sail's draft or camber.

belly button — a patch, located in a spinnaker's center, that a light line attaches to. The line is used during a spinnaker takedown. Prohibited in some classes. Also known as a pull down patch, recovery point, retriever patch, or takedown patch.

bend — 1) To attach and make ready for use, as in "bend on a sail." 2) A category of knots used to join two lines together to form a longer line.

beneath — to leeward of.

Bermuda High — a large subtropical semi-permanent center of high atmospheric pressure found near Bermuda, in the Western Atlantic Ocean at the Horse latitudes (i.e., sub-tropic latitudes between 30 and 35 degrees North). When this weather system moves farther east it is referred to as the Azores High or, generally, as the North Atlantic High.

Bermuda rig — a configuration of mast and rigging featuring a tall, triangular mainsail and a raked mast. The mainsail is set aft of the mast with its head raised to the top of the mast; its luff runs down the mast and is normally attached for its entire length; its tack is secured at the base of the mast; its foot controlled by a boom; and its clew attached to the aft end of the boom, which is controlled by a mainsheet. Also known as a Bermudian rig or Marconi rig. The later in reference to the inventor, Gulielmo Marconi, whose wireless radio masts the Bermuda rigs are said to resemble. The vast majority of racing monohull yachts are Bermuda-rigged sloops. See also: aspect ratio, fractional rig, and masthead rig.

Bernoulli's Principle — as the speed of a fluid flow increases its pressure decreases; one of the fundamentals of fluid dynamics. So, for example, airflow (i.e., the fluid) over a curved sail's leeward side has to travel a greater distance than air that flows over the windward side. Since airflow over the leeward side has to travel farther, it has to travel faster in order to reach the trailing edge at the same time as the air that flows over the windward side. The faster-flowing air on the leeward surface has a lower pressure than the slower-moving air on the sail's windward surface. This pressure difference generates lift and pulls the boat to leeward and forward. This is also known as Bernoulli's Equation and the Longer Path Explanation. The Bernoulli's Principle is from Daniel Bernoulli's book, *Hydrodynamica*, published in 1738.

berth — 1) A place to sleep onboard a boat. See also: pilot berth, pipe berth, quarter berth, settee, and v-berth. 2) A location in a harbor to secure a vessel, such as a dock or moor. 3) A safe and cautious distance, as in "a wide berth." British and Commonwealth sailors use berth to mean position, as in "the inside berth at the mark."

BFD — an initialism for "black flag disqualification." The scoring abbreviation used to indicate that a boat has violated the Black Flag Rule (*RRS-2009* 30.3) and has been disqualified. The boat has the maximum points allowed assessed against her when the race is scored using a Low Point System. See *RRS-2009* Appendix A. The applicable *Notice of Race* or *Sailing Instructions* may also modify the number of points assessed.

bight — 1) An open loop in a line. "The bight" is the potentially dangerous area within a bight of line that is under load. For example, anyone sitting inside the bight of a working spinnaker sheet run through a turning block would likely be severely injured by both the sheet and shrapnel if the block's sheave separated from its frame. 2) The sea area between two promontories.

bikes — slang for a winch grinding pedestal, a device used to provide turning power to one or more deck-mounted winch drums. Either a single crew member or two crew members that work in tandem operate what look like bicycle pedals mounted atop the pedestal. See also: grinding pedestal.

bilge — the lower, internal part of a hull. Space at the very bottom of a boat where water leaks collect. Bilge pumps evacuate the water.

bilge brothers / bilge buddies — slang for the crew members sent below when the winds are really light, to relax on the leeward cushions near the mast. This offers many advantages: wind drag is reduced, the slot is not clogged, and their weight is concentrated closer to the boat's center of gravity. Low centered weight also helps reduce pitching in leftover waves and swell. Being sent below is not always fun for the crew, but they can get out of the sun, have some food, and catch up on some reading. Also known as being mushrooms or putting dogs in the doghouse.

binnacle — a stand for a ship's compass and binnacle light mounted in front of or incorporated into the wheel's pedestal.

bitter end — the last part of a rope or chain. The end that is opposite the end in use. An anchor rode's inboard end. The tail. Compare to: standing part.

black band — a colored band that indicates one of three limits while a boat is racing, depending on where the band is located. At a masthead, the black band's lower edge is the limit that a sail's head may be hoisted to. At a gooseneck, the black band's upper edge is the limit that a sail's tack may be pulled down to. The limit a sail's clew may be pulled out to is indicated by the forward edge of the black band at a boom's aft end. These bands may not actually be black, but in a contrasting color to the spar on which it is placed. Also known as the outer limit mark.

black flag rule — *RRS-2009* rule 30.3 states, "If a black flag has been displayed, no part of a boat's hull, crew, or equipment shall be in the triangle formed by the ends of the start line and the first mark during the last minute before her starting signal. If a boat breaks this rule and is identified, she shall be disqualified without a hearing…." The black flag rule imposes a severe penalty on any boat that crosses the start line before her starting gun. See also: BFD.

black water — any sewage or fluids discharging from a head/toilet on a boat. Federal and State laws cover when and where black water can be discharged overboard. In general, untreated black water discharge into inland or coastal waters is prohibited.

blade / blade out — to make a sail as flat as possible (i.e., with minimum draft) by using mast bend, sail trim, and other controls to completely de-power it or to allow for attached, laminar flow in very light air. The opposite of bag. Blade is also used as slang for the rudder or leeboards on dinghies.

blanket — a tactical maneuver where a boat uses her sails to block a competitor's wind and slow the competitor down. See also: dirty air, gassing, herding, slam dunk, and tight cover.

blast reacher — a flatter, smaller sail than a jib top reacher, made from heavy material, with a high-cut clew that prevents water from being trapped if the boat heels. Used in heavy winds and when apparent wind angles are between 60 and 80 degrees, it keeps a boat from heeling excessively.

bleeding — purging air from a fuel or hydraulic system, such as getting air out of a diesel engine's fuel lines after the engine has run out of fuel.

block — a frame or casing (i.e., a cheek) that holds one or more sheaves rotating on a pin or on ball bearings. Blocks allow lines to change direction or gain mechanical advantage. There are many types of blocks, including becket blocks, bullet blocks, cheek blocks, foot blocks, and turning blocks.

blooper — a full staysail set leeward of the main. Sometimes referred to as a big boy or shooter. An antiquated sail setup.

blow — to rapidly release a loaded halyard, sheet, or guy and let it run free. Often done by opening the clutch holding it, without its tail being wrapped on a winch. An example is to blow the halyard on the spinnaker during a leeward douse. Variations include burn and blow off. Blow off is also used as slang for douse.

blow a hoolie — slang used by British and Commonwealth sailors to describe either a particularly intense storm or, metaphorically, someone's intensely negative reaction to an event.

blowboat — a disparaging term for a sailboat.

Blue Water Classic — an alternative name for the Sydney-to-Hobart annual race run since 1945 on December 26 from Sydney Harbor across the Tasman Sea into Storm Bay and up the Derwent River to Hobart. For more information, browse to http://rolexsydneyhobart.com.

BN — an initialism for "boat nanny." An under-recognized and under-appreciated employee who crews, cleans, and maintains a race boat. Performs such jobs as scrubbing and painting the bottom, polishing brightwork, and fixing dings and scratches. Before sailors became enlightened, they referred to this invaluable person by using another insensitive, demeaning, and derogatory racial reference. Other initialisms used include BM for "boat manager" and BMW for "boat maintenance worker."

board — as in "we were faster on the other board," a colloquialism for the tack a boat is or was on.

boat — due to sailboat racing's expensive nature, an acronym for "bring over another thousand (dollars)."

boat-for-boat — competing without any time-allowance handicap adjustments.

boat hook — a short bar with a fitting on one end that contains one or more hooks. A boat hook is used to help put a line over a piling, recover an object dropped overboard or provide an extended reach.

boatswain's chair — (pronounced "bosuns chair.") A canvas or leather seat made fast to a halyard. It is for a person to sit on while working aloft.

boat wind — wind created by a boat's forward movement. It is in the opposite direction of a boat's heading and equal to boat speed.

bobstay — a rod or wire that runs from a bowsprit's outboard end down and aft to the hull's stem. It balances a headstay's upward force.

bog — a compound used to fill in low spots or to build up areas when fairing a hull, keel, or rudder. Made from a mixture of epoxy and microscopic glass beads, tiny hollow plastic spheres, or another low-density filler so that it can add volume but not weight. Microlight is West Marine's brand of fairing compound. Awlfair is Awlgrips' brand. Also called builder's bog, fairing compound, or fairing putty.

boltrope — a reinforcing rope sewn along a sail's luff or foot. Allows the luff or foot to be secured in a grooved head foil, mast, or boom and takes the principal strain when the sail is flying. Boltrope is the only thing referred to as rope aboard a boat. Also called luff tape. See also: dual-groove head foil.

Bonine — an over-the-counter antiemetic medication used to treat and prevent motion sickness, nausea, and vomiting. Bonine is a registered trademark of Insight Pharmaceuticals Corp. Its generic name is meclizine hydrochloride. See also: Dramamine and Transderm-Scop.

Bonus Point (scoring) System — a methodology used to select the winner of a race or of a series of races. In a Bonus Point System, a finisher receives an increasing number of points, based on a non-linear scale, for each earlier finisher. The assignment of points is more favorable towards earlier finishers, as the competition is assumed to be more intense among those participants. The boat with the fewest cumulative points at the end of a race or series of races is the winner. This is the less used of two scoring systems defined by *RRS-2009*, unless the applicable *Notice of Race* or *Sailing Instructions* identifies a non-*RRS*-defined scoring system. The alternative defined scoring method is the Low Point System. The Bonus Point System was formerly known as the Olympic scoring system. See also: Cox-Sprague Scoring System and High Point System.

boom vang — a device connected between a mast and boom. It is used for maintaining proper mainsail shape, particularly when running or broad reaching. There are two types: block & tackle and solid. Block & tackle vangs have a 3:1, 4:1, or higher purchase and exert only a downward pull on the boom. Solid boom vangs use a purchase system to exert a downward pull and a coil spring or gas-filled ram to provide upward support. Often referred to simply as the vang. Sometimes referred to as a boom kicker, kicker, or kicking strap.

bosun's bag — a sail repair kit.

bosun's chair — a more modern spelling for what a crew member sits on while working aloft. See also: boatswain's chair.

bottom mark — a mark at the end of a windward-leeward racecourse's downwind leg, or at the end of the second of two reaching legs of a triangle or Olympic racecourse. Also called the leeward or lee mark.

bow — (pronounced "bou.") 1) The front of the boat; the pointy end. In traditional nautical terms, a bow is one side of a boat forward of the beam to the stem. A boat has a port bow and a starboard bow. So, in traditional terms, the pointy end would be the bows. Also referred to as the foredeck. 2) The crew member whose core responsibilities include preparing headsails and spinnakers for hoisting and dropping, and rigging their associated sheets, lines, and guys. When jibing, the foredeck crew swaps the guys at the spinnaker pole's outboard end. Also acts as the eyes at the front of the boat during pre-start and starting phases, calling the start line, traffic, and overlaps and relaying distance information to the afterguard through hand signals. Also known as the foredeck crew.

Example Hands Signals from the Bow

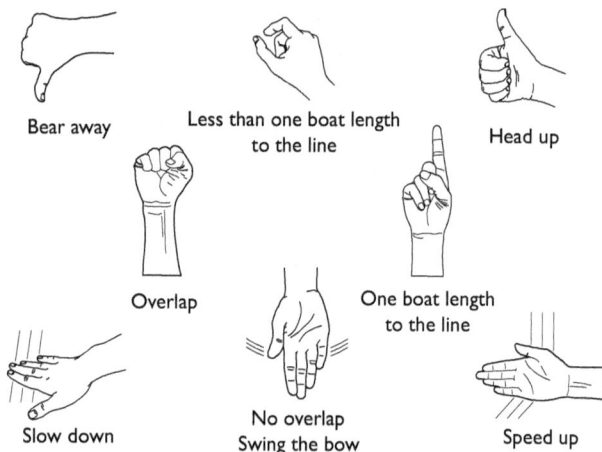

Bear away

Less than one boat length to the line

Head up

Overlap

One boat length to the line

Slow down

No overlap
Swing the bow

Speed up

bow chick — a self-referential term for a female crew member who works the foredeck position.

bow chocks — fittings on deck at the bow. Mooring or anchor lines are led through them.

bow down / bow up — a comparison between one boat and another's pointing ability. The boat this is bow up is pointing higher than the boat that is bow down.

bow horn — 1) A U-shaped metal bracket that is attached to the deck at the stemhead. The upper arms of the U are bent to resemble upside-down Js and are bent slightly aft. A heavy metal ring (i.e., cringle) sewn into a headsail's tack is hooked onto one of the Js before the sail is hoisted. 2) The semi-circular bracket, located at the stemhead, that contains shackles used to capture a headsail's tack or that a shackle on a headsail's tack fastens to. See also: tack ring.

bow line — a docking or mooring line leading from the bow.

bowline — (pronounced "boh-lin.") A knot used to form a line into a closed loop. A bowline does not contract and it is easily opened.

bow out — a comparison between one boat and another's position relative to windward. The boat that is bow out is more windward than her competitor. A bow out position offers clean air and the opportunity to gain more leverage in a favorable wind shift. See also: leg out. Compare to: height.

bow pulpit — the stainless steel tubing that forms a safety rail around a boat's bow, including vertical supports and usually double horizontal rails. On a boat using lifelines, the lifelines usually connect to each aft end of the bow pulpit as part of a continuous safety perimeter.

bowsprit — a spar projecting forward from the bow to support headsails or asymmetrical spinnakers. Supported laterally by shrouds, by the headstay from above, and by a bobstay from below. Some boats have a retractable bowsprit used only to support an asymmetrical spinnaker's tack. Also known by the shorthand sprit and the slang prod.

bow team — the group of crew members who work forward of the mast. On a smaller boat, the mast and bow crew; on a larger boat, the mast, mid-bow, and bow.

box — jargon for the area that boats may enter only during their start sequence and that they must stay clear of at all other times. This area is contained within the starting area boundaries as defined in the applicable *Sailing Instructions* or otherwise. Boats that travel within the box outside of their starting sequence are subject to race committee or competitor protest.

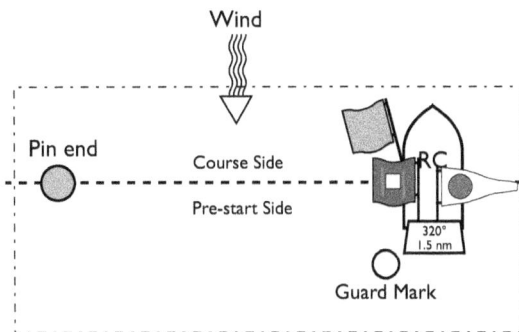

Box

box-rule — a measurement-based rule, similar to one-design, where boats are built to certain pre-defined standards or rules with minimums and maximums for specific parameters, although there is some latitude for design and outfitting. Boats compete boat-for-boat without any time-allowance handicap ratings, the theory being that any boat that fits within the box is acceptable and anything is permitted unless the rules specifically prohibit it.

brag flag — a pennant or burgee that commemorates a winning finish in a race or regatta. Often flown from the winning boat's headstay.

braided line — a line composed of multiple strands of interwoven fiber, rather than fibers that are twisted or laid up. A line composed of an inner braided core and outer braided cover is called double-braid or braid-on-braid. Braided line is easier on the hands than twisted line and is resistant to stretching and kinking, so it is used for sheets, halyards, and control line. Class II or core-dependent double-braid derives all of its strength from the inner core—the outer cover provides no strength, only wear protection. Class I double-braid relies on both the core's and the cover's strength.

bread & butter — basic, ordinary, or routine, as in bread & butter rules, bread & butter tactics, or bread & butter moves. The basic rules, tactics, or maneuvers.

break — 1) Describes when a spinnaker's edge collapses or curls in. Also known as a reverse curl. See also: leech break and luff break. 2) Describes when a telltale's loose end is lifting, twirling, or fluttering.

breaking wave — a wave crest that is too steep or too large to remain stable, so it violently breaks away from its base and collapses. Can occur when a storm imparts more energy into a body of water than can be dissipated, when two wave trains collide or when a strong wind opposes a running tide or current. See also: pooped.

breast line — a short line leading directly from a boat to a dock.

brick — 1) To tightly flake and then fold a sail into a compact shape, such as for long-term storage or vehicular transport. See: sailmaker's flake. 2) To crunch up a sail as fast and as best you can, to clear it off the deck quickly. Compare to: luff tie flake.

bridle — two or more lines that are grouped together and are used for hoisting or rigging; e.g., the bridles used to hoist and hold down an end-for-end spinnaker pole. Sometimes used to refer to the line between the topping lift and the spinnaker pole's outboard end on a dip-pole setup.

brightwork — the varnished woodwork on a boat. The stuff that takes much effort to beautify.

broach / broaching — an uncontrolled and unintended event where a boat is turned broadside to the wind and waves. Can be caused by, among other things, strong wind gusts that overpower a boat or by a large wave that the helmsman and trimmers either ignore or cannot respond to because of a stalled rudder. The boat may roll, laying her mast horizontal, perhaps causing the boat to be swamped or capsize. Under the worst conditions, a boat knocked on her ear can end up with her crew overboard, with her sails destroyed or upside down. Also referred to as a knockdown, rollout, or wipeout. In addition, a broach may be referred to as a round down or round up, depending on whether it is to leeward or windward.

broad reach — a point of sail where a boat is sailing away from the wind, but not directly downwind. A boat is broad reaching when she is heading towards 12:00 and the wind is coming from between either 3:15 to 5:00 or 7:00 to 8:45. When broad reaching, a boat is flying an asymmetrical or symmetrical spinnaker or her jib is eased all the way out and her boom is set about three-quarters of the way to leeward. See also: barber hauler, power reaching, and reaching sheet.

BSA — 1) Bahamas Sailing Association. For more information, browse to http://www.bahamassailing.org. 2) Bermuda Sailing Association. For more information, browse to http://www.bermudasail.bm.

bug — slang for a kink or knot that is in a sheet or halyard and that prevents it from running freely through a fairlead or block.

bullet — slang for winning a race and scoring a single point, when the race is scored using a Low Point System; e.g., 1 point for first, 2 for second, etc. The competitor with the fewest points at the series end is the overall winner.

bullet block — a small block or pulley.

bump — to pull or haul vigorously. For example, to stand at the mast and quickly pull down on a halyard or to pull a bight of halyard outwards from the mast, as another crew member winches it in—tails it—to hoist a sail.

buntline — a line used to secure the loose cloth at a reefed sail's foot. Buntlines run around the gathered sailcloth, through reef point grommets, and around the boom. On square-riggers, a buntline is used to pull up a square sail's foot.

buoy — a float that is anchored in the water and that marks a location. It indicates a navigational route or a warning of danger. See also: mark.

buoy racing — racing on a course of two or more legs that are denoted by marks. Also referred to as can racing, harbor racing, in-port racing, inshore racing, or mark racing. The strategic priorities of buoy racing are to stay between any opponents and the next mark or wind shift, and to consolidate any leverage gained. Compare this to offshore racing, where the strategic priorities are to find the most favorable weather pattern, to get to the weather pattern before the competition and to be better placed within that weather system. Some will argue that inshore racing is conducted in unprotected waters but within sight of land, while buoy racing is conducted in protected waters. To others there is no difference.

burdened vessel — an antiquated term for the boat that must yield when boats meet or cross, or when one boat is overtaking another. Was also known as the keep-clear vessel. Currently referred to as the give-way vessel. In general, a boat on port tack or that is overtaking another boat is the give-way vessel. See also: *COLREGS* and rules of the road. Compare to: stand-on vessel.

burgee — a flag that is flown from a boat and that indicates which yacht club the boat's owner belongs to.

burnish — to polish hard-finish bottom paint to make the paint smoother.

burp — as in "burp the main, " a slang way of asking for the main halyard, for example, to be eased an inch or less. A line such as a halyard will slip through a clutch cleat slightly as its cam locks onto the line. Therefore, to burp the main halyard when the mainsail is hoisted, snug the halyard on a winch and then open and close the clutch.

burrito — as in "burrito the main, " an alternative method to flaking for storing a main on a boom. You do this by folding the head over the upper third of the sail, rolling it from the fold towards the foot, and then sail tying it to the boom. Doing this is easier than flaking for inexperienced crew, or when the deck is rolling and the wind is blowing. An alternative method is to lower the main about 10 feet, form the loose sailcloth into a cradle, drop the rest of the main into the cradle, and then tie the package to the boom. A few people refer to this as a joynt or a taco.

butt cleat — slang referring to someone sitting on a line that needs to be trimmed or eased, making the adjustment more difficult.

butterfly — Two headsails flying simultaneously. See also: dual-groove head foil and poor man's twin.

by the lee — sailing with the wind coming from behind, and on the same side the mainsail is on. Also known as running by the lee.

C

---

cabin sole — the bottom surface of the enclosed space under a boat's deck. The cabin or saloon floor.

cabin top — a structure raised above deck, over the cabin, to provide headroom in the cabin. Also called the coachroof. Occasionally called a deckhouse or hood.

caddy — a crew member whose core responsibility is to be an extra hand as needed. Often selected as much for his or her strength and agility as for his or her sailing ability. British and Commonwealth sailors are likely to use this term. See also: floater.

calm — little or no wind pressure. Wind velocity between zero and one knots (zero to one miles per hour). Force zero on the Beaufort wind scale.

camber — the amount or degree of curvature in a sail's horizontal cross-section. See also: draft.

cam cleat — a pair of spring-loaded cams that come together to clamp their teeth on a line rove between them. Example uses include securing the boom vang, downhaul, and jib car control lines.

can — 1) An odd-numbered green buoy. Sailors use the memory aid "seven-up cans are green" to remember the color and numbering scheme for cans. A can that marks a channel's left side when a boat is returning to harbor—within the United States and other territories using the region B lateral buoyage system. Compare to: nun. 2) Can is also slang for a mark.

Canada's Cup — a match race between one United States boat and one Canadian boat battling one on one. Long known as "America's Cup of the Great Lakes," the race is held periodically on the Great Lakes. Named for the yacht that won the first-ever match race on Lake Erie in 1896, the cup has crossed the lakes several times since.

canard — one or more retractable hull appendages that are mounted on the centerline and are lowered to supply lateral resistance. A boat may have one canard forward of the keel, or one forward and one aft of the keel. Compare to: daggerboard.

canoe stern — a pointed stern such as on a canoe. A boat with a canoe stern is also referred to as a double-ender.

can racing — inshore racing around the marks of a multi-leg racecourse. See also: buoy racing.

canting keel — a ballast bulb keel hinged at the bottom of a hull and swung from side to side by powerful hydraulic rams. The crew swings the keel to the windward side to counteract the sails' heeling force. Boats that use canting keels for their improved righting ability often also use daggerboards to make up for canting keels' less effective leeway resistance. A canting keel offers the heel-resistance advantage of water ballast, without having to add the additional weight. Also known as a swing keel.

cap shrouds — parts of the standing rigging that help support a mast laterally. Composite fiber, or stainless steel wire or rod, run from hull-mounted chain plates on the beams through any number of spreader tips, to their attachment points on the masthead. Cap shroud tension is typically adjusted with turnbuckles located just above the chain plates. Also referred to as V1s or vertical 1s. Also called sidestays. See also: chicken stays, continuous rigging, discontinuous rigging, Loos gauge, and mast jack. Compare to: diagonals.

capsize — to turn a boat over on her side in the water. A boat can get capsized by excess power in her sails, excess weight on the wrong side of the boat or powerful waves. See also: broach.

car — an adjustable slide, fairlead, or block that runs on a track or traveler. Examples are jib lead car, traveler, and spinnaker pole car.

carbon fiber — graphite fibers embedded within epoxy resin (i.e., glue) and formed into strong and light material for spars, structural members, hulls, or sails.

Carbo Racing Foil — Harken's brand name for its dual-groove head foil. A device that is fitted over the headstay or forestay and that contains one or more luff grooves to accommodate and provide continuous support for headsails that use boltrope. The device is usually made from aerodynamically shaped extruded aluminum or plastic. A headsail is secured at the luff by sliding its luff tape/boltrope through a pre-feeder and then into the head foil's feeder and up its luff groove. A dual-groove head foil allows for hoisting a second headsail in the second groove before dousing the first, so a boat can avoid running bare headed and losing performance. Schaefer Marine's brand is called Tuff Luff. Also known as forestay track.

cardinal heading / cardinal points — the four principal compass points: North, East, South, and West.

Caribbean Sailing Association Rating — a handicap rating for boats racing in the Caribbean. The rating is based on a boat's hull, rig, sail, and weight measurements, and a subjective evaluation of her performance potential. For more information, browse to http://www.caribbean-sailing.com. Compare to: IRC and ORR.

category 0-4 offshore race — refers to the *ISAF Offshore Special Regulations* used to classify an event and establish minimum safety regulations for each category. As the racing conditions become more intense, the category ratings move from four to zero and the safety regulations become more stringent. The applicable *Notice of Race* or *Sailing Instructions* may modify any requirements.

category 5 or 6 inshore race — refers to the *ISAF Special Regulations for Inshore Racing* used to classify an event and establish minimum safety regulations for each category. The racing conditions are less favorable for category 5 than category 6, so the safety regulations are more stringent. The applicable *Notice of Race* or *Sailing Instructions* may modify any requirements.

category A or C — refers to former classifications contained within the *ISAF Regulations, section 20-Advertising Code*, pertaining to advertising displayed on boats or on competitors' uniforms. Rules covering advertising are exclusionary—anything not specifically permitted is prohibited. The applicable *Notice of Race* or *Sailing Instructions* may modify any requirements.

cat-in-the-hat — slang for the postponement flag, because of its color scheme. Known formally as the AP flag or Answering Pennant.

cavitation -- the hydrodynamic effect from a vortex around a foil - usually the rudder – that allows air from the surface to mix with the water around the foil and reduce its effectiveness. See also: ventilating the rudder.

cat's paw — the downdraft or outflow winds that ripple the water surface in a dark, paw-shaped pattern. The winds are diverging at the leading edge of a gust. A good turbulence and wind shear indicator. Also referred to as a fan puff.

CBYRA — Chesapeake Bay Yacht Racing Association. For more information, browse to http://www.cbyra.org.

celestial navigation — a method for determining position using the sun, planets, or stars. A sextant is used to determine the selected object's angle above the horizon—a sextant shot. The exact time and the object's angle are compared to a set of tables to determine a boat's position.

centerboard — a retractable hull appendage, attached approximately on the hull centerline and rotating about a single transverse axis that may move in relation to the hull, and that is primarily used to affect leeway. A boat utilizing a centerboard does not have a keel. A daggerboard that retracts into the hull is sometimes generically referred to as a centerboard.

center of effort (CE) — the point where all wind forces concentrate; the point on the sail plan that is the balance point for all aerodynamic forces.

center of lateral resistance (CLR) — the theoretical underwater pivot point around which a hull swings.

chafe — the damage to one object caused by rubbing against another object.

chafing gear — the material applied to an object to prevent or reduce chafing. So it really should be called chafe prevention gear.

chain plates — the metal plates to which shrouds, lines, and stays are attached. These plates are located on either side of the deck near the beam and are attached to the hull. Also referred to as deck plates.

change mark — a mark that indicates the new end of a leg when a course has been changed. Usually of a contrasting color or shape to the original mark. At the mark previous to the one being changed, the mark boat will display a "C" flag along with at least one other visual signal, and will make repetitive sounds. The other visual signals include a placard that indicates the compass bearing to the new mark; a green triangle for a change to starboard; a red rectangle for a change to port; a "-" if the leg has been shortened; and a "+" if the leg has been lengthened.

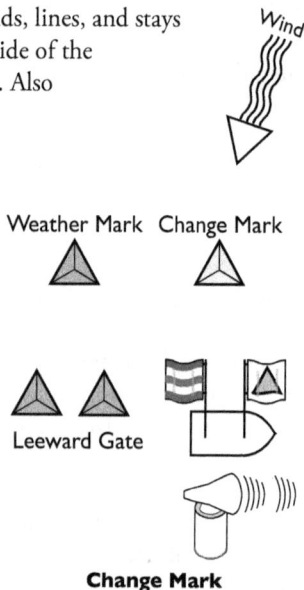

Weather Mark   Change Mark

Leeward Gate

Change Mark

changing down — dousing or peeling a larger jib for a smaller one to de-power the sail plan.

changing sheet — a line used to temporarily control a sail while its primary sheet is being re-rove to a new location or the sail is being peeled. A line to temporarily hold the tack of a new spinnaker that is being hoisted either inside or outside one already flying, or to hold the tack of the spinnaker already flying, during a spinnaker peel—in this case, the line is more correctly called a changing strop. One version consists of a medium length of nylon webbing with trigger-release snap shackles at either end. One shackle is connected to a bow cleat or stemhead, while the other end is clove-hitched to the headstay at shoulder height, with the snap shackle hanging two feet down. This version allows you to free the old spinnaker from the pole, so the pole can be used for the new chute. Another version consists of a 12-inch line with a trigger-release snap shackle at one end and a clip at the other. (See also: handcuffs.) This version allows you to keep the old spinnaker attached to the pole but to free the guy, so it can be connected to the new spinnaker. With either version, the snap shackles are under considerable load, so trigger-release versions are used. You can spike off the old chute with a fid when the new one is hoisted and drawing. Also referred to generally as a strop. Sometimes called a stripper line or tag line.

chart — a graphical representation of the Earth's surface, or a portion thereof, such as oceans, lakes, rivers, canals, locks, harbors, dams, and adjacent coastal regions. Charts indicate landmasses and other physical features, currents, water depths, and other unique characteristics, including detailed and accurate representations of the coastline, that take into account varying tidal levels and local details of the Earth's magnetic field. Charts also provide detailed information on the normally obscured area beneath the water surface. This information is critical for safe and efficient navigation. Charts are used to plot courses for navigators to follow in order to transit a certain area. They take into account special conditions required for boats, such as draft, bottom clearance, wrecks, and obstructions that can be hazardous. Waypoints and aids-to-navigation are identified to indicate relative position and points where specific maneuvers, such as changing course, must be performed. Nautical charts come in many forms, including printed on paper or computerized electronic navigational charts (ENCs) for chart plotters and GPS receivers.

chart plotter — a specialized navigation computer that overlays GPS and other data on electronic navigational charts (ENCs). It is used to perform route planning and navigation functions, including real-time display of a boat's location on the appropriate chart. A chart plotter may also display a boat's speed and course, as well as the time, distance, and bearing to the destination or next waypoint, all in real time. Other data that may be displayed includes information from radar, automatic information systems (AIS), depth sounders, and thermometers. See also: tactical/routing software.

chart table — the table a navigator uses to review charts and plot courses. See also: nav station.

cheater — a spinnaker staysail. A small, lightweight headsail set under (i.e., to weather of) a spinnaker. See also: daisy.

cheater flake — a single bight or fold in a sail. This fold is parallel to its foot and extends from either the tack or clew to the middle of the foot. When a sail is flaked after you take a cheater flake to its tack, its luff ends up gathered directly over its tack—a luff flake. A sail ends up with its leech gathered directly over its clew—a leech flake—when it is flaked after you take a cheater flake to its clew. Also known as a half flake or starter flake.

checkstay — a device adjusted to prevent a mast from over-bending or pumping. It is run between each quarter and a point on the mast significantly below and astern of the forestay attachment point. A checkstay may be rigged separately or jointly with a running backstay. It is part of the running rigging.

cheek block — a block or pulley with one flat or concave side so that it can be mounted on a spar, on deck or on another flat surface. Its cheek is mounted to something; e.g., a block to redirect a jib sheet up to a winch. Also generically called a turning block.

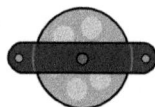

Cheek Block

Chicago Mac — Chicago Yacht Club's Race to Mackinac. An annual 333-mile race from Chicago's lakefront to Mackinac Island in Lake Huron. Billed as the longest annual freshwater race in the world. For more information, browse to http://www.chicagoyachtclub.org.

chicken — slang for the wind direction indicator vane (i.e., Windex) or masthead fly (i.e., fly) at the masthead. The vane swivels to show the apparent wind direction. British and Commonwealth sailors call it a wind hawk. See also: paddles.

chicken chute — an unusually small spinnaker set in a strong wind. Named so because only those who are said to be too chicken to sail a conventional-sized spinnaker use it.

chicken jibe — a 270-degree tack from one broad reach to another. Used when the winds are blowing so hard that you are afraid of breaking something when the boom slams across during a conventional jibe.

chicken stay — a temporary side stay or shroud run from the gooseneck or other attachment point on the mast to a chain plate or the rail at mid-foredeck. Used to counteract side loads on the mast.

China Coast Race Week — Asia's premiere sailing event. A regatta held over two successive weekends in the waters of the South China Sea, adjacent to Hong Kong. On the first weekend, boats complete on various windward/leeward and inshore courses. On the second weekend, boats compete on an offshore course that meanders around several islands. For more information, browse to http://www.chinacoastraceweek.com.

chine — a hull design with its sides and bottom being on distinct planes. Hard chine describes little or no rounding where the planes meet. Soft chine describes some rounding while still maintaining distinct planes.

Chinese jibe — a specific variety of accidental jibe where a boat is steered or the wind shifts such that the boat's stern involuntarily passes through the eye of the wind. Additionally, the main's leech has considerable twist—usually because of too little vang tension, and the boom is prevented from swinging. (e.g., by a preventer, or the boom is trapped by a backstay or runner.) The upper half of the main jibes and fills, while the lower half remains by the lee. The excessive forces at the masthead can cause a boat to roll on her side or broach. This is an insensitive and derogatory ethnic reference that should be avoided, as should the event.

chord — the hypothetical straight horizontal line from a sail's luff to its leech; an aerodynamic shape's baseline.

chord depth — the horizontally perpendicular measurement from a sail's chord to its maximum draft point. See also: bag and blade.

chute — one of many colloquial terms for a spinnaker, in this case because it resembles a parachute in both construction and appearance. See also: a-sail, kite, and round head.

cirrocumulus — a high-level cirriform cloud with extensive vertical development. It appears as a thin sheet of small white puffs that give it a rippled effect. Cirriform clouds often create what is referred to as a "mackerel sky," because the ripples look like fish scales and indicate upper-level wind patterns. Sometimes they are confused with altocumulus. However, cirriform clouds have smaller individual masses and do not cast a shadow on other elements. Cirrocumulus are the least common cloud type. They often form from cirrus or cirrostratus and are composed almost exclusively of ice crystals. The individual cloud elements that reflect the red or yellow light of a setting sun make them one of the most beautiful of all clouds.

cirrostratus — a high-level cloud that typically appears thin and white but that can produce a magnificent array of colors when the sun is low on the horizon. Cirrostratus are cirriform clouds that develop from cirrus spreading out into a thin layer, creating a flat, sheet-like appearance. Cirrostratus can give the sky a slightly milky or veiled look and usually cover a large portion of the sky. When viewed from the Earth's surface, these ice crystals can create a halo effect around the sun or moon. Cirrostratus clouds are good precursors of precipitation; they indicate that rain may occur within 12 to 24 hours.

cirrus — a high-level cloud that typically appears thin and white but that can produce a magnificent array of colors when the sun is low on the horizon. Cirrus comes from the Latin term for "curl" or "wisp of hair." Strong westerly winds aloft can blow cirrus clouds into streamers known as "mares' tails." They generally move from west to east across the sky and usually indicate fair weather.

clam cleat — a quick-release cleat that uses mechanical jamming action to hold a line in place without slipping. The line is held in place between two narrowing, toothed jaws. Pulling the line up and out of the cleat releases it. You use a clam cleat to secure a leech cord, for example. Ronstan calls this a v-cleat.

class — a general category of similarly designed boats or boats that have similar PHRF ratings and that are grouped together for racing.

class flag — the flag that indicates in which class or section a boat is competing. Sometimes the code flag for the number corresponding to the class's starting order is used as the class flag. At other times, solid-color flags in differing colors are used. There is often a requirement to fly a class flag from the backstay on each competing boat, although on one-design boats it's often optional to fly a class flag. The applicable *Sailing Instructions* indicate the starting order for multi-class races.

clear ahead — a boat is clear ahead of another when the aftermost point of her hull and equipment (in their normal position) are forward of a line abeam (i.e., perpendicular) from the forward-most point of the other boat's hull and equipment (in their normal position). The other boat is clear astern. These terms apply only to boats on the same tack unless *RRS-2009* rule 18 (concerning rounding and passing marks) applies, or if both boats are sailing more than ninety degrees from the true wind. See also: overlap.

clear air — natural wind flow that is free from any turbulence created by flowing over a boat and its sails, or by flowing over another object. Disturbed air reduces sail efficiency, so a boat will sail faster in clear air than in disturbed air.

Clear Ahead
Clear Astern

clear astern — a boat is clear astern of another when her hull and equipment (in their normal position) are behind a line abeam (i.e., perpendicular) from the aftermost point of the other boat's hull and equipment (in their normal position). The other boat is clear ahead. These terms apply only to boats on the same tack unless *RRS-2009* rule 18 (concerning rounding and passing marks) applies, or if both boats are sailing more than ninety degrees from the true wind. See also: overlap.

clearing mark — a landmark or buoy that lies upon a clearing line. Along one side of the line is a hazard; along the other, a boat can safely sail.

cleat — 1) A fitting that has one or two horns to which a line can be made fast by taking turns under and over the horns. Examples are a deck cleat, horn cleat, and jam cleat. The line is secured with a cleat hitch. 2) To cleat is to secure a line to a cleat.

cleat boots — the covers put over the ends of deck cleat horns to prevent lines from getting caught, fouled, or snagged. Made from wood or molded rubber and usually joined into pairs by shock cord. Also called Bartz blocks, chock blocks, or cleat guards.

clevis pin — a shaft or shank that closes a shackle or the jaws of another fitting. Some clevis pins are screwed into place; others are held in place by a safety ring or cotter ring—commonly referred to as a "ring ding." See also: mouse.

clew — a sail's lower, rear corner where its foot meets its leech. On a jib or spinnaker, sheets are attached to the clew. An outhaul and Velcro safety strap attach to the clew of a mainsail.

clinometer — an instrument used to determine a boat's heel angle or fore and aft pitch angle. Also called an inclinometer or tilt gauge. Lev-o-gage from Sun Company is a popular brand.

close cover — a tactical maneuver where a windward boat impedes a leeward boat's wind by keeping the leeward boat in the covering boat's wind shadow. This is done to slow down the leeward boat or to force her to change course. At the same time, the covered boat can time her tacks to stay in phase with wind shifts and diminish any lead the covering boat has. Also referred to as hard cover or tight cover. See also: herding.

closed — when referring to a sail's leech, closed means that the top third of a sail has little or no more twist to leeward than the bottom two-thirds of the sail. When referring to the distance between a jib's leech and a mainsail's luff, closed means that the gap or slot is very narrow. Compare to: open.

close-hauled — a point of sail where a boat is sailing as close to the apparent wind as possible while keeping her sails full and drawing. If a boat is sailing towards the 12:00 position, the wind is coming from approximately either 11:00 or 1:00. Her jib is sheeted in tight, and her boom is at the boat's centerline. See also: forereaching, inhauler, and luffing.

close reaching — a point of sail where a boat is sailing towards the wind but lower (i.e., farther from the wind) than when a boat is close-hauled. If a boat is sailing towards the 12:00 position, the wind is coming from between either 1:30 to 2:45 or 9:15 to 10:30. Her jib is eased slightly, and her boom is up to a quarter of the way leeward of the boat's centerline. Also known as fine reaching, shy reaching, or tight reaching. See also: barber hauler and power reaching.

cloud — a visible cluster of minute water droplets or ice crystals in the atmosphere above the Earth's surface. See also: high clouds, low clouds, and middle clouds.

clove hitch — a knot used to temporarily fasten a line to a piling or spar.

club racer — 1) A competent, experienced amateur race crew member. 2) A small sailing dinghy or keelboat that is usually owned by a sailing club and sailed by club members.

club racing — amateur sailing competitions where the participants are from one club or from the local area.

clutch cleat — a clamping device used to secure a line under load, often after it has been snugged with a winch. Lines can be trimmed through the clutch without having to release the clutch. Lines can also be released under load. Some clutch cleats can have their mechanism locked open with their handle in the closed position. Also referred to as a sheet stopper or stopper. Clutch cleats are often grouped in banks on each side of a coachroof. These banks are referred to as clutch banks, the keyboard or piano, or stopper banks.

CNYSA — Central New York Sailing Association. For more information, browse to http://www.centralssailing.org.

coachroof — a structure raised above deck, over the cabin, to provide headroom in the cabin. Also called the cabin top. Occasionally called a deckhouse or hood.

coaming — a raised border that is around a cockpit or hatch and that keeps water out. May be made wide enough and sturdy enough to support a winch.

cockpit — a recessed area in a boat's deck in which the crew works and from which the boat is steered. Located amidships or aft.

cockpit drop — a spinnaker douse where the sail is brought down a boat's leeward side and into the cockpit. See also: letterbox drop.

code 0 — a hybrid sail designed to work like a large, loose-luffed genoa for very tight reaching, but classified under racing rules as a spinnaker. It is an asymmetrical sail with the most upwind capability. The luff is as straight as possible, and the sail is flatter than other spinnakers. Also called a gennaker.

code flags — short for International code flags or signaling flags. A set of flags in different colors and shapes and with various markings that, when used singly or in combination, have different meanings. They also have different meanings when used for racing than they do for fishing or shipping. The flags include 26 square flags that depict the letters of the alphabet, ten numeral pendants, one answering pendant, and three substituters or repeaters. See also: cat-in-the-hat, class flag, prep flag, recalls, and warning flag.

coffee grinder — slang for a winch grinding pedestal with mechanically operated, dual-opposing hand cranks. Occasionally used as slang for a winch. See also: grinding pedestal.

cold eddie – a whirlpool of water that has separated from the main body of the Gulf Stream and that is colder than the surrounding water. Cold eddies circulate in a counter-clockwise direction and can be up to 180 miles (300 km) in diameter. Cold eddies form off a southward bending meander (lobe) and are found south of the Gulf Stream. Also known as a cold core eddie or cold core ring. Compare to warm eddie.

cold front — the boundary between an advancing cold air mass's forward edge and a retreating warm air mass's rear edge.

collision mat — a tarpaulin with lines that lead from its corners. It is used to cover a breach in a hull below the waterline from the outside.

COLREGS / 72 COLREGS — collision regulations. The *COLREGS* or 72 *COLREGS* are the *International Regulations for Preventing Collisions at Sea*, developed by what is now the International Maritime Organization (IMO) at its convention in 1972. A term often incorrectly used to refer to both the *International Regulations for Preventing Collisions at Sea* and the *Inland Navigation Rules* as presented by the United States Coast Guard. *COLREGS* are applicable outside of established lines of demarcation. *Inland Navigation Rules* differ slightly from *COLREGS* and are applicable inside the lines of demarcation.

committee boat — a boat that contains the race officials who manage a race. The committee boat, also known as the RC boat, displays placards or flags that indicate the selected course and a placard that indicates the direction and bearing to the first mark. The committee boat may also display other flags that indicate modifications to the races or rules listed in the *Sailing Instructions*. In addition, attention, start, warning, and sequence sounds and flags originate from the committee boat. Also referred to as the race committee boat, RC boat, or signal boat. Compare to: mark boat.

companionway — a staircase or ladder that connects a cockpit and cabin. See also: doghouse.

compass — a device that indicates direction or bearing in degrees relative to a fixed point, such as the magnetic North Pole. A circular compass face, known as the card, is divided into 360 equally spaced graduations, known as degrees. Zero, usually indicating North, is at the top of the card, and the remaining degrees are numbered consecutively clockwise around the card. The cardinal compass points (i.e., North, East, South, and West) are also indicated. There are many compass types, including gyrocompasses, which show true degrees that are oriented to the Earth's True North; fluxgate compasses, which are highly accurate electro-magnetic compasses that can be connected to navigation instruments; steering compasses, which are used for steering; and bearing compasses, which are for taking bearings. A hand-bearing compass is a handheld compass for taking bearings. A telltale compass is a compass located below decks, where other crew members can keep track of courses steered. A sidereal compass uses stars to determine orientation.

cone of protection — a theoretical safety zone protected against lightning strikes provided by a boat with her mast, engine, and other large metal objects electrically bonded together and well-grounded. It is a cone extending from the masthead to the water's surface, out to a radius approximately equal to the mast's height. Known in the world of physics as a Faraday's Cage. For more information, see the American Boat and Yacht Council's standards and technical report on lightning protection TE-4, available at http://www. abycinc.org.

consolidate — to maneuver in such a way as to realize any gain made through leverage, by closing the lateral distance to a competitor while staying closer to the intended mark.

constant pressure chart — an alternate term for Isobaric Chart; a weather map that represents conditions on a surface of equal atmospheric pressure. For example, a 500-millibar (mb) chart will display conditions at the level of the atmosphere where the atmospheric pressure is 500 mb. The height above sea level for a constant pressure may vary from one location to another at any given time, and may vary with time at any location, so it does not represent a surface of constant altitude or height. That is, the 500-mb level may be at a different height above sea level over Chicago than over New York at a given time, and may be at a different height over Chicago from one day to the next.

contender — a boat whose position or cumulative score offers her a reasonable chance of being a top finisher. Also known as being "in the hunt." See also: podium finish.

continental air mass — an air mass that originated over land.

continuous rigging — a rigging configuration where each shroud runs from its attachment turnbuckle at a chain plate through any number of spreader tips without termination, to its attachment point on the mast, as one continuous tensile element. With composite rigging, a bundle of stays attach to a chain plate. One element splits off at each spreader tip and attaches to the mast to form a diagonal, with the last element attaching to the masthead as the cap.

convection — describes heat transfer by fluid motion. In a meteorological sense, generally by vertical air currents. See also: advection fog.

convective cloud base — the altitude where convective clouds begin to form. The altitude where dry-adiabatic rate and dew point rate lines meet.

convergence — the phenomenon of air flowing to a point within an atmospheric layer. Since this air cannot be collected at the convergence point, a vertical exhaust current develops.

convict — a derogatory term a New Zealander uses in reference to an Australian.

core — the braided strands of fiber at the center of double-braid or braid-on-braid line. Class II or core-dependent double-braid line derives all its strength from the inner core. The outer cover provides no strength, only chafe protection, so the cover is sometimes stripped away to reduce the line's weight.

Corinthian — an amateur or a boat without a paid professional skipper. The term implies a high level of good sportsmanship and conduct. See also: *RRS-2009* rule 2.

Coriolis Effect — the apparent deflection to the right, in the northern Hemisphere, of any free body in motion. In a meteorological sense, the Coriolis Effect is most often applied to apparent wind deflection, with maximum effect at the poles and none at the equator. The deflection is referred to as apparent because the free body appears to change direction as the Earth rotates out from underneath it.

corner — a racecourse leg's lateral extreme, where the extended layline from the start line or previous mark meets the extended layline of the next mark. See also: bang the corner.

Cornersville — a place all the way to one side of a racecourse where a boat goes in search of a mythical strategic advantage, and where the population is usually 1. Also called banging the corner.

corrected time — the official running time of a race, for a particular boat, after any relevant handicap time-on-distance or time-on-time correction formula has been applied.

cotter pin — a small, double-pronged metal pin used to keep another part from changing its position, such as keeping a nut from turning or a clevis pin from falling out. The pin is secured in place by separating the prongs' ends. Also called split pins. Circular cotter rings are also called ring-dings.

course — 1) Shorthand for racecourse. A course is made up of two or more legs that are denoted by marks. 2) A boat's actual travel direction, as opposed to her heading (the compass reading for where the boat's bow is pointing) or bearing (the direction to or from a particular location). Wind effects, current, and leeway are what cause heading and course to be different. Generally expressed in degrees or a cardinal heading.

courtesy hike – an extra hard hike to compensate for someone who is temporarily off the rail.

cover — 1) A tactical maneuver where a lead boat maintains an advantaged position by staying between the trailing boat and the wind or the next mark. This often requires tacking or jibing each time the trailing boat does, in order to maintain position. 2) The outer jacket of double-braid or braid-on-braid line composed of multiple strands of interwoven fiber.

Cox-Sprague Scoring System – a modified high point scoring system that awards scores based on both the number of earlier finishers and later finishers. See also: Bonus Point System, High Point System and Low Point System.

Cowes Week — an event billed as the largest and longest-running regatta in the world. Held in early August every year since 1826, except during the two World Wars. Over 1,000 boats participate in up to 40 races per day during Cowes Week. For more information, browse to http://www.cowesweek.co.uk.

crack / crack off — to ease the sheets and bear away, fall off, or foot.

crash boat — a small motorboat used to set, change, and retrieve inflatable marks on a racecourse. Also known as a mark boat. Compare to: committee boat.

crash jibe — whether a jibe is planned or accidental, the boom swings violently and in an uncontrolled manner from one side of the boat to the other.

crash tack — a sudden, unplanned, often graceless tack done to avoid a collision.

crest — the highest part of a wave.

crew — a competitor or team of competitors that operate a boat. A crew member.

cringle — a heavy metal ring or rope loop at a sail's edge. Used to secure the sail to a line or halyard.

CRO — an initialism for "club race officer." A US Sailing designated position. See also: race officer.

cross — 1) To pass ahead of a competitor on the opposite tack or jibe. Compare to: duck. 2) An indication or verbal confirmation from a boat on starboard tack to a competitor on port tack that they should cross in front instead of ducking behind. Also known as waving. British and Commonwealth sailors would say to "carry on."

cross hauler — a sail control used to angle a jib sheet's lead more toward a boat's centerline. This reduces the headsail's sheeting angle, increases the sail's angle of attack, and improves pointing ability. A basic rule of thumb is to be very wary of ever hauling the jib clew inboard of 7 degrees. Also known as an inhauler. See also: barber hauler, outgrabber, and twinger.

crossover block — a horizontally oriented sheave, mounted behind the clutch bank on either side of a coachroof, that is used to route a line to a winch on the opposite side. Also called a halyard turning block, winch feeder or winch turning block.

cross-sheeting — trimming a jib sheet from the weather rail either by using a turning block near the leeward primary winch to redirect the working sheet to the windward primary winch, or by holding the tail of the working sheet wrapped on the leeward primary winch turned by a winch grinding pedestal. Cross-sheeting keeps weight off the low side and on the high side, where it is needed most.

CRYA — Columbia River Yachting Association. For more information, browse to http://www.crya.us.

CSSA — Central States Sailing Association. For more information, browse to http://www.cssasailing.org.

cumuliform — describes clouds with vertical development in the form of rising mounds, domes, or towers.

cumulonimbus — a vertically developed cumulus cloud that extends through all altitude levels. It has a dark base and is often capped by an anvil-shaped cirriform cloud. Also called a thunderstorm cloud, a cumulonimbus is frequently accompanied by heavy showers, lightning, and thunder, and is sometimes accompanied by hail, tornadoes, or strong, gusty winds. Cumulonimbus clouds are heavy, dense clouds made up of water droplets in their lower portions and ice particles in their upper portions. The cumulo prefix suggests that the cloud is bumpy and unstable, while the nimbus part suggests that the cloud contains rain.

cumulus — low clouds composed of water droplets. Cumulus clouds look like white fluffy cotton balls. They usually have flat bases and lumpy tops. Small, separate cumuli are associated with fair weather (cumulus humilis). Cumulus clouds can form on fair weather days with daytime heating or with frontal passage, but if the atmosphere becomes unstable and strong upward air currents form, cumulus clouds can grow into cumulus congestus, or towering cumulus. These cloud tops can easily reach 20,000 feet or more into the troposphere and may produce a rain shower. Further development may create a cumulonimbus. Cumulus is derived from the Latin for "heap" and suggests that the cloud is bumpy and unstable.

cunningham — a sail control used to adjust the shape in a mainsail's lower third. It consists of a line passing through a loop or cringle in a mainsail's luff, just above its foot. Trimming a cunningham, usually through a block & tackle, alters a sail's luff tension and its maximum draft position. Named after Briggs Swift Cunningham Jr., the 1958 America's Cup winning captain. Also called a downhaul because it hauls down on the sail. Some cruising boats use a cunningham on their jib, too. Often referred to by cunni for short.

current — water flowing in a given direction due to wind, a venturi effect or gravity, such as river flow. British and Commonwealth sailors refer to the horizontal movement of water due to the rise and fall of the tide as the stream. See also: drift and set.

current wind — wind created by a boat's current-induced movement.

cutter — a sailboat with a single mast that is stepped more than one-third of the way aft from the bow and fitted with both a fore- or headstay and an inner stay. A cutter usually carries more than one headsail.

CYA — Canadian Yachting Association. For more information, browse to http://www.sailing.ca.

cyclone — a low-pressure area within which the wind is spiraling outward. In the northern Hemisphere, this is in a counter-clockwise pattern.

D

---

daggerboards — a pair of retractable keel-shaped appendages, but without fins or ballast bulbs, that are usually located forward of the keel on either side of the centerline. When a canting keel is swung to windward to keep the boat upright, the leeward daggerboard is lowered to supply lateral resistance, stopping the boat from slipping sideways. Compare to: canard.

daisy sail / daisy staysail — a high-aspect ratio, high-clewed, loose-luff sail, usually made from lightweight material. A wire or Spectra line in the luff allows it to be tensioned enough to resist sagging to leeward in strong winds. As a staysail, it is set to weather of a spinnaker or reacher, adding more power to the foretriangle. Set alone, it is used as a windseeker. A daisy's LP measurement is typically 85% of the boat's J measurement. Also referred to as a cheater.

danbuoy — a floating safety device thrown from a boat when a crew member goes overboard. It gives a visual reference to where the victim is located. It optionally has a light on top for reference at night.

DCYRA — Deep Creek Yacht Racing Association. For more information, browse to http://www.dcyra.org.

dead ahead — directly in front of.

dead downwind — directly to leeward. Often abbreviated DDW.

deadman — a colloquialism for a spinnaker made from heavyweight cloth and used during heavy winds. See also: chicken chute.

death roll — to run nearly dead downwind and experience a sea or steering-induced violent roll in combination with increasing wind strength; i.e., velocity. The rolling intensifies until either the crew reacts appropriately and regains control of the boat, or the boat capsizes. See also: broach.

de-bone — jargon for removing battens from a sail.

deck — a permanent horizontal structure that forms the cover over the hull and that acts as the primary working surface. Also known as the working deck.

deck organizer — a collection of turning blocks used to redirect and sort halyards and control lines coming from disparate angles or locations through to a clutch bank or to cleats. A deck organizer is often mounted on the coachroof and consists of a bracket that contains two or more horizontally oriented sheaves or turning blocks. The turning blocks may form a single layer or be in multiple layers, depending on how many lines the deck organizer needs to accommodate. Sometimes referred to as a collector.

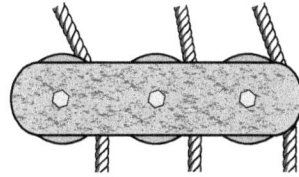

Deck Organizer

deck sweeper — slang for an overlapping headsail. See also: genoa.

delaminating — a failure in the bond between two layers, such as the inner and outer hull skins, or the overlapped seams of composite sail panels.

delivery crew — a limited number of paid or volunteer personnel who assist in operating a boat that is being repositioned to a race location, or back to her home port after a race. May be the same or different people than the race crew.

delivery sails — old or marginal sails that are used on a boat that is being delivered from one location to another. Doing so saves wear and tear on better sails, which are reserved for practice or racing.

delivery skipper — the paid or volunteer crew member who is in charge of a boat's crew and responsible for a boat and her crew's safety as she is being repositioned to a race location, or back to her home port after a race.

de-power — to luff and reduce a sail's power—pointing the boat too close to the wind, so the wind no longer fills the sails; to ease the sheet so that a sail flutters or flogs; or to sheet a sail in so hard that the airflow over it stalls. Compare to: feather.

dew point — the temperature at which dew would form from a volume of air, with its current moisture content. The point at which a volume of air is completely saturated with moisture.

DFL — an initialism for "dead … last." Slang for coming in dead last in a race. Use your imagination to figure out what the F stands for.

DGM — an initialism for "disqualification for gross misconduct and not excludable." The scoring abbreviation used to indicate that a boat showed up for, but is disqualified from, a scheduled race under *RRS-2009* rule 90.3(b). The boat has the maximum points allowed assessed against her when the race is scored using a Low Point System, and this race must be included with the boat's finishes, even if throw-outs are allowed.

diagonals — slang for the shrouds that run from a chain plate on deck to the lowest spreader's base, or the intermediate sets that run from a lower spreader's tip to the next highest spreader's base. Also known as Ds.

diamond shrouds — one or more sets of shrouds that attach to a mast equidistant above and below a spreader and that extend through the spreader tip. Diamond shrouds give extra strength to the mast. Some diamond shrouds attach to the mast via shroud tensioners run to the mast base. Also known as jumpers.

digital N course – a five-legged team racing course comprised of a windward leg followed by a reach, a run, another reach and a finish to windward.

dip pole jibe — one of two methods for jibing a symmetrical spinnaker. Done in several steps: raise the inboard spinnaker-pole-end to a pre-determined height, release the spinnaker pole from the working guy, ease the topping lift to allow the pole to dip down at the outboard end and swing through the foretriangle, place the new working guy into the pole's jaw, and then trim the topping lift to hoist the outboard pole end to the correct height on the new side, all as the boat is jibed and rotated under the spinnaker. Compare to: end-for-end jibe.

dip start — a starting maneuver where a boat remains on the course side of the start line and then dips behind the line just before the starting gun sounds, taking advantage of midline sag. If certain flags are displayed, this tactic will result in having to restart, getting a 20% scoring penalty or being disqualified. For penalties that are applied for rule violations at the start, see: *RRS-2009* I Flag Rule 30.1, Z Flag Rule 30.2, and Black Flag Rule 30.3. See also: ZFP.

directional puff — the remnants of a cat's paw or fan puff after its winds stop diverging and instead move in the source upper air mass's direction. If a directional puff comes from aft of the prevailing wind direction it is a lift or a lifted puff. If a directional puff comes from forward of the prevailing wind direction, it is a header or a headed puff.

dirty air — natural wind flow made turbulent by flowing over a boat and her sails, or by flowing over another object. Dirty air reduces sail efficiency, so a boat sailing in dirty air will sail more slowly than one in clear air. Sailing in dirty air on a beat allows boats ahead to pull farther ahead; sailing in dirty air on a run lets those behind catch up. Also called disturbed air. See also: blanket and wind shadow.

discard — the worst one or more individual race scores for a competitor are excluded from the scores used to calculate that competitor's overall score, if a certain number of races have been completed in a series. Individual scores subject to a DNE (i.e., disqualification not excludable) or DGM (i.e., disqualification for gross misconduct and not excludable) must be included in the overall score. Whether any scores are excluded, and if so, how many, are discussed in the applicable *Sailing Instructions*. Also known as a throw-out.

discontinuous rigging — a rigging configuration where shrouds are made up of relatively short rod or cable lengths, and where each span between spreaders, between a spreader and the mast, or between a spreader and the deck is terminated in a tang, turnbuckle, or other link.

dismast — to fully or partially lose a mast due to a critical component failure. A catastrophic event.

displacement hull — a boat hull type that plows through the water and displaces water equal to its own weight, rather than planing on top of the water without regard to the maximum amount of power added. Monohull keel racing boats are typically designed with displacement hulls. See also: hull speed and sled. Compare to: planing hull.

displacement/length ratio (DLR) — a comparison of how heavy a boat is compared to her waterline length. DLR is calculated by dividing a boat's displacement in long tons (2,240 pounds) by one one-hundredth of her waterline length in feet, cubed. Boats with a DLR under 150 are considered racing boats. Racer/cruisers have displacement to length ratios that generally fall in the range of 150 to 200. Modern cruising boats are typically in the range of 200 to 300. Boats with a DLR above 300 are considered heavy cruisers.

distance race — a race that is conducted on a large body of water or across several bodies of water and that lasts an extended period of time—from a few hours to several days or more. Distance races can begin near one port and finish near another, or they can return to the starting port after covering considerably more miles than a buoy race. Distance race strategy evolves as a race progresses. Early in the race, the strategic priorities are to find the most favorable weather pattern, to get to the weather pattern before the competition and to be better placed within that weather system. Of course, as competitors approach the finish mark, tactics shift more towards those of a buoy race, where the priorities are to stay between any opponents and the next mark or wind shift, and to consolidate any leverage gained. Also referred to as an offshore race or port-to-port race. See also: Chicago Mac, Newport-Bermuda, and Transpac.

disturbed air — natural wind flow made turbulent by flowing over a boat and her sails, or by flowing over another object. Disturbed air reduces sail efficiency, so a boat sailing in disturbed air will sail more slowly than one in clear air. Also called dirty air. See also: wind shadow.

ditch bag — an emergency survival kit. A supply of essential equipment, food stores, and water to be taken into a life raft if the crew has to abandon ship. Also known as an abandon ship bag or grab bag.

divergence — the expansion of an air mass's volume over a region. One cause of divergence is that the air aloft sinks. The opposite of convergence. Divergence at the atmosphere's upper levels enhances upward motion, and with it the potential for thunderstorm development—if other factors are also favorable.

dive the boat – to go in the water and clean a boat's bottom. Usually done while wearing fins, mask, and snorkel or while using scuba or snuba gear.

dive the clew — jargon for the act of pulling an overlapping genoa's clew around the mast, past the shrouds, and holding it down to keep it inside the lifelines, while the jib trimmer or grinder tails the jib sheet. It is possible to sit inboard of the new working jib sheet and to hold the sheet against the shroud until the clew reaches the shroud and then pull it back and down. When you jibe an asymmetrical spinnaker, you pull the clew from the headstay and run aft. The mast crew is often the person who dives the clew. Also known as tractoring. See also: tailer.

DIYRA — Dixie Inland Yacht Racing Association. For more information, browse to http://www.diyra.org.

DNC — an initialism for "did not compete." This scoring abbreviation is used to indicate that a boat failed to compete in a scheduled race. The boat has the maximum points allowed assessed against her when the race is scored using a Low Point System. The maximum allowed points may be equal to the total number of registered entrants, or it could be the number of entrants plus one or more points. See *RRS-2009* Appendix A. The applicable *Notice of Race* or *Sailing Instructions* may also modify the number of points assessed.

DND — an initialism for "disqualification not discardable." This is a no-longer-used scoring abbreviation that indicates a boat was disqualified from a race, had the maximum points allowed assessed against her, and could not discard or throw out those points from her overall score in a race series that allowed throw-outs. DNE has replaced this ruling.

DNE — an initialism for "disqualification not excludable." This scoring abbreviation is used to indicate that a boat showed up for, but is disqualified from, a scheduled race under *RRS-2009* rule 90.3(b). The boat has the maximum points allowed assessed against her when the race is scored using a Low Point System, and this race must be included with the boat's finishes, even if throw-outs are allowed. The applicable *Notice of Race* or *Sailing Instructions* may also modify the number of points assessed.

DNF — an initialism for "did not finish." This scoring abbreviation is used to indicate that a boat failed to complete a scheduled race or failed to complete the race within the allotted time. The boat has the maximum points allowed assessed against her when the race is scored using a Low Point System. The maximum points allowed might be different for an individual race than for a race that is part of a series longer than a regatta. See *RRS-2009* Appendix A. The applicable *Notice of Race* or *Sailing Instructions* may also modify the number of points assessed.

DNS — an initialism for "did not start." This scoring abbreviation is used to indicate that a boat showed up for, but failed to properly start, a scheduled race. The boat has the maximum points allowed assessed against her when the race is scored using a Low Point System. The maximum points allowed may be different for an individual race than for a race that is part of a series longer than a regatta. See *RRS-2009* Appendix A. The applicable *Notice of Race* or *Sailing Instructions* may also modify the number of points assessed.

dock — 1) To put a boat into a shore-side space at a man-made structure. 2) An artificially enclosed area where the water depth inside can be controlled. Compare to: pier and wharf. Note: Definitions of dock, pier, and wharf vary from person to person and place to place, with much overlap and confusion. In broad terms, each refers to a man-made structure that extends from land over or parallel to water, with piles or pillars for support, or floating on a buoyant platform that is constructed for foot or vehicle traffic and where boats can moor. British and Commonwealth sailors use the term slipway. See also: slip.

dockominium — a boat slip purchased like real estate. It grants the owner perpetual ownership and tax write-offs for interest paid, if the docked boat is used as a second home.

dodger — a canvas or hard-shell structure erected over a coachroof to protect the cockpit and the crew within from wind and sea spray.

doghouse — slang used for both the coachroof—or, more specifically, the cover over the companionway— and the saloon.

dogs in the doghouse — jargon for the act of sending a few crew members down below when the winds are really light. There, they can relax on the leeward cushions near the mast. This eliminates the wind drag from their being on deck (and clogging the slot), while their weight is concentrated closer to the boat's center of gravity. This also helps to reduce pitching in leftover waves and swell. Not always fun for the crew, but they can get out of the sun, have some food, and catch up on some reading. Crew sent below are also sometimes referred to as bilge buddies or mushrooms, because it is dark and wet below. See also: sewer.

dog the watch / dog watch — a way of rotating crew through the worst hours of standing watch by either having an odd number of watches per day, or dividing one watch in half and requiring crew to stand only half a watch. For example: having three 4-hour watches between 6:00 am and 6:00 pm and four 3-hour watches between 6:00 pm and 6:00 am.

donuts — slang for shackle guards, which are large-diameter plastic line guards that are placed around an eye-spliced spinnaker guy at a snap shackle. These prevent the shackle from jamming in the spinnaker pole's jaw. Smaller-diameter plastic balls are also used on halyards to prevent shackles from jamming in their sheaves.

double-handed — describes sailing with only two crew aboard. Some races are limited to only double-handed entrants, while others may have specific double-handed classes. See also: Chicago Mac and Transpac.

double-headed — describes sailing with two sails set forward of the mast. For example, a cutter rig with a jib on the headstay and a staysail on the innerstay, or a sloop with a spinnaker flying forward of the headstay and a loose-luff spinnaker staysail tacked to a mid-bow D ring.

double rights — a boat in a controlling position because she has gained the privilege of right-of-way from two or more rules simultaneously. For example, a boat on the inside of an overlap and to leeward as she approaches a weather mark gains right-of-way from *RRS-2009* rule 11 (i.e., windward/leeward overlap) and *RRS-2009* rule 18.2(a) (i.e., inside of an overlap). With double rights, a boat can perform a more advantageous tactical rounding as opposed to a seamanlike rounding.

douse — to lower a sail quickly. The opposite of hoist. Also known as a drop, strip, or takedown.

dousing leash — a line connected around the sheet of, or connected onto the clew of, a spinnaker about to be doused after a peel. It is used as an aid in dousing the chute as the lazy guy normally used in a douse is being used for the peel. Also called a stripper leash.

down — away from the direction from which the wind blows. To head down is to turn the bow away from the wind.

downburst — a severe localized downward rush of air that produces a damaging wind blast on or close to the surface of the water. Downbursts occur in severe thunderstorm regions, where the air is accelerated downward by exceptionally strong evaporative cooling (i.e., a dry downburst) or by very heavy rain that drags dry air down with it (i.e., a wet downburst). When the rapidly descending air strikes the ground, it spreads outward in all directions. See also: microburst.

downdraft — a small-scale column of rapidly sinking air. Often accompanied by precipitation. See also: updraft.

downhaul — 1) A line used to control the vertical movement of a spar or boom's outboard end. On a spinnaker pole, this line is sometimes referred to as a foreguy, though guys typically control a spar in a horizontal or inclined position. A downhaul is adjusted in unison with the afterguy, spinnaker sheet and topping lift to form the spinnaker into the most efficient shape and to position the spinnaker at the most effective angle to the wind. A downhaul is part of the running rigging. 2) The device that pulls down on a sail's luff, such as on a cruising jib, is sometimes referred to as a downhaul instead of a cunningham.

down-the-mine — slang for the bow of a boat getting buried in the back or bottom of a wave. British and Commonwealth sailors are likely to use this term.

downwind — away from the direction from which the wind blows. The opposite of upwind. Also known as offwind. See also: leeward.

downwind leg — a racecourse leg where a boat sails a series of reaches or sails on a downwind run, and may need to jibe one or more times to arrive at the leeward mark. Also called the offwind leg.

draft — 1) The amount or degree of curvature in a sail's horizontal cross-section; its camber. Draft is measured perpendicular to the chord, a straight line that runs between the leech and the luff. Also called belly or depth. 2) How deep a boat is immersed when she is bearing a given load. Measured vertically from the waterline to the lowest part of a boat's keel. A boat's draft depth plus a safety factor is the minimum water depth in which she can stay afloat.

draft lines / draft stripes — a sail's horizontal lines or stripes and vertical ticks that are used as visual references for adjusting sail shape, for example as an aid in positioning draft location and determining draft depth. Also called camber stripes.

draft location / draft position — the point on a sail where the draft is the greatest. This point is measured along the sail's chord line and is expressed as a percentage of the chord length from the sail's luff; e.g., 40% back. See also: cunningham and jib lead car.

Dramamine — an over-the-counter antiemetic medication used to treat and prevent motion sickness, nausea, and vomiting. Dramamine is a registered trademark of McNeil-PPC, Inc. Its generic name is dimenhydrinate. See also: Bonine and Transderm-Scop.

drift — a reference for the speed at which current flows. See also: set.

drifter — 1) Winds so light that a boat under sail cannot maintain steerage. See also: becalmed, parked up, and zephyr. 2) A genoa that is made from lightweight material and is used when a boat is reaching or running in light air. See also: light sails.

drogue — a device that is deployed off the stern of a boat to slow her forward motion and to keep her hull parallel to the wind and perpendicular to the waves, when she is being driven before the wind while underway. See also: warp. Compare to: sea anchor.

droop hiking — sitting with your posterior and upper body extended beyond the outer edge of a boat's deck, with only your legs inside the boat and usually with your feet hooked under a strap. Done to counteract excessive heeling. Also known as legs-in hiking.

drop — to lower a sail quickly. The opposite of hoist. Also known as a strip or takedown. A colloquial term for douse.

drop-in buoy — an inflatable buoy that is held in place by one or more anchors and that is temporarily set as a mark. See also: mark.

dry line — the boundary that separates warm, dry air from warm, moist air. The difference between the two air masses may be significant. A dry line is usually a boundary of instability along which thunderstorms form.

DRYRA — Detroit Regional Yacht Racing Association. For more information, browse to http://www.drya.org.

dry sailing — 1) When boats are kept on shore instead of anchored or moored in the water. This practice prevents undesirable marine growth and the attendant absorption of moisture into it. 2) Dry sailing is also a colloquialism for describing sailing maneuvers by using your hands to represent courses, heel angles, and tactics, usually as part of a postmortem conducted in a drinking establishment.

drysuit — an exterior protection clothing layer made with a waterproof outer shell, watertight zippers and seams, watertight hood, face seal for wind and water protection, detachable mitts, and neoprene wrist and ankle seals. All to prevent water from getting in. Some models come with attached boots or latex socks. Used in severe conditions to enable crew to work in heavy spray or on-deck waves without suffering too severely from cold or hypothermia. Drysuits are more comfortable to move around in and easier to get into and out of than wetsuits. They keep clothing dry but provide little insulation. Warmth is controlled with insulating layers worn under the drysuit.

DSQ — an initialism for "disqualified." The scoring abbreviation used to indicate that a boat showed up for, but is disqualified from, a scheduled race. The boat has the maximum points allowed assessed against her when the race is scored using a Low Point System. The maximum points allowed may be different for an individual race than for a race that is part of a series longer than a regatta. See *RRS-2009* Appendix A. The applicable *Notice of Race* or *Sailing Instructions* may also modify the number of points assessed.

dual-groove head foil — a slotted headstay system that contains two luff grooves to accommodate and provide continuous support for jibs or genoas that use boltrope. Usually made from aerodynamically shaped extruded aluminum or plastic and fitted over the headstay or forestay. A headsail is secured at the luff by sliding its luff tape/boltrope through a pre-feeder and then into the head foil feeder and up a groove. A dual-groove head foil allows for hoisting a second headsail in the second groove before dousing the first, so a boat can avoid running bare headed and losing performance. Harken's brand is called Carbo Racing Foil. Schaefer Marine's brand name is Tuff Luff. See also: jib peel and spinnaker peel.

duck — to pass behind an opponent who is crossing on the opposite tack. If this is done well and early enough, the ducking boat accelerates as she bears off to a reach to pass behind the other boat and then heads up to close-hauled (for example, if sailing upwind) by the time she crosses the other boat's stern. The main is eased to allow the boat to bear off, and then the jib is eased for proper trim. As you head up, the main is trimmed to help the turn, and then the jib is trimmed after the bow comes up. Also known as dipping or taking a stern. Compare to: cross.

dummy jibe — a tactical maneuver where the helmsman initiates a jibe, but returns to the original course as the boat approaches dead downwind. A fake-out. Also called a false jibe or half jibe.

dummy tack — a tactical maneuver where the helmsman initiates a tack, but returns to the original course either as the bow approaches head-to-wind or just before the headsail begins to fill on the new side. A fake-out. Also called a false tack or half tack.

dying wind — a steadily diminishing wind pressure.

E

---

ease — to loosen or let out whatever is being eased, while keeping it under control. To pay out. Sometimes the phrase free off is used. Compare to: blow.

ease & squeeze — the process of easing the sails as a puff approaches, which allows you to gain more power, and then trimming in (i.e., squeezing the leeches) as the boat accelerates, which allows you to point higher. Compare to: scallop.

EBYRA — Eastchester Bay Yacht Racing Association. For more information, browse to http://www.ebyra.org.

ECSA — Eastern Connecticut Sailing Association. For more information, browse to http://www.ecsa.net.

elephant ass — a descriptive term for a spinnaker's head that folds in or collapses along its center seam. Causes include having the pole set too high or having the lead set too far back (both of which can be adjusted), and material that is stretched out on either side of the center seam (requires a re-cut).

ELISA — Eastern Long Island Sailing Association. For more information, browse to http://www.elisailing.org.

E measurement — the length of a boom from its tack ring to its outer limit mark or black band. A mainsail's foot length from tack to clew.

emergency tiller — a tiller designed for use if wheel steering fails.

ENC — an initialism for "electronic navigation chart." A nautical chart for use in chart plotters and GPS receivers.

end-for-end jibe — one of two methods for jibing a spinnaker. Done in several steps: release the spinnaker pole from the working guy and from the mast simultaneously, rotate the pole end-for-end, place the end previously on

the mast onto the new working guy, and then connect the end previously on
the guy onto the mast, all as the boat is jibed and rotated under the spinnaker.
Compare to: dip pole jibe.

envelope — a reference to the amount you are able to steer to either side of a
boat's current optimal sailing angle without diminishing velocity made good
(VMG). Depending on conditions and sail shape, the envelope upwind can
be as narrow as one or two degrees, or as wide as five degrees. Downwind, the
envelope can be as wide as 25 degrees. Also called the groove, steering envelope
or steering groove.

envelope drop — a leeward spinnaker douse, where the kite is brought under
the main's loose foot and then down the companionway. See also: letterbox
douse.

EPIRB — an acronym for "Electronic Position-Indicating Radio Beacon."
An emergency signal beacon that can be triggered manually or automatically
when a rescue is needed. It uses a radio signal and a unique digital code to alert
Cospas-Sarsat satellites or passing airplanes to a person or a boat's position.
The digital code is used to locate pre-registered information about the EPIRB's
possessor, such as vessel name and type, owner's name, and contact information.
An EPIRB can be a floating canister carried aboard a boat. Individual crew can
wear one as a watch, within their clothing, or around their neck, so they can be
located if they get washed overboard. See also: GPIRB, PLB and VPIRB.

equatorial air mass — an air mass that originates and derives its temperature
and moisture characteristics from the region near the Equator.

Equipment Rules of Sailing — the rules, as published by the International
Sailing Federation (ISAF) and as adopted by each national authority, that
govern how and what equipment is used in yacht races.

establishing a range — aligning two or more objects, such as a mark and an
object on shore, and observing whether the relationship between the objects
remains constant. Used as a way to judge your position. Also called a line sight,
ranging or transit.

exclusion zone — an area that the applicable *Sailing Instructions* designate
as off-limits or out-of-bounds to competitors. An exclusion zone may be
established for the competitors' safety, to avoid commercial traffic, or for other
reasons. The area may be defined by geographic points, GPS coordinates, or
any other means. If a competitor violates an exclusion zone, another entrant
or the race committee may protest, resulting in a penalty for the competitor.
Compare to: scoring gate.

exercise the halyard — to ease or trim a sail's halyard a few inches, usually on a spinnaker that has been flying for several hours, in order to spread chafing effects over a greater part of the line. After some time has elapsed, someone is sent up the mast to swap halyards and bring down the old one. Its shackle is then re-spliced to an un-chafed halyard portion.

external halyard — a halyard, usually for a spinnaker, run along an external surface of a mast instead of within the mast. It touches only sheaves and a winch. This is done to reduce chafing on the halyard where it passes through the mast entrance and sheave box. Used with a wing block, the halyard can double as a spare for a jib or main, too.

eye candy — an attractive crew member who is onboard just for his or her looks. Also referred to as boat fluff, bow candy, deck fluff, deck jewelry, dock pop, or fashion statement.

eye splice — a permanent loop formed in a line's end, sometimes around a thimble or bail.

F

---

fairing — maximizing a keel, rudder, or hull's performance by grinding down high spots, filling in low spots, and matching the foil's shape to a template. This is done to make the foil symmetrical, uniform, and matched to the designer's intended shape. See also: fairing compound.

fairing compound — the material used to fill in low spots or to build up areas when fairing a hull, keel, or rudder. The compound, made from a mixture of epoxy and microscopic glass beads, microspheres, tiny hollow plastic spheres, or other low-density filler, adds volume without adding weight. Microlight is West Marine's brand of fairing compound. Awlfair is Awlgrips' brand. Also called bog, builder's bog, or fairing putty.

fairlead — 1) A device used to maintain or change a line's direction without chafing or fouling, and with minimal friction. 2) Describes what a line possesses when it can run smoothly to its destination. "It has a fairlead."

fairway — the middle of a channel.

fair wind — wind from a direction that allows a boat to sail to a desired destination without the need to tack, or wind that allows a boat to sail on her desired heading. Winds that fair change to a true wind direction more aft on a boat's sail plan. See also: free and lift (wind).

fall off — to steer away from a close-hauled or upwind course. To bear away or bear off. See also: footing.

falls — a reference to the line rove between the blocks of a block & tackle. When jibing a mainsail, some suggest grabbing the mainsheet by the falls to pull the boom to the other side. In more traditional nautical terms, falls describe the bitter end of a line rove through a block & tackle.

false jibe — a tactical maneuver where the helmsman initiates a jibe but returns to the original course as the boat approaches dead downwind. A fake-out. Also called a dummy jibe or half jibe.

false tack — a tactical maneuver where the helmsman initiates a tack but returns to the original course either as the bow approaches head-to-wind or just before the headsail begins to fill on the new side. A fake-out. Also called a dummy tack or half tack.

fan puff — downdraft or outflow winds that ripple the water's surface in a dark, paw-shaped pattern—the winds are diverging at the leading edge of a gust. A fan puff is often preceded by a lull. A good turbulence and wind shear indicator. Also referred to as a cat's paw.

fantasyland — a jocular term for the cockpit because the afterguard (typically stationed in the cockpit) must be dreaming if they think the crew can pull off the suggested tactics in the time allotted.

fast — secured. As in "make that line fast."

Fastnet — a 608-nautical-mile race that has been run in odd-numbered years since 1925. The race goes from Cowes, on the Isle of Wight in the United Kingdom; along the south coast; past the Scilly Isles; across the Irish Sea; around Fastnet Rock south of Ireland; and on to the finish line at Plymouth, England. See also: Cowes Week and Solent.

fat — a reference to a sail that is over-trimmed or a boat that is footing. See also: heavy. Compare to: light, luffing, and skinny.

fat head main — a mainsail with an oversized roach. The sail is designed with much more sailcloth aft of a straight line between its head and clew than a typical sail that comes to a point; i.e., a pin top. The head is also squared-off. This greatly increased roach makes the sail more elliptical and more efficient, and puts more sail area where the wind is both stronger and more consistent. The result is more sail power both upwind and downwind. The upper end of the leech automatically compensates for gusts with this design of sail, because of its tendency to twist off in a gust. A permanent backstay interferes with the over-dimensioned roach when you tack or jibe, so to swing the boom across, either reef the sail before the maneuver and shake the reef out after, or use top-mast backstays. Also known as a square-top main. See also: Chinese jibe and flicker.

favored end — the end of the start line that is positioned farther upwind than the other or that benefits from geographic shifts or currents more than the other. It also refers to the end of the finish line that can be reached sooner than the other due to beneficial current, wind shifts, or positioning. For example, if the wind is blowing perpendicular to the start line, then neither end is favored.

If the wind is blowing at an angle narrower than 90 degrees to one end, then that is the favored or biased end of the line. Absent other environmental factors, the race committee often sets the pin end more favored to discourage boats from bunching up at the committee-boat end. The favored end of the line may not be on the same side as the favored side of the course.

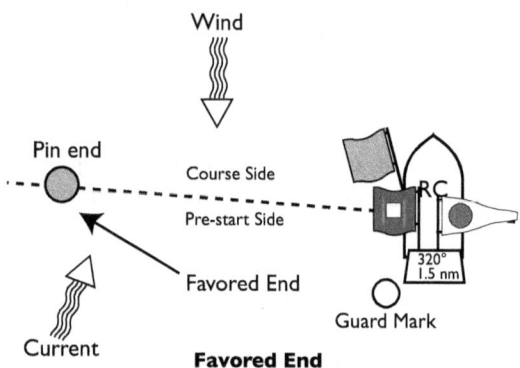

Favored End

favored side — one side of a course always offers an advantage over the other, due to one or more factors, including a persistent wind shift, the onset and subsequent veering of a sea/lake breeze, the dominance of a particular phase of a series of oscillating wind shifts, by favorable current, stronger wind, or smaller waves. Before the start, evaluate the conditions and decide which side is advantaged and then develop a plan to get to that side first. The favored side of the course may not be on the same side as the favored end of the line. See also: strategy and tactics.

feather — to steer closer to the wind during a puff to convert excess power in the sails into better pointing ability. See also: scallop.

feeder race — an informal or formal race among entrants to a regional or national regatta, while they travel from their home port to a major event. See also: SORC.

fender — an air- or foam-filled cushion, pad, or other protective object placed alongside a boat's hull, or between a boat and a pier, to prevent damage.

fend off — to use a fender or a board (or, dangerously, a body part) to push away from or as a cushion between a boat and an object (such as a deck, a pier, or another boat) with which the boat is about to collide.

fetch — 1) The ability to pass a mark to weather and leave it on the required side, without the need to tack. 2) A surface area over which waves are generated by a wind from a constant direction and speed. 3) Fetch is also the name given to the length of the fetch area—the effective distance the waves have traversed in open water, from their point of origin to the point where they break.

fid — 1) A tapered tool used to open trigger-release snap shackles, such as Tylaska, Wichard, or Gibb brands. Sometimes called a spike or tripping fid. See also: plug fid. 2) A hollow tool that has a tapered point and that is used for splicing line.

fid drop — a spinnaker douse where a fid or spike is used to open a trigger-release snap shackle at the sail's tack. Also called a spike drop. This dousing method is used during a spinnaker peel or during a letterbox drop.

figure-eight knot — a knot formed to look like the number eight; a stopper knot. It is tied into a line's end to prevent it from passing through a block, grommet, or cam cleat. You can release a figure eight with a bight under load, unlike with a regular figure-eight knot.

fine reaching — a point of sail where a boat is sailing towards the wind but lower (i.e., farther from the wind) than close-hauled. See also: close reaching.

fine-tuner — the second part of a two-part mainsheet trimming system. For example, a very powerful 16:1 tackle handles the fine-tuning while fast, primary mainsheet trim is done through the first part, a tackle with a 4:1 purchase.

finger dock — a narrow pier set at an angle to a larger pier. Also known as a finger pier.

finish — according to *RRS-2009*, a boat finishes when any part of her hull, crew, or equipment (in their normal position) crosses the finish line in the direction of the course from the last mark, either for the first time or after taking a penalty under rule 44.2 or under rule 28.1, after correcting an error made at the finishing line.

finish line — an invisible line usually designated as between a pole with a flag on the Race Committee boat and a white buoy that marks the line's pin end, though other marks may be used. The finish line is theoretically set perpendicular to the last leg of the racecourse. The suggested line length is 5 to 6 times the length of the largest boat in the fleet. See also: favored end.

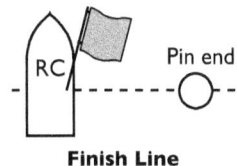

Finish Line

flag 'em — slang for protesting another boat. You signal a protest by promptly displaying a red protest flag and shouting, "Protest!" See also: protesterone and the room.

flake — to prepare a sail for storage by forming it into bights or folds in layers parallel to its foot. Doing so allows the sail to lie flat, while still allowing it to be hoisted quickly and easily without tangling. A sail that has no battens and that has been luff flaked and stored in a bag can be folded to one-third of its length for easier stowage without damaging the sail. A sail with battens has to be leech flaked if it is to be folded in thirds for stowage. See also: cheater flake, sail maker's flake, and z-fold. Line is also flaked into a single-layer coil to keep it neat and ready to run. A flat coil of line with its end in the center is known as a Flemish coil or Flemish flake.

flat — describes minimum draft in a sail, the opposite of full. See also: blade.

flattening reef — a sail control used to adjust the shape in a mainsail's lower third. A flattening reef consists of a line passing through a loop or cringle in a mainsail's leech, a short distance up from its clew. Tensioning a flattening reef removes fullness from a sail's lower third and has a similar effect to pulling the clew out past the black band. This is a control similar to a cunningham, but it is rarely used with masts that can bend. Also called a flattener.

fleet — the collection of boats in a class, section, or area. For tactical purposes, after the start the fleet consists of only those boats that are most threatening and close enough to attack or be attacked. Also referred to as the pack.

fleet racing — a race format where all competitors sail against each other at once. This format uses either a handicap system, or a system where boats compete boat-for-boat, such as with a one-design fleet. Compare to: match racing and team racing.

flicker — 1) a bent fiberglass arm that is connected to a masthead crane and hooked onto a permanent backstay. Used to lift the backstay out of the way of an over-sized roach on a mainsail during a tack or jibe, when tension on the backstay is eased. May be prohibited under some class or box rules. Also known as a whip. A product of Selden Mast. For more information, browse to http://www.seldenmast.com. 2) Flicker is also one of the many slang terms for a telltale.

float douse / float drop / float takedown — a spinnaker douse where the sail is brought down on a boat's leeward side. The foredeck gets control of the spinnaker—either by the foot or the lazy guy— and the halyard is blown. The sail's upper half floats out over the water and the foot or lazy guy is used to pull the spinnaker under the jib and onto the deck or down the forward hatch. A stretch & blow douse is a heavy air float drop, where the sheet is trimmed on hard to enable the foredeck to get the spinnaker under control and to keep the clews out of the water.

floater — a crew member whose core responsibility is to be an extra hand as needed. A floater may be asked to help repack spinnakers and organize and stow sails below decks. On deck, this crew member works with the foredeck, mast, and pit crew to help hoist and drop sails and may assist with the spinnaker pole during jibes. A floater is selected as much for his or her strength and agility as for his or her sailing ability. This crew member is also known by several other terms, some with more positive connotation than others, including caddy, mid-bow, runner, sewer, sewer rat, squirrel, and sweeper.

flog — describes a sail's uncontrolled, violent flapping in the wind. Flogging damages sailcloth, reduces sail performance, and shortens a sail's life. Ragging and slatting have similar meanings. See also: luff.

flop — slang for coming about or tacking, as in, "flop over to the other board."

flossing — using a soft line to clean weeds, lobster pots, or other flotsam from a keel or rudder's leading edge. Done by looping a line under the bow and working the line back and forth as it drifts aft. One alternative method is to tie knots in the line to aid in cleaning the hull and to dislodge trash. Another method is to work the line towards the keel, then drop one side and hold the other side firm, while water pressure pushes the line down the keel's leading edge and (you hope) sweeps the trash off the keel's leading and bottom edges. See also: weed stick.

fly — shorthand for masthead fly.

flyer — to take a significantly different course than the rest of the fleet or to execute a risky tactic or maneuver, in a desperate attempt to catch an advantageous lift and make big gains. The bigger the risk, the bigger the potential gain—or loss! Also spelled flier. See also: bang the corner and unobtainium.

flying block — a block secured by a length of line or a block at an adjustable control line's end. Examples are outgrabbers and twingers.

fog — water droplets suspended in the air at the Earth's surface. A cloud that has its base on the surface and that reduces visibility. If visibility is frequently reduced to 1/4 of a mile or less, the fog is termed dense fog.

foil — a daggerboard, keel centerboard, or rudder. Any shaped surface designed to maximize lift while minimizing drag in a given range of conditions. A foil may be designed to operate in any fluid, such as air or water, though generally in yacht racing, only surfaces that operate in water are referred to as foils. Surfaces directed into airflow are referred to as sails. The exception is a head foil: a device that contains one or more luff grooves to accommodate and provide continuous support for a jib or genoa's luff that uses boltrope. A head foil is usually made from aerodynamically shaped extruded aluminum or plastic fitted over the headstay or forestay.

following seas — sea swell that comes from astern and that does not overtake a boat. It is very difficult to control any boat when swell overtakes her and shoves her forward, causing the boat to skew broadside on to the wind and swell. See also: pooped.

follow-me flag — when the L flag is raised on a committee boat, competitors are notified to come within hailing distance or to follow the boat that is displaying the flag.

foot — 1) A sail's lower edge, opposite the head, between its luff and leech, and its tack and clew, on a trilateral sail—a sail with only three edges. Sometimes referred to as the skirt. 2) To sail a lower course or to bear off.

foot block — a large-diameter turning block.

foot cleat — slang referring to someone standing on a line that needs to be trimmed or eased, making the adjustment more difficult.

foot cord — an adjustable cord that runs inside a hollow hem along a sail's foot. Tightening the cord prevents the foot from fluttering. Also called a foot line or foot string.

footing (foot off) — sailing lower than close-hauled; to sail to windward slightly below an optimum course; to turn away from the wind. A boat picks up speed as her pointing angle decreases. The opposite of heading up. See also: fall off and fat.

foot mode — to trim and steer a boat for increased speed, usually by bearing off. Pointing ability is traded for speed. Also known as acceleration mode, drive mode or overdrive.

foredeck — a politically correct and gender-neutral term for the crew member who is involved in hoisting, dropping, and controlling headsails, etc. See also: bow.

foredeck drop — a windward spinnaker douse where the kite collapses against the jib (i.e., gets backwinded) and piles onto the deck as its halyard is eased.

Usually done after a no-pole jibe or after the pole is tripped and put on deck. See also: Mexican. Legend has it that during the 1992 America's Cup, Peter Isler coined the phrase "Casper douse" for when a crew member gets wrapped in the spinnaker during a foredeck drop.

foreguy — a line used to control a spar in a horizontal or inclined position. A part of the running rigging. Some people use the term to refer to the line that controls a spinnaker pole's outboard end. Compare to: downhaul.

forepeak — the forward-most unfinished storage area on a boat. On a racer/cruiser, the place where the forepeak has upholstery and cabinetry is referred to as a v-berth.

forereaching — a point of sail where a boat is sailing so close to the wind that her sails are partially luffing. If the boat is headed towards the 12:00 position, the wind is coming from either between the 11:00 and 12:00 position or between the 12:00 position and 1:00 position. Forereaching is used to slow a boat's motion while still maintaining some steerage, such as during heavy winds. See also: pinching. Compare to: in irons.

forestay — a composite fiber, or stainless steel wire or rod, that extends from a point below the masthead to a point on the foredeck at the stem or bow. A forestay is used for mast support and for carrying a headsail. Part of the standing rigging on a fractional rig set-up.

forestay track — a device that contains one or more luff grooves to accommodate and provide continuous support for a jib or genoa's luff that uses boltrope. A forestay track is usually made from aerodynamically shaped extruded aluminum or plastic fitted over the headstay or forestay. Also known as the head foil.

foretriangle — the triangle formed by the forestay or headstay, mast, and foredeck.

foretriangle dam — an alternative term for a spinnaker net, an object that fills the upper half of a foretriangle and prevents a spinnaker from wrapping around the headstay.

fornicatorium — slang for the cabin where the skipper takes his or her date... Also called the honeymoon suite.

forward — towards the front or the bow.

foul — an infraction of the *Racing Rules of Sailing.*

fouled — any device, item, or line that is entangled, jammed, or clogged. Examples are a line that is overwrapped on a winch, a liquid that is contaminated, and a boat's surface that is covered with undesirable marine growth.

foulies — slang for foul-weather gear. See also: drysuit, salopettes, shell, spray suit, and survival suit. Sailors from Britain and the Commonwealth use the term oilskins or waterproofs.

foul weather gear — an exterior layer of clothing protection that is waterproof and windproof. It keeps the wearer warm and dry in stormy conditions, and lets perspiration evaporate. The best-constructed clothing repels water and provides excellent ventilation, comfort, and breathability. It is flexible enough to allow unconstricted movement and sturdy enough to withstand the wear and tear of racing. Available in varying thicknesses for various temperature ranges and conditions. Also referred to as oilskins or waterproofs and by the slang term foulies.

fractional rig — a rigging configuration with the forestay, and sometimes the shrouds, attached to the mast at a point below that of the backstay. A fraction is used to designate the point on the mast where the forestay is connected. For example, 8/10 means that the forestay is connected eight-tenths of the way up the mast from the deck, or at 80% of mast height.

fraculate — to rake a mast forward while sailing downwind. This is done to get a deeper draft in the main and to get the spinnaker out from behind the main to allow more wind into the spinnaker.

fraculator — a line primarily used to help fraculate the mast, but that is also used to prevent a jib that has been teed-up from catching the wind and rising too soon or from interfering with a spinnaker jibe. A fraculator consists of a line connected to the stemhead at one end and with a clip or quick-release shackle at the other. The clip or shackle is connected to the bail on a jib halyard's shackle after the jib has been run through the pre-feeder and into the head foil. The mast can be raked forward by tensioning the jib halyard. Also referred to as a defraculator, fracalator, fractionator, frapilator, or magic string. Its abbreviated form is frac. Fraculator is probably derived from frapping—the drawing together of the several parts of a tackle that have already been tensioned.

frankenchute — slang for a spinnaker that has undergone many repairs.

freeboard — the distance from the waterline to the lowest point where water can enter a boat. Some racing boats have low freeboard for reduced weight, reduced wind resistance, and improved stability, but low freeboards allow waves to more easily wash over the deck. See also: coaming and topsides.

free — when referring to wind, from a true direction aft of abeam. A wind that frees changes to a true wind direction aft of abeam. See also: fair wind and lift.

fresh / freshen — when referring to wind, to be brisk or strong, or to grow stronger. See also: heavy air.

fresh breeze — wind velocity between 17 and 21 knots (19 to 24 miles per hour). Force 5 on the Beaufort wind scale. See also: heavy air.

frizzle line — an endless loop of light line or shock cord used to uncross a fouled spinnaker halyard without the need to climb the mast. The line runs around either sheaves or blocks at the top and base of a mast, with the exposed portion running down a mast's forward face. Alternatively, the line is completely exposed on the mast's forward edge, looping from the center to a mast's outer edge. A spinnaker halyard runs through a ring attached to the loop. The ring is normally positioned at the halyard sheave, to keep it out of the way. The ring is large enough that a halyard will easily pass through it, yet small enough that a shackle will not. There is typically a frizzle line for each spinnaker halyard. If a spinnaker halyard gets crossed over another halyard, its shackle is skied—pulled to the masthead—and the frizzle line is used to pull the halyard back down to its stowed position. A frizzle line is also used to free a halyard stuck behind the spreaders, or one that is accidentally skied. A temporary frizzle line can be made from a light line more than twice as long as the mast is high and run around the working halyard, with both ends tied to the fouled halyard's shackle. When you use fully exposed line on a masthead rig, the ring gets attached to the frizzle line with a short leash to allow the halyard to fly straight out from the sheave. A frizzle line is best utilized when you are sailing short- or single-handed. Possibly named for the frizzle mutation of chicken feathers; such mutated feathers grow curved outward instead of lying smoothly along the bird's body. One halyard crossed over another is also curved outward, instead of lying smoothly along the mast's face. Maybe a better term for this device is a defrizzle line, since it removes the outward curve.

frog legged — slang for a spinnaker that has each corner stopped or banded so it can be hoisted and pre-fed to the pole end without filling prematurely. So named because of the way the foot looks as it is folded and stuffed into a turtle. See also: spinnaker bands / spinnaker stops.

front — the boundary or transition zone between two air masses of different characteristics. A moving front is named for the advancing air mass; e.g., a cold front if colder air is advancing. A front moves at a speed proportional to the pressure gradient wind at right angles to it. A cold front moves at about 90% of the pressure gradient wind speed, and a warm front moves at about 75%.

frontal passage — the transition of a front over a specific point on the Earth's surface. A change in dew point and temperature, a shift in wind direction, and a change in atmospheric pressure indicate frontal passage. Precipitation and clouds may accompany a frontal passage.

frontsail — a jocular term for a headsail: any sail tacked aft of the headstay or forestay and forward of the forward-most mast, such as a genoa, jib, or storm jib.

FSA — Florida Sailing Association. For more information, browse to http://www.floridasailingassociation.org.

fuel scrubbing — pumping fuel through several filters to separate any water and to remove sludge, sediment, and biological organisms. Done to salvage a large quantity of contaminated fuel while simultaneously cleaning the fuel tank. The fuel is drawn from a tank by a hose directed into each corner, scrubbed, and then returned to the tank under pressure, which is used to power wash the tank's interior. The filtering process is repeated until the fuel appears clean. Also known as fuel polishing.

full and by — an antiquated term meaning to sail close-hauled with all sails full and drawing.

fully battened — having battens that run the full horizontal width of a sail.

furl — to wrap or roll a sail around the mast, spar, or stay to which the sail is attached.

furniture barge — a disparaging term for a cruising boat.

FVQ — Fédération de voile du Québec; Quebec Sailing Federation. For more information, browse to http://www.voile.qc.ca.

G

---

gale — on the Beaufort wind scale, a wind with speeds from 28 to 55 knots (32 to 63 miles per hour). For marine interests, gales are categorized as moderate or near (28 to 33 knots), fresh (34 to 40 knots), strong (41 to 47 knots), or whole (48 to 55 knots).

> "He that will not sail till all dangers are over must never put to sea."
>
> Dr. Thomas Fuller (1654 - 1734)
> British physician, preacher, and scholar

gardener — a crew member who is paid by a boat owner's business to supposedly work at that business but who in reality is paid to crew. Done as a way to get around rules that prohibit paid crew.

gaskets — nylon webbing in various lengths, often with a loop sewn into one end. Used to secure a flaked mainsail to a boom, to secure a jib flaked on deck after a douse, and for a million other uses. More commonly known as sail ties.

gassing — maneuvering your boat in such a way as to disturb the air flowing over another boat's sails—whether by design or not. The affected boat is "getting gassed." See also: disturbed air and lee bow. Compare to: herding, slam dunk, and tight cover.

gate — a pair of marks theoretically set perpendicular to the wind and set some width apart. A boat can choose to round either mark as long as the boat passes between them first from the proper direction. Gates are supposed to eliminate congestion at a mark when a fleet or class contains many competitors. Often, one mark is favored—because it is closer, less crowded, or towards the favored side of the course. Gates are most often used at the leeward end of a course but may be used at the windward end. The distance between the marks is approximately 8 to 10 times the boat length of the longest boats racing. Compare to: offset mark and scoring gate.

gate keeper — a boat that is in a controlling position, such as the inside boat at a mark or the leeward boat at a start line.

gauge — the lateral separation between two boats. Also known as the gap. See also: height and lane.

gear — a generic term for sailing equipment.

gel coat — the smooth outer skin of a hull built from fiberglass or carbon.

general recall — a recall that occurs when the race committee is unclear which competitors violated the starting sequence rules, or when there is an error in the starting sequence. The race committee initiates a general recall by displaying the First Substitute flag and by firing two sounds.

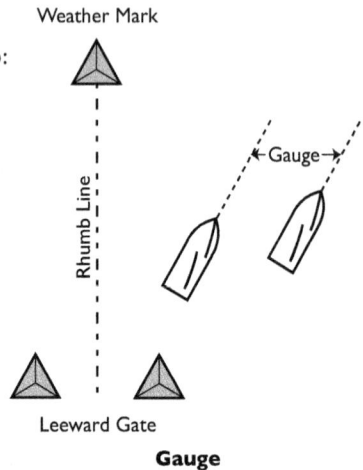

Weather Mark

Gauge

Rhumb Line

Leeward Gate

Gauge

genny / jenny — slang for a genoa. Occasionally used as slang for a generator.

genoa — a headsail (pronounced "headsul") or foresail: a triangle-shaped sail that is tacked aft of the headstay or forestay and that extends aft of the mast. An overlapping headsail. Also referred to as a deck sweeper, genny or jenny. In British and Commonwealth slang, it is called a lapper. See also: LP.

genoa staysail — an overlapping staysail designed for use upwind. Set under (i.e., to weather of) a genoa, the staysail's luff profile is adjusted to match that of the genoa, and is usually hoisted on a spinnaker topping lift.

geostrophic scale — the scale used to estimate pressure gradient wind speeds from a weather map that shows isobars at 4-millibar intervals.

GHCYBC — Greater Huntington Council of Yacht & Boat Clubs. For more information, browse to http://www.huntingtonboatingcouncil.org.

ghost — to make little forward progress due to a lack of wind. See also: becalmed, drifter, parked-up and zephyr.

girth — a measurement applied to an asymmetrical spinnaker that expresses the a-sail's width from its luff midpoint to its leech midpoint. The ratio of girth to foot also determines whether the sail is classified as an a-sail or a headsail. Also known as mid-girth.

give-way vessel — the boat that must yield when boats meet or cross, or when one boat is overtaking another, as specified in the *International Regulations for Preventing Collisions at Sea*, the *Inland Navigation Rules*, or the *Racing Rules of Sailing*. Also known as the burdened or keep-clear vessel. In general, a boat on port tack or that is overtaking another boat is the give-way vessel. Compare to: stand-on vessel.

GMT / Greenwich Mean Time — the time at the prime meridian in Greenwich, England. Now referred to as Universal Time, Coordinated (UTC).

Gold Cup course — the former name for the racecourse configuration that includes a right triangle, followed by windward and leeward legs, with the finish to leeward. This course is now referred to as a windward-leeward-triangle course.

gooseneck — a double-hinged connection on a boom's forward end, where it attaches to the mast. The gooseneck is the pivot that allows a boom's aft end to move from side to side or up and down in relation to the mast. A gooseneck commonly has a tack shackle or tack fitting to accommodate the mainsail's tack, and, optionally, a reefing hook.

government marks – government aids-to-navigation used as a mark.

GPIRB — an acronym for "GPS-equipped Electronic Position-Indicating Radio Beacon." An emergency signal beacon that can be triggered manually or automatically when a rescue is needed. Using a radio signal to transmit its exact location along with a unique digital code, it alerts Cospas-Sarsat satellites or passing airplanes to a person or a boat's position. The digital code is used to locate pre-registered information about the GPIRB's possessor, such as vessel name and type, owner's name and contact information, etc. A GPIRB can be a floating canister carried aboard a boat, or individual crew members can wear one as a watch, within their clothing, or around their neck, so they can be located should they be washed overboard.

GPS — an initialism for "global positioning system." A navigation system that determines the latitude and longitude of a receiver on Earth through the signals received from a satellite constellation in orbit approximately 12,000 miles above the Earth. GPS units determine their speed and travel direction from calculated position changes. GPS works in all weather conditions, anywhere in the world, 24 hours a day. The official United States Department of Defense name for GPS is NAVSTAR. GPS is currently the most technologically advanced electronic position fixing system, replacing LORAN and Radio Direction Finder.

grab bag — an emergency survival kit. See also: ditch bag.

grabbing a tow — the maneuver of riding in the wake trough of a faster boat ahead.

grab rails — handhold fittings mounted on a cabin's top and sides. Used for personal safety when you are moving about a boat.

gradient wind — steady horizontal air motion along curved parallel isobars or contours in an unchanging pressure or contour field, assuming a lack of friction, divergence, and convergence. Gradient wind blows parallel to the isobars shown on weather charts and at speeds inversely proportional to the distance between the isobars. Tightly spaced isobars indicate strong winds. Widely spaced isobars indicate weaker winds. Also referred to as pressure gradient wind.

grand-prix class — rules and specifications for boats that compete without time allowance handicaps, such as box-rule boats, as established by the Offshore Racing Congress (ORC).

grand-prix racing — professional racing teams that compete in a series that comprises several events.

Grand Ram — a term of affection for a sailor who has completed 50 Bayview Mac races.

great circle route — the shortest path between two points across the surface of the Earth, with those points lying along the arc of a great circle. A great circle has both the *same circumference* and the *same center* as the Earth. All meridians of longitude are great circles. The Equator is the only parallel of latitude that is a great circle. All other parallels are semi-great circles (also known as small circles). A great circle route appears as a curve when plotted on a Mercator chart. Between any two distant points, a great circle route is shorter than a rhumb line course. And, unless you are sailing directly North, South, or along the Equator, a great circle route is sailed as a series of intermediate rhumb line courses.

green water — large amounts of water, as opposed to spray, that washes over a deck.

grey water — any water that discharges from a sink or shower on a boat. There are no Federal restrictions on grey water discharge. State laws may be more restrictive.

GRIB — an acronym for "Gridded Binary" data files. GRIBs are computer-generated weather- and sea-condition forecasting models assembled in a commonly used data format. These data files are considerably more compact than regular weather charts. This makes them well suited for download via wireless means, but to use them, you need a computer and special display software. Forecast data can include wind speed and direction, current set and drift, tidal information, and sea temperature. The largest producer of GRIB files is the National Oceanic and Atmospheric Administration (NOAA), although the military, research institutions, and private companies also generate GRIB files. NOAA and some other providers offer their forecasts without charge, while some charge a subscription fee. These forecasts are typically published without human review.

grind — to turn a winch with a winch handle or to operate the handles on a grinding pedestal.

grinder — a crew member whose core responsibilities include grinding. The beneficial qualities of a grinder are strength and speed.

grinding pedestal — a device used to provide turning power to one or more deck-mounted winch drums. Either a single crew member or two crew members work in tandem to operate dual-opposing hand cranks that are arranged like bicycle pedals mounted atop the pedestal. Turning power is transferred to the winch drums through belts or shafts and gearboxes, or through a hydraulic system mounted below the cockpit floor. A grinding pedestal can operate at various speed-to-mechanical-advantage ratios.

grommets — metal eyelets in a sail, such as for bunting lines or reefing rings. See also: luff grommets.

groove — how sensitive boat performance is to helm movement. The amount you are able to steer to either side of a boat's current optimal sailing angle without negatively affecting velocity made good (VMG). Depending on the conditions and sail shape, the groove upwind can be as narrow as one or two degrees, or as wide as five degrees. Downwind, the groove can be as wide as 25 degrees. Flatter headsails and spinnakers create a narrower groove. As the draft in a headsail is moved forward the groove becomes wider and more forgiving. Headsails with a rounder entry offer a wider groove, but at the expense of pointing ability. The groove is also wider and a boat has more feel when the boat is heeled over. Also called the envelope, steering envelope, or steering groove.

gross tonnage rule — an unofficial, though no less persuasive, safety advisory that suggests smaller vessels, regardless of their rights under the formal Navigation Rules, stay clear of larger vessels.

ground fog — the fog created when radiational cooling at the Earth's surface lowers the temperature of the air near the ground to or below its initial dew point—the temperature at which it becomes completely saturated with moisture. Primarily takes place at night or early morning.

grounding — 1) Running aground. Where any part of a boat impacts the seabed or lakebed, and the boat's forward progress is halted. Sometimes done intentionally for bottom maintenance or temporary moorage. When done unintentionally, damage to the hull is possible. 2) Connecting electrical current to the Earth to dissipate static electricity or lightning strikes. See also: cone of protection.

GRP — an initialism for "glass reinforced plastic." Fiberglass. See also: gel coat.

GSBYRA — Great South Bay Yacht Racing Association. For more information, browse to http://www.gsbyra.org.

gsm — sailcloth weight expressed in grams per square meter.

guard — when referring to a VHF channel, to stand by and monitor that channel for radio announcements from the race committee.

guard mark — a small inflatable buoy whose purpose is to keep competitors away from the RC boat. It is set off a race committee boat's quarter, on the same side as the start or finish line, and is considered an extension of the boat. All boats must pass between the guard mark and the line's pin end, and must avoid touching the mark. Also known as a keep-away buoy or limiting buoy. See also: *RRS-2009* rule 31. Compare to: inner distance mark.

guide mark – a flag or buoy set approximately in the center of a long start line. A guard mark is used as a reference by competitors to estimate the start line's location. See also: line sight.

gunwales — pronounced "gunnels" to rhyme with "tunnels." The sides of the hull above the waterline and below the deck. See also: freeboard.

gust — a short-duration increase in true wind speed, on a scale of seconds or minutes. See also: velocity lift.

gust front — the leading edge of the cool, gusty surface winds produced by thunderstorm downdrafts.

guy — a line that supports or is used to control a spar in a horizontal or inclined position; e.g., the afterguy for the spinnaker pole.

GYA — Gulf Yachting Association. For more information, browse to http://www.gya.org.

gybe / gybing — British and Commonwealth sailors' way of spelling the maneuver of turning a boat so that her stern passes through the eye of the wind; to bring the wind that was once over one quarter now over the opposite quarter. In addition, the mainsail and headsail (or spinnaker) are brought to the opposite side. A boat is considered on the new tack once her stern passes through the eye of the wind. Also spelled jibe or jibing, but never jive or jiving. See also: accidental jibe. Compare to: tacking.

gybe drop — a gybe and spinnaker drop performed simultaneously, or in rapid succession, with the chute doused on the windward side. See also: Mexican.

gybe mark — a mark on a triangle or Olympic course; it is set at a 90-degree angle to the rhumb line and halfway between the windward mark and leeward mark. It is the turning point between the two downwind-reaching legs of the racecourse. Sometimes referred to as the reach or reaching mark.

gybe set — to round a weather mark, gybe, and then set a spinnaker. Compare to: bear away set.

gybing duel — to repeatedly gybe in an attempt to escape from a covering boat or to continue to cover an opponent. Usually happens between the two lead boats during the last downwind leg, or between two boats battling for overall position in the standings.

gybulator — a stiff, 6-inch-long tongue that protrudes upwards and that is tilted outward from an asymmetrical spinnaker's tack. This tongue's purpose is to keep a lazy sheet from dropping down over the bow, sprit, or pole when a spinnaker is configured for outside jibing.

H

---

half jibe — a tactical maneuver where the helmsman initiates a jibe but returns to the original course as the boat approaches dead downwind. A fake-out. Also called a dummy jibe or false jibe.

half tack — a tactical maneuver where the helmsman initiates a tack but returns to the original course either as the bow approaches head-to-wind or just before the headsail begins to fill on the new side. A fake-out. Also called a dummy tack or false tack.

halyard — a line or wire that is attached to a sail's head and that is used to hoist or raise it. An antiquated alternative is uphaul.

halyard lock — a device to hold a sail's head in place at the masthead. Can be as simple as a ferule that is on a halyard and that rests in a bracket with a tapered slot, or as complicated as a ratchet system with a trip line. The main advantages of using a lock are reducing mast compression; ensuring the mainsail is always hoisted to the black band, with the hoist position being unaffected by mast bend; eliminating luff load variations due to halyard stretch; and being able to reduce the halyard's size, which results in reduced weight aloft. On some installations, the sail's head is shackled to a permanent bracket at the masthead, which takes the entire load off the halyard and virtually eliminates halyard chafe. Someone has to ascend the mast to attach the shackle, but a trip line can be used to remotely open the shackle. Also referred to as a skyhook. Southern Spars calls theirs a strop lock.

hand — 1) How a line feels to the touch—its roughness, slipperiness, etc. 2) An antiquated term for a crew member.

hand bearing compass — a handheld compass used to take bearings. British and Commonwealth sailors call it a pork pie; United States sailors call it a hockey puck.

handcuffs — two trigger-release snap shackles that are joined at their bails or joined with a very short length of webbing and that are used in spinnaker peels. One snap shackle is connected to the spinnaker's tack and the other to a bracket or ring underneath the spinnaker pole's jaw. Once

Handcuffs

they are connected, the working guy/lazy sheet is spiked off with a fid and connected to the new spinnaker. One alternative is to use handcuffs with a slightly longer piece of webbing and connect one snap shackle directly around the guy, aft of the pole. Another alternative is to attach the snap shackle to the lazy sheet's bail. Also referred to as linked shackles or peeling shackles, and generally referred to as a peeling strop.

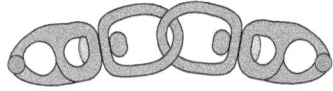

hanging locker — a storage place for clothing, especially wet clothing.

hanks — metal or plastic spring-loaded clips that are used to attach a sail's luff to a stay and that allow the sail to travel up and down the stay. For example, a staysail is hanked to an innerstay, and a jib is hanked to a headstay.

harbor — a man-made or natural location that is deep enough for boats to dock or moor and that provides protection from wind, current, and waves. Also known as a boat basin. See also: marina, pier, and wharf.

harbor racing — inshore racing around the marks of a multi-leg racecourse. See also: buoy racing.

harbor start — a directive that is in the *Notice of Race* or *Sailing Instructions* but that is not defined by the *Racing Rules of Sailing*, so the definition varies from place to place and regatta to regatta. May indicate the time the Race Committee intends to leave the harbor for the race course. May also indicate that all boats must remain at the dock until the specified time. A harbor start may also indicate that a race's start line will be located within the harbor.

hard cover — a tactical maneuver where a windward boat impedes a leeward boat's wind by keeping the leeward boat in the covering boat's wind shadow. This is done to slow the leeward boat down or to force her to change course. The covered boat can time her tacks to stay in phase with wind shifts and diminish any lead the covering boat has. Also referred to as tight cover.

harden up — to steer closer to the wind, usually by trimming; i.e., pulling in on the sheets.

hard over — to turn the helm or tiller as far as possible in one direction. See also: lock it up.

hard thrash — close-hauled sailing in rough water. A phrase used mostly by ocean racers. See also: Newport-Bermuda.

hatch — a sliding or hinged opening in a deck or coachroof. It provides passengers and crew access to the cabin or space below; an opening in a boat's deck fitted with a watertight cover.

Hawaiian rounding — a windward mark rounding where the inside boat (i.e., the one with rights) forces the outside boat a considerable distance farther outside—as in all the way to Hawaii. See also: proper course.

head — 1) Both the room where a toilet is housed as well as the toilet itself. Head derives from beakhead or knighthead, a grated working platform forward of the bow and below the bowsprit on ships built in the 16th century and later. The constant wave action washing over the grate made this an ideal location for sailors to relieve themselves. 2) A sail's top corner—the one that a halyard is connected to. On a trilateral sail—a sail with only three edges—the corner where the luff and leech meet.

headboard — the rigid, flat plates that are sandwiched onto a sail's head and fitted with a cringle. Designed to resist chafe from a metal shackle on a halyard rubbing through the sail's softer material.

head down — to turn away from the direction from which the wind blows. The opposite of head up. See also: bear away, fall off, and foot.

headed jibe — a downwind course that is affected by a header, which allows you to bear off and point more directly at the leeward mark.

headed puff — a short-duration increase in true wind speed with a shift in true wind direction more forward than the prevailing wind direction; e.g., fewer than 45 degrees aft of a close-hauled sailing course. See also: header. Compare to: lifted puff.

headed tack — an upwind course that is affected by a header, which causes you to either bear off and point farther from the direct course to the windward mark, or to tack.

header — a shift in true wind direction more forward on a boat's sail plan, which makes the apparent wind stronger and more forward. Upwind, a header causes you to bear off and to point farther from the direct course to the windward mark. Downwind, a header has the same effect, which causes you to bear off and to point more directly at the leeward mark. If you are sailing upwind and want to point as close as possible to the windward mark, sail on lifts and tack on headers. If you are sailing downwind and want to sail tighter and faster down the rhumb line, sail on headers and jibe on lifts. A header usually arrives in a puff moving laterally across a boat's course from forward of the prevailing wind direction; e.g., fewer than 45 degrees aft of a close-hauled sailing course. The opposite of a lift.

head foil — a slotted headstay system that accommodates and provides continuous support for a jib or genoa's luff that uses boltrope. A head foil is usually made from aerodynamically shaped extruded aluminum or plastic fitted over the headstay or forestay. A headsail is secured at the luff by sliding its luff tape/boltrope through a pre-feeder and then into the feeder for the head foil and up the groove. A dual-groove head foil allows for hoisting a second headsail in the second groove before dousing the first, so the boat can avoid running bare headed and losing performance. Tuff Luff is Schaefer Marine's brand name of twin groove headsail foil. Harken's brand is called Carbo Racing Foil. Also known as forestay track.

heading — the compass direction a boat's bow is pointing, as opposed to the course, which is a boat's actual travel direction, or bearing, which is the direction to or from a particular point. The effects of wind, current, and leeway are what cause the difference between heading and course.

headsail — (pronounced "headsul.") Any sail tacked aft of the headstay or forestay and forward of the forward-most mast, such as a genoa, jib, or storm jib. Sometimes referred to as a foresail.

headsail trimmer — a crew member whose core responsibility is to control the sheets and other control lines that set a headsail's shape for maximum performance. The same person may trim both upwind and downwind, or one trimmer may be responsible for headsails upwind while a different trimmer may be responsible for spinnakers downwind. Depending on a boat's size or just during starts, one trimmer may trim when the boat is on starboard tack and another trimmer may trim when the boat is on port tack.

headstay — a composite fiber, or stainless steel wire or rod, that extends from the masthead to a point on the foredeck at the boat's bow or stem. A headstay is used to support the mast and to carry a headsail. It is part of the standing rigging on a masthead rig set-up.

Headstay Tension

Less ◄— — — — — — — —► More

Less	More
•Light air	•Heavy air
•Increase sag	•Increase speed & point higher in flat water
•Increase draft depth (fuller)	•Decrease sag
•Increase power & drag	•Decrease draft depth (flatter)
•In waves & for acceleration	•Decrease power & drag
•Closes slot	•Opens slot
•Decrease twist - draft moves aft	•Increase twist - draft moves forward
•Rounder entry--reduced pointing with wider steering groove	•Flatter entry--better pointing with narrower steering groove
•With more sag, trim sheet to maintain trim	•With less sag, sheet must be eased to maintain trim
•With more sag, ease the halyard to maintain entry shape	•With less sag, trim the halyard to maintain entry shape

headstay sag — a headstay that deflects to leeward and aft due to the wind force on a sail hoisted on the headstay. Shortening or lengthening the headstay and adjusting the backstay affect sag. As headstay sag increases, a jib or genoa's draft depth increases and the luff's entry becomes more round. Headstay sag has a greater affect on a headsail's upper third because of that portion's narrow width.

head up — to turn the bow towards the wind, such as to a close-hauled course from a reaching course. If a boat heads up too much, she begins to pinch or luff and lose speed. See also: feather, forereaching, and point mode. Compare to: fall off or foot off.

heat it up — a directive to sail a higher sailing angle to increase boat speed.

heavy — refers to a sail that is over-trimmed or a boat that is footing. See also: fat. Compare to: light, luffing, and skinny.

heavy air — wind velocity that exceeds 12 knots (14 miles per hour). When racing in heavy air, taking advantage of wind shifts is a priority because puffs blow through so quickly that getting into a beneficial wind shift will do more to get a boat to the next mark sooner than will looking for more pressure. See also: fresh breeze.

heel — 1) a boat that temporarily leans to one side or the other along her longitudinal axis in response to any combination of wind pressure on her sails, wave action against her hull, or unbalanced crew or cargo weight. A repeated inclination to first one side and then the other is known as rolling; a continuous inclination is known as listing. 2) The bottom of a mast; its foot.

height — the comparative distance between one boat and another's relative distance to the next mark. The boat closer to the mark has height on the one farther away. See also: gauge and lane. Compare to: bow out.

height mode — trimming sails and flattening a boat to make the most progress to windward in moderate to heavy air and smooth water. Height mode can be achieved only after the boat attains full speed by trading speed for pointing ability. Also known as point mode. See also: feather and scallop.

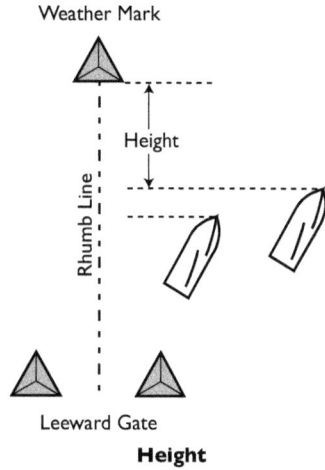

Weather Mark

Rhumb Line

Height

Leeward Gate

Height

helm — both the function of and the wheel used to steer a boat. See also: trick.

helm's alee — an alert by the helmsman to the crew that he or she is beginning a tacking maneuver. Sometimes the expression "Hard alee" is used for the same purpose, though this is really a command to the helmsman.

helmsman — the crew member whose core responsibilities include driving the boat as fast as possible and who works with the tactician to formulate tacks, jibes, and other maneuvers. With a short crew, the helm may also act as tactician. A helmsman's ability to maintain intense concentration for long durations is beneficial. A member of the afterguard. Also called the skipper. See also: stern ballast.

herding — any technique that encourages other boats to go the way the attacking boat wants them to go and that punishes the other boats for going where the attacking boat does not want them to go. An attacking boat herds other boats when she is fearful of what may happen if they get away. Herding reduces the leverage of both the attacking boat and the attacked boat. Also called corralling.

high — a comparatively high-pressure area with winds that spiral downward and outward—clockwise in the Northern Hemisphere and counterclockwise in the Southern Hemisphere. Compare to: low.

high clouds — cirriform clouds that are composed of ice crystals and that generally have bases between 16,500 and 40,000 feet (5-13 km) above the ground in the mid latitudes. The main high cloud types are cirrocumulus, cirrostratus, and cirrus.

High Point (scoring) System — a methodology used to select the winner of a race or series of races. In a High Point System, a finisher receives one point for each later finisher. The boat with the most cumulative points at the end of a race or series of races is the winner. The *Racing Rules of Sailing* does not define this rarely used scoring method. See also: Bonus Point System, Cox-Sprague Scoring System and Low Point System.

high-pressure system — a region of air where the barometric pressure is higher than the pressure in the area that surrounds it. In this weather system, the air is subsiding; has diverging, out-flowing winds; and rotates opposite the Earth's rotation—clockwise in the Northern Hemisphere and counterclockwise in the Southern Hemisphere. It is the opposite of a low-pressure system or cyclone. The winds are lighter near the center and increase in speed as they move towards the outer edge of a high-pressure system. To remain in wind when sailing near a high pressure system, stay at least two isobars (8 mb) away from the peak pressure. Known as an anti-cyclone to British and Commonwealth sailors.

High Pressure Center Wind Flow

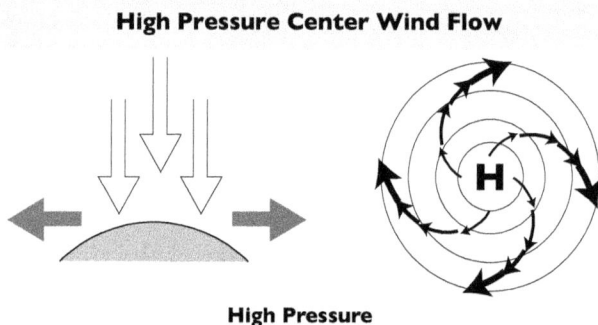

High Pressure

hike (hike out); hiking — to counteract excessive heeling by sitting on the toe rail with your legs extended outboard and leaning out to windward. Also, to lean out to leeward to induce heeling in very light air. *RRS-2009* rule 49.2 states, "When lifelines are required by the class rules or the *Sailing Instructions*, they shall be taut, and competitors shall not position any part of their torsos outside them, except briefly to perform a necessary task." The rule does allow the following: "On boats equipped with upper and lower lifelines of wire, a competitor sitting on the deck facing outboard with his waist inside the lower lifeline may have the upper part of his body outside the upper lifeline." Also called legs-out hiking. The British and Commonwealth term for this is "sit out." Compare to: dogs in the doghouse and droop hiking.

hiking stick — an extension added to a tiller that enables a helmsman to steer while hiking. Used when you want improved visibility or stability. Also called a tiller extension.

hip — a reference to a competitor positioned near a boat's windward quarter, overlapped or nearly so astern, as in "on our hip." A boat with another on her hip is limited in her ability to tack. See also: pin.

hitch — a family of knots used to secure a rope to another object. Examples are clove hitch, half hitch, and rolling hitch.

hockey puck — slang for a hand-bearing compass, a hand-held compass fitted with a sight. The compass is held near the eye with the sight pointed at a distant navigational aid, landmark, or object. The magnetic bearing to that object is displayed in a magnified window or on a digital screen. The name comes from the compass's size, shape, and weight. Known as a pork pie to British and Commonwealth sailors.

hole — a short-duration decrease in true wind speed, with the apparent wind direction moving forward on the boat's sail plan. Also called a lull.

hood — the structure raised above deck, over the cabin, to provide headroom in the cabin. Also called the coachroof or deckhouse.

Hook Race — Racine Yacht Club's Race to Door County. An annual 197-mile race along Lake Michigan's western shore. Also known as the Death's Door Challenge or the Poor Man's Mac. For more information, browse to http://www.racineyachtclub.org.

horizon job — hyperbole that implies a particular boat is so far ahead of the others that all the trailing boats can see is a small blip on the horizon.

horse collar — a horseshoe- or horse collar-shaped life-saving float that is thrown to someone who has fallen overboard. Its shape allows a person to wrap the device around his or her body, under the arms, and to float with his or her head well above water. A horse collar is typically mounted on a bracket attached to the stern pulpit, which makes it easily accessible during an emergency. A type of life preserver generally referred to as a ring buoy. Also known as a horseshoe buoy.

hot angles — when you sail at a higher sailing angle while on a reach or run. Provides increased boat speed compared to a lower sailing angle.

hot bunking — while a boat is on an overnight race, crew from different watches share one bunk because there are fewer bunks than crew.

hounds — the fittings used to connect a forestay and shrouds to a mast. See also: tang.

hourglass — describes when the middle section of a spinnaker gets twisted or tangled around itself while the upper and lower sections fill with air and expand. The situation becomes worse when the mid-section gets twisted around the headstay. The upper and lower sections fill and tighten the wrap. In either case, the spinnaker is creating more drag than driving force. Also known as a kite wrap or wineglass.

HRYRA — Hudson River Yacht Racing Association. For more information, browse to http://www.hryra.org.

HSA – initialism for headsail area. A calculation used to obtain a rating certificate.

hull factor — a value that represents the rating authority's assessment of a boat's features and her character and efficiency when compared to a basic cruising configuration. It is an attempt to incorporate otherwise unrated elements of a boat to determine where she fits on a scale with a pure cruiser on one end and a pure racer at the other. A boat with a hull factor of 7.5 or below is considered a cruiser. See IRC rule 27.2.

hull speed — the fastest a single hull displacement boat will go without the benefit of waves or current. Froude's Law (William Froude, 1810-1879) states that a displacement-hulled boat will go no faster than the wave length created by the hull as it moves through the water. This wave length is equal to 1.34 times the square root of the length of the hull at the waterline (LWL). Many boats can be overpowered or sail down the back of a wave and exceed this calculated maximum for short durations.

human banding — holding a spinnaker as it comes out of its turtle to keep it from filling too soon. Can be dangerous because a large spinnaker can carry away someone tangled within it.

human guy — a crew member who manually pushes the afterguy out abeam after a spinnaker pole has been tripped and put on deck. This is done to keep the spinnaker clews as wide as possible, to present more surface area to the wind, and to keep the spinnaker drawing as much as possible. Often done in preparation for a Mexican or other windward spinnaker douse. Human pole is an alternative and more accurate term.

human preventer — a crew member who stands on the cabin top and leans his or her butt against the boom to dampen its movement.

humidity — the measure of the atmosphere's water vapor content. Is expressed as a percentage of the air's current capacity.

HWJ — an initialism for "heavy weather jib." A headsail intended to provide minimal propulsion for a boat when sailing in extremely heavy air; it is not intended to be a racing sail. It is the same size as, or only slightly larger than, a storm jib. An HWJ lacks the orange panels of a storm jib, but often has a secondary method for attaching the luff, like with a storm jib. Usually not made with carbon fibers.

HYRA — Hawaii Yacht Racing Association. For more information, browse to http://www.hyra.us.

I

I flag rule — *RRS-2009* 30.1 states, "If flag I has been displayed, and any part of a boat's hull, crew or equipment is on the course side of the start line or one of its extensions during the last minute before her starting signal, she shall thereafter sail from the course side across an extension to the pre-start side before starting." Dipping the line is inadequate. If a boat is on the course side for any reason during the last minute of a start sequence (such as being over early), to start properly, she must sail around either end of the line before restarting. Also referred to as the round-an-end rule.

I measurement — the mast height above the deck. On fractional rigged boats, the height from the deck to the forestay attachment point.

ILYA — 1) Inland Lake Yachting Association. For more information, browse to http://www.ilya.org. 2) Inter-lake Yachting Association. For more information, browse to http://www.i-lya.com.

IMOCA — an acronym for the "International 60-foot Monohull Open Class Association." Established in 1991 and recognized by ISAF since 1998, it is the governing body for the Ocean Racing World Championships, which include the Vendée Globe, the Route du Rhum, and the Transat Jacques Vabre. IMOCA is an open class, so anything is permitted unless the rules specifically prohibit it. See also: *Equipment Rules of Sailing for 2009-2012* C.2.3. For more information, browse to http://www.imoca.org.

impeller — a rotor or wheel with blades mechanically driven or driven by fluid that flows past them. An impeller is used to pump water or propel objects through water or other fluids.

IMS — an initialism for "International Measurement System." A predictive rating system based on a boat's hull, rig, and weight measurements; her sail inventory; and the results of a velocity prediction program (VPP)—a complex computer program that estimates a specific boat's performance over a range of wind speeds and sailing angles. See also: ORR and PHRF.

inches of mercury (Hg) — the barometric pressure measurement unit related to the height of a column in a mercurial barometer, usually in a range between 27.00 and 31.00 inches. One inch of Hg equals 25.40005 millimeters. One inch of Hg equals 33.8637526 millibars.

inclining — short for inclining measurement, a stability test used to determine the vertical center of gravity of a boat and its ability to remain upright or return to its normal upright position after weight movement, waves, wind, etc. heel it over.

inclinometer — an instrument used to determine a boat's heel angle or fore and aft pitch angle. Also called a clinometer or tilt gauge. Lev-o-gage from Sun Company is a popular brand.

inhauler — a sail control used to angle a jib sheet's lead more toward a boat's centerline. This reduces the headsail's sheeting angle, increases the sail's angle of attack, and improves pointing ability. A basic rule of thumb is to be very wary of ever hauling the jib clew inboard of 7 degrees. Also known as a cross hauler. See also: barber hauler, outgrabber, and twinger.

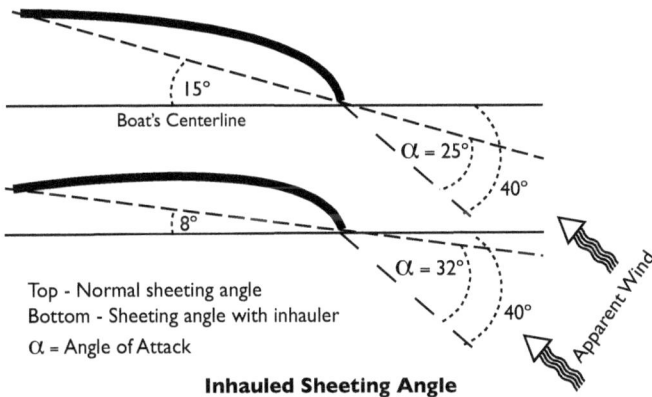

15°
Boat's Centerline
$\alpha = 25°$
40°

8°
$\alpha = 32°$
40°

Top - Normal sheeting angle
Bottom - Sheeting angle with inhauler
α = Angle of Attack

Apparent Wind

Inhauled Sheeting Angle

in irons — a point of sail where a boat has turned head-to-wind or has lost the wind, and is stuck and unable to make headway. If a boat is headed towards 12:00 and the wind is coming from 12:00, the boat is in irons. Compare to: forereaching and pinching.

Inland Navigation Rules — the rules of the road for boat operations in harbors, and on certain rivers, lakes, and inland waterways. See also: *COLREGS* and rules of the road.

inner distance mark — a small inflatable buoy set abeam of a race committee boat. Its two purposes are to keep race boats from scratching the RC boat, and to afford the race committee a better view of the line. When on the same side as the start line, an inner distance mark is set on or slightly to leeward of the line. When set on the same side as the finish line, it is set on or slightly to weather of the line. All boats must pass between the inner distance mark and the line's pin end or outer distance mark, and must avoid touching the mark. Mostly used at British- and Commonwealth-based races. Compare to: guard mark.

inshore racing — racing on a course of two or more legs that are denoted by marks. Also referred to as buoy racing, can racing, in-port racing, or mark racing. Some will argue that inshore racing is conducted in unprotected waters but within sight of land, while buoy racing is conducted in protected waters. The strategic priorities of inshore racing are to stay between any opponents and the next mark or wind shift, and to consolidate any leverage gained. Compare this to offshore racing, where the priorities are to find the most favorable weather pattern, to get there before the competition, and to be better placed within that weather system.

inside — between a competitor and a mark. As regards sails, the one in front of another, from the crew's perspective.

inside jibe — where an asymmetrical spinnaker's clew passes between its tack and the headstay or forestay during a jibe. Compare to: outside jibe. The deciding factor between doing an inside versus outside jibe may be the a-sail's size. On a large boat, such as an SC70 with an extremely large a-sail, there may not be enough room to complete an inside jibe. An outside jibe is the only option.

inside overlap — when two or more boats are on approach to a mark and are overlapped at the time the boat closest to the mark reaches the zone, the boat between a competitor and the mark (without regard to which one is closer to the mark) has an inside overlap. Any boat to the outside of a boat with an inside overlap must give the inside boat room to sail around the mark without regard to any other rules. See also: double rights and *RRS-2009* rule 18.2.

inside set / outside douse — to hoist a new sail inside or to windward of the working sail, and then douse the outside or leeward sail as a way to maintain speed and respond to wind shifts and wind velocity changes. See also: dual-groove head foil, jib peel, and spinnaker peel.

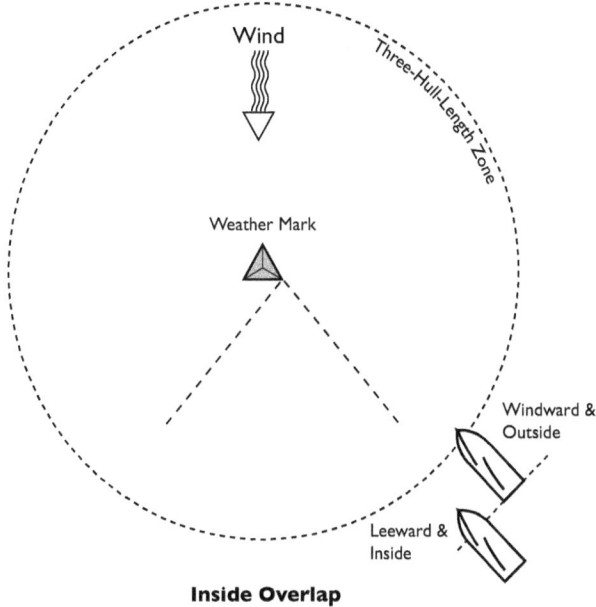

Inside Overlap

instability — 1) An atmospheric state where the vertical temperature distribution is such that an air parcel, if set in vertical motion, tends to move away from the parcel's original position with increasing speed. 2) A boat's inability to naturally return to its original waterline position after being disturbed.

instrument pod — two or more instrument displays within a single bracket. Often located on the aft face of a mast, just below the boom. See also: 007 and jumbo.

instrument repeater — a large, flat, lightweight, and low-power Liquid Crystal data display device (LCD) that displays information such as wind speed or direction, depth, or heading. Instrument repeaters are mounted within view of the helm, such as in an instrument pod or on the cabintop.

insulating layer — a middle clothing layer designed to keep heat in and cold out by creating a still or dead air layer between the fibers. Usually put on over a wicking or base layer. Two popular insulating materials are wool, which naturally wicks away moisture, and fleece, a synthetic material that maintains its insulating ability even when wet and that spreads the moisture out so the material dries quickly.

International Sailing Federation (ISAF) — the governing body for the sport of sailing in all its forms and throughout the world. ISAF is responsible for developing the rules and regulations applicable to sailing competitions and for training judges, umpires, and race administrators. ISAF is the organization responsible for overseeing an international sailor classification system—whether a sailor is an amateur (Category 1) or is employed in some capacity in the marine industry (Categories 2 and 3). ISAF publishes the *Racing Rules of Sailing*, the *Equipment Rules of Sailing*, and several codes and regulations. ISAF was formed in Paris 1907 and before 1996 was known as the International Yacht Racing Union. For more information, browse to http://www.sailing.org.

intertropical convergence zone — a zone within the tropics where the Northern Hemisphere's northeasterly trade winds meet the Southern Hemisphere's southeasterly trade winds. The zone lies within the equatorial air mass, which is near, but usually not on, the Equator.

in the hunt — a boat whose position or cumulative score offers her a reasonable chance of being a top finisher. A contender. See also: podium finish.

in their kit — a term used by British and Commonwealth sailors to mean "with their gear on."

intracoastal waterway — a 3,000-mile (4,800-km) waterway along the United States Atlantic and Gulf coasts, in two segments. One segment is the Gulf Intracoastal Waterway, which extends from Brownsville, Texas, to Carrabelle, Florida. The other is the Atlantic Intracoastal Waterway, which extends from Key West, Florida, to Norfolk, Virginia. Sometimes referred to as "the ditch," or, incorrectly, the intercoastal waterway.

inversion — 1) A departure from the usual increase or decrease of an atmospheric property with altitude. Inversion usually refers to an increase in temperature with an increase in altitude, which is the opposite of the usual temperature decrease with height. 2) A capsized boat that is completely inverted in the water.

inversion wrinkles — wrinkles that are in the mainsail and that extend from mid-mast to farther aft than mid-boom. Inversion wrinkles are usually caused by over-bending the mast. Inversion wrinkles rob the boat of valuable power. Also called over-bend wrinkles. See also: speed wrinkles.

IRC — a measurement-based handicap rating system that is subject to performance-based modifications. The rating is based on a boat's hull, her rig and weight measurements, her sail inventory, and the results of a velocity prediction program (VPP), a complex computer program that predicts a specific boat's performance over a range of wind speeds and sailing angles. Her rating may be modified as a result of the boat's actual performance. US Sailing is the IRC Rule Authority in the United States. In the United Kingdom, the Royal Ocean Racing Club's ratings office administers the ratings. The initials IRC do not expand to individual words. For more information, browse to http://www.rorcrating.com. See also: ORR, PHRF, and TCC.

iron genny / iron spinnaker — an auxiliary engine.

IRPCAS — an initialism for "*International Regulations for Preventing Collisions at Sea,*" what are more commonly referred to as the *COLREGS.* Navigation rules for boats operating in international waters outside of established lines of demarcation.

ISAF — an acronym for "International Sailing Federation."

island goat — a member of the Island Goat Sailing Society, whose members have sailed in the Chicago to Mackinac race 25 times or more. Also known as an old goat. A woman who has completed 25 Macs is called a nanny goat.

isobars — lines that are drawn on a weather map and that connect points of equal barometric pressure. Isobars extend around areas of high and low pressure. Pressure gradient wind speeds are inversely proportional to the distance between the isobars. Tightly spaced isobars indicate strong winds. Widely spaced isobars indicate weaker winds.

isochrone / isochrone curve — a curved line that connects points at which events occur at the same time at various locations. In route planning analysis, it is a curve that connects the distance a boat can travel by sailing on various sailing angles from a common starting point and for the same amount of time. See also: polar diagram, target boat speed and VMC.

isotherms — lines drawn on a weather map that connect points of equal air or water temperature.

J

jack line — a safety line. It runs from bow to stern, along both sides of the deck and inside the rail. Usually made of nylon webbing or, occasionally, wire rope. To minimize the risk of falling or being swept overboard, crew members clip into the jack line with a lanyard run from their harness. British and Commonwealth sailors use the term jackstay.

jam cleat — a horn cleat with a tapered lands under one horn. It uses mechanical jamming action to hold a line in place without slipping.

jet stream — a meandering, tube-like system of high-velocity (50 to 300 knots or 57 to 345 miles per hour) winds. The tube's width may exceed 100 miles and it may be one or more miles high. The jet stream is a westerly (i.e., flows east) and usually occurs between 30,000 and 40,000 feet in altitude. Two jet streams exist in each hemisphere: polar and subtropical.

jib — a headsail (pronounced "headsul") or foresail: a triangle-shaped sail that is set forward of the mast but that does not extend aft of the mast. A non-overlapping headsail. Compare to: genoa.

jib club — a small, moveable spar used on a jib's foot to enable self-tacking.

jibe — to turn a boat so that her stern passes through the eye of the wind, bringing the wind that was once over one quarter now over the opposite quarter. In addition, the mainsail and headsail (or spinnaker) are brought to the opposite side. A boat is considered on the new tack once her stern passes through the eye of the wind. Spelled gybe by British and Commonwealth sailors. See also: accidental jibe. Compare to: tacking.

jibe broach — a downwind, leeward broach, where the bow turns away from the wind and the boat heels considerably. Also referred to as a round down. See also: broach.

jibe drop — a jibe and spinnaker drop performed simultaneously or in rapid succession, with the chute doused on the windward side. See also: Mexican.

jibe mark — the turning point between two downwind reaching legs of a racecourse. For example, on a triangle or Olympic course, a mark set at a 90-degree angle to the rhumb line and half way between the windward mark and leeward mark. Sometimes referred to as a reach or reaching mark.

jibe set — to round a weather mark, jibe, and then set a spinnaker. Also called gybe set. Compare to: bear away set.

jibing duel — two competitors, one covering the other, repeatedly jibing. The covered boat jibes in an attempt to lose the covering boat. The covering boat jibes to maintain coverage. Usually happens during the last downwind leg between the two lead boats, or between two boats in a battle for overall position in the standings.

jib lead car — a device used to change a jib's sheeting angle fore and aft so that the sail has a more efficient shape. Lead cars travel on jib tracks that run parallel to a boat's centerline. The lead's position controls the tension on the leech and foot, as well as the draft location in the sail's upper third. The lead position also has an effect on the draft in the sail's lower third, though to a lesser degree. You adjust the car's position by manually operating a locking pin and sliding the car or by using a block & tackle or purchase system. See also: closed, open and twisted. Compare to: barber hauler and inhauler.

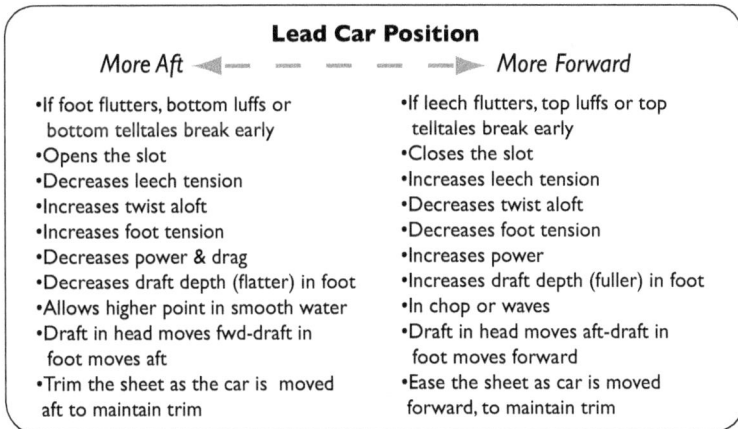

Lead Car Position

More Aft ◄◄━ ━ ━ ━ ━► More Forward

More Aft	More Forward
•If foot flutters, bottom luffs or bottom telltales break early	•If leech flutters, top luffs or top telltales break early
•Opens the slot	•Closes the slot
•Decreases leech tension	•Increases leech tension
•Increases twist aloft	•Decreases twist aloft
•Increases foot tension	•Decreases foot tension
•Decreases power & drag	•Increases power
•Decreases draft depth (flatter) in foot	•Increases draft depth (fuller) in foot
•Allows higher point in smooth water	•In chop or waves
•Draft in head moves fwd-draft in foot moves aft	•Draft in head moves aft-draft in foot moves forward
•Trim the sheet as the car is moved aft to maintain trim	•Ease the sheet as car is moved forward, to maintain trim

jib peel — to set a second headsail before dousing the first as a way to maintain speed and respond to wind shifts and wind velocity changes. The new sail is hoisted either outside (behind, from the crew's perspective) or inside (in front of) the working sail. As the new sail is trimmed in, the old sail is doused. Also referred to as a peel, a running change, or a straight-line headsail change. See also: inside set and outside set. Compare to: bare headed.

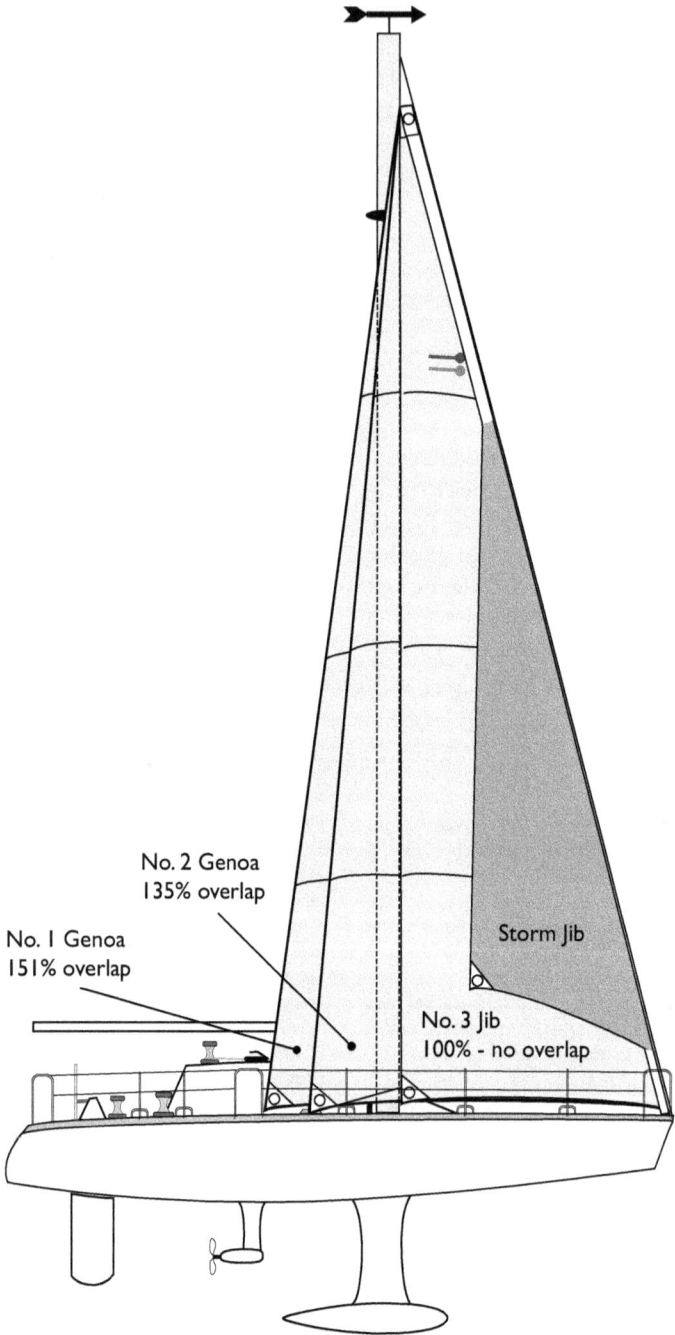

No. 2 Genoa
135% overlap

No. 1 Genoa
151% overlap

Storm Jib

No. 3 Jib
100% - no overlap

Jib Size Indications

jibsheet — a control line used to adjust a jib or genoa's shape and angle of attack to the wind.

jib size indications — headsails are sometimes referred to by a number (e.g., #1, #2, #3) to indicate their relative sail area as opposed to their specific size; a lower number indicates a larger sail area. Thus, a #1 is the largest jib or genoa on a boat, and is larger than a #2, etc. The description of light, medium, or heavy is sometimes added to indicate the sailcloth weight used and, by inference, the designed draft depth and relative wind speed for which the sail is designed. On a boat with an extensive suit of sails, sails may be referred to as J1, J2, J3, etc.; G1, G2, G3, etc.; and R1, R2, R3, etc., for the various sizes of jibs, genoas, and reaching sails, respectively.

jib top reacher — a large headsail used when a boat is sailing off the wind but not far enough down to set a spinnaker. Usually cut with a high clew (i.e., the foot angled upwards from tack to clew) to avoid catching the boat's bow wave at speed. The initialism "JT" is also used to refer to a jib top reacher.

jib tracks — the pathways on which jib lead cars travel and that run parallel to a boat's centerline. Boats may have a single track or an inner and outer track.

jib trimmer — a crew member whose core responsibility is to control the sheets and other control lines that set a headsail's shape for maximum performance. The same person may trim both upwind and downwind, or one trimmer may be responsible for headsails upwind while a different trimmer may be responsible for spinnakers downwind. Depending on a boat's size or just during starts, one trimmer may trim when the boat is on starboard tack and another trimmer may trim when the boat is on port tack.

J measurement — the foretriangle base, measured along the deck from the forestay pin to the mast's forward edge.

jockey pole — a short spar attached to the mast and set abeam (i.e., athwartships) just above the lifelines. Used to hold a spinnaker guy outside the lifelines, to keep the guy off the shrouds, and to provide a better angle for controlling a spinnaker pole's position—especially when it is close to the headstay while you are reaching. Also called a reaching strut.

JT — an initialism for "jib top reacher."

judge — a protest committee member. US Sailing certifies US Sailing judges. The International Sailing Federation certifies international judges. A judge is impartial and free of direction from race organizers or any other party.

jumbo — a large, flat, lightweight, and low-power Liquid Crystal data display (LCD) that displays information such as wind speed or direction. It is often within an instrument pod attached to a mast's aft face just below the boom. Also known as an instrument repeater.

jump — as it relates to halyards, to stand at a mast and quickly pull down on a halyard or pull a bight of halyard outwards from the mast, as another crew member winches it in—tails it—to hoist a sail. Also known as bumping or sweating.

jumpers — one or more sets of shrouds that attach to a mast equidistant above and below a spreader and that extend through the spreader tip to give extra strength to the mast. Some jumpers attach to a mast via shroud tensioners run to the mast base. Also known as diamond shrouds.

K

karate yachting — a colloquialism for describing sailing maneuvers by using your hands to represent courses, heel angles, and tactics, usually as part of a postmortem conducted in a drinking establishment. Also known as bar sailing, dry sailing, and hand sailing.

keel — a large ballast-filled beam or foil that gives a boat greater stability, additional lift, and resistance to sideways motion—leeway. It is often fixed and is located under the hull centerline. There are several designs for keels, including bulb, fin, full, and winged. A bulb keel is a fin keel with a teardrop-shaped ballast-filled bulb at the bottom. A bulb keel is designed to place the ballast as low as possible, therefore gaining the maximum possible leverage and thus the most righting moment in a comparatively shallower keel. The rudder is mounted separately from the keel. A fin keel is a narrow blade or foil whose fore-aft dimension is less than 50% of the hull's waterline. The rudder is mounted separately. A full or continuous keel runs nearly the entire length of the hull, beginning below the waterline at the bow or knuckle, back to the stern, and with a rudder integral to the keel's aft end. Winged keel design calls for horizontally oriented lead-filled winglets at the bottom of a fin. This places the ballast lower, like with a bulb keel, and provides additional lift to aid stability and heel, with reduced drag.

keelboat — a sailing vessel with a fixed keel, which provides lift, stability, and resistance to leeway.

keep clear vessel — an antiquated term for the boat that must yield when boats meet or cross, or when one boat is overtaking another. Was also known as the burdened vessel. Currently referred to as the give-way vessel. In general, a boat that is on port tack or that is overtaking another boat is the give-way vessel. See also: *COLREGS* and rules of the road. Compare to: stand-on vessel.

kelp cutter — a blade set into the leading edge of a keel or rudder, or a U-shaped cutter wrapped around the leading edge. A push rod is used to operate the cutter—either through a watertight seal or through a tube that extends above the waterline.

kelp stick — a long, flexible rod used to clean weeds, lobster pots, or other flotsam from a keel or rudder's leading edge. See also: weed stick.

kelp windows — small windows placed in a hull's bottom, just forward of the keel and to either side. Used to visually check whether kelp or other flotsam is fouling the keel. Usually not very informative as kelp tends to ride very high on a keel, while the view from these windows is farther down. A window placed directly over the keel's leading edge offers a more informative view. Another version, referred to as an endoscope, is a miniature, freely rotating periscope that extends downwards through hull fittings located at various places along a boat's bottom. This lets the crew view the boat's entire bottom, keel, rudder, and propeller.

Kevlar — a man-made, yellow/brown aramid fiber used for sails or composites for building hulls because of its exceptionally high tensile strength. In sails, Kevlar retains its shape better and is lighter than Dacron, but it is more expensive. It loses its good properties when exposed to the sun for extended periods. Kevlar is Dupont's brand name.

keyboard — a term used variously for the pit crew member, for the location where this crew member works, and for the clutch banks or stopper banks that hold halyards and control lines. Piano is also a term used. See also: pit and stopper bank.

Key West Race Week — an annual event, held in late January that hosts grand-prix and club racers from around the world. For more information, browse to http://www.premiere-racing.com.

king spoke — a mark on a helm or wheel; it indicates when the rudder is centered (i.e., in line with the keel). Often a piece of tape wrapped around a wheel's top center. Refers back to wooden sailing ship days, when an ornamented spoke on a ship's wheel indicated a centered rudder.

kite — a colloquial term for a spinnaker, because of the way it flies from strings on the wind. See also: spinnaker.

Kiwi — a colloquial term for a New Zealander or something from New Zealand.

Kiwi douse — a type of windward spinnaker douse. See also: Mexican.

knock — a wind shift that forces a boat to sail below her mean wind course. See also: header.

knockdown — slang for broaching. See jibe broach, leeward broach, or round down.

knockout – a match and team racing format in which the boats race until one has won a majority of the scheduled races. Single- or double-elimination rounds may also be used.

knot — 1) A speed measurement equal to one nautical mile per hour. See also: nautical mile. 2) To interweave one line with another, or to interweave a line through or around another object and onto itself to connect the line to the other object.

knot meter — a boatspeed indicator. Also known as the fun meter. See also: log.

knuckle — on a hull, the point where the bow meets the waterline. A reference point used to judge a boat's fore/aft balance.

L

ladder – a match and team racing format in which the winner or the top finishers from one round advance to the next round of competition.

lake breeze — a local wind that blows from a lake to the adjacent land near the surface; an onshore breeze. A lake breeze is caused by the temperature differential between relatively warmer land and a cooler adjacent body of water. The warmer, unstable air rising over the land draws air in from the water. The rising air is then re-circulated by a higher-level gradient wind that blows offshore. Predominant during the day, such a breeze reaches its maximum during early- to mid-afternoon. It blows in the opposite direction of a land breeze. See also: sea breeze.

lake effect — an air mass's change in temperature, humidity, stability, or momentum as it blows across a large lake, and the resulting weather phenomena over downwind areas.

Lake Ontario 300 — Port Credit Yacht Club's race around Lake Ontario. Also billed as the longest annually held fresh-water sailing race in the world. It is conducted over two courses: the 300-mile Duck Island course, and the shorter, more cruiser-friendly Scotch Bonnet course. For more information, browse to http://www.lo300.org.

laminar flow — fluid, such as air, that flows in smooth, parallel layers with no disruption between the layers. The opposite of turbulent flow. Attached, laminar fluid flow across the two sides of a foil at different speeds is what creates lift—Bernoulli's Principle. See also: attached flow and stall.

lance cleat — a spring-loaded cam set next to a toothed wedge. The cam and wedge come together to clamp their teeth on a line rove between them. See also: cam cleat.

land breeze — a coastal breeze that blows offshore, from the land to the sea. It is caused by the temperature differential between the relatively warmer sea surface and the cooler adjacent land. Predominant during the night, a land breeze reaches its maximum about dawn. A land breeze blows in the opposite direction of a sea breeze. Also referred to as a drainage breeze. Often a diurnal event; i.e., an action or event that occurs during a twenty-four hour cycle or that recurs every twenty-four hours.

lane — a boat's clear air position between two competitors: one to windward and one to leeward. A boat can maintain clear air and avoid both competitors' wind shadows by staying in the lane and not heading up or down. See also: gauge and height.

latitude — a reference to a position on the Earth's surface. It is expressed as so many degrees north or south of the Equator. Circles of latitude are imaginary lines around the Earth, are parallel to the Equator, and represent one degree of arc. The Equator is zero degrees, the North Pole is 90 degrees north, and the South Pole is 90 degrees south. Degrees of latitude can be further subdivided into minutes and seconds: with 60 minutes per degree and 60 seconds per minute. One degree of latitude is equal to approximately 60 nautical miles, one minute of latitude is equal to approximately one nautical mile and one second is equal to approximately 100 feet. A position is expressed as degrees, minutes, and seconds; or degrees and decimal minutes. Also known as a parallel. Compare to: longitude.

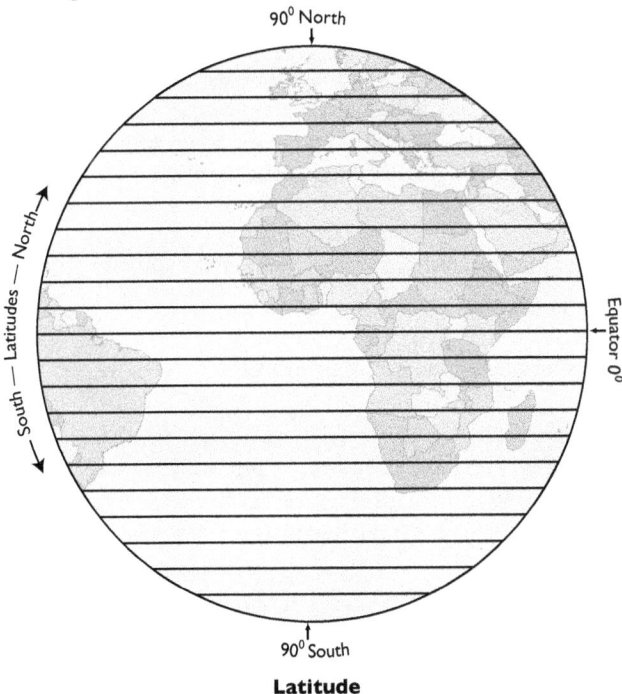

Latitude

lay / laying — sailing a course that will clear a mark or obstacle without any need to tack or jibe. See also: fetch.

layline — an imaginary line that leads up to a windward mark and along which you can sail an optimum close-hauled course and clear the mark on the desired side in the existing wind. Also refers to the line down to a leeward mark and along which you sail fastest to the mark. When you reach this point, you are said to be "on the layline." Going beyond the layline means you are sailing a greater distance to reach the mark or finish line, which is referred to as overstanding. The two marks that make up a leeward gate would each have their own laylines, as would each mark that makes up a start or finish line. Laylines move as the winds shift.

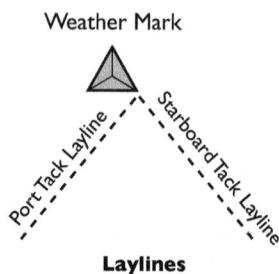

Weather Mark

Laylines

lazarette — a small storage locker at a boat's stern. Often a cockpit seat base.

lazy guy / lazy sheet — a non-loaded line that is run for later use. Examples are a lazy spinnaker afterguy, a non-loaded spinnaker afterguy that is rigged and connected to a spinnaker's clew that carries an active spinnaker sheet; a lazy spinnaker sheet, a non-loaded spinnaker sheet that is connected to a spinnaker's tack that carries a working spinnaker guy; and a lazy jib sheet, a non-loaded jib sheet that is on a boat's weather side and that is connected to a jib's clew that is being controlled by a working jib sheet on a boat's leeward side. A lazy sheet is also referred to as a weather sheet. Compare to: working guy / working sheet.

LBIYRA — Long Beach Island Yacht Racing Association. For more information, browse to http://www.lbiyra.org.

lead — to pass a line through a fitting or block. See also: reeve.

lee bow — to be in a covering position on an opponent's leeward bow. Tacking ahead of, and one or two boat lengths to leeward of, a competitor has a devastating effect because of the turbulence created to windward. Lee bowing is possible only if the lead boat is far enough ahead to cross. Otherwise, the attacked boat is too likely to pull ahead during the attacker's tack. See also: wind shadow.

leech — a sail's back or trailing edge that is between its head and clew.

leech break — describes when a spinnaker's trailing edge collapses or curls in. A properly trimmed spinnaker shows a smooth curve along its leech. If the leech begins to break, the pole should be pulled back, the sheet eased, or a higher course steered. Compare to: break and reverse curl.

leech cord — an adjustable cord that runs inside a hollow hem along a sail's leech. Tightening the cord prevents the leech from fluttering. The leech cord on a mainsail can also be used to fine-tune leech twist. Also called a leech line or leech string.

leech flake — a sail that is flaked so its leech is gathered directly over its clew by either first taking a cheater flake at the clew or by making wider folds towards the clew and narrower folds towards the tack. A sail that has battens and that has been leech flaked and stored in a bag can be folded to one-third of its length for easier stowage without damaging the sail. Compare to: luff flake and sail maker's flake.

lee cloth — material attached to a sea berth to prevent the occupant from falling off the berth when the boat heels or during rough conditions.

lee helm — a boat's tendency to steer herself away from the wind when her rudder is in a neutral position. This tendency increases as the center of effort moves farther forward in relation to the center of lateral resistance—the sail plan becomes out of balance. An example is when you use a #1 jib with a reefed main. The helmsman counteracts lee helm by holding the wheel to weather or the tiller to leeward. The opposite of weather helm.

lee shore — a shore that the wind is blowing towards.

leeward — a boat's leeward side is the side that is or was (when she is head-to-wind) away from the wind. However, when a boat is sailing by the lee or directly downwind, her leeward side is the side on which her mainsail lies. The other side is her windward side. When two boats on the same tack overlap, the one on the leeward side of the other is the leeward boat. The other is the windward boat.

leeward! — something a leeward boat that wants to assert her rights shouts to a competitor to windward.

leeward boat — a boat that is overlapped with and downwind of another boat. The other boat is the windward boat. A leeward boat has certain rights over a windward boat. See also: *RRS-2009* rule 11.

leeward broach — where the bow turns away from the wind, and the boat is turned broadside to the wind and waves. A downwind, leeward broach is the most dangerous kind of broach. The boat may roll, laying her mast nearly horizontal, which creates the possibility that the boat could be swamped or capsized. There is usually a violent, uncontrolled jibe, and unless the spinnaker pole is immediately put on the headstay, it will bury in the water and place extreme loads on the mast. These two forces combined offer a high probability of dismasting the boat. To recover, ease the mainsheet, vang, runners, spinnaker sheet, and afterguy. A good rule of thumb to remember is to "ease the wet side." Once the boat is brought back under control, the sails are trimmed back in again. Just as you de-power the boat from back to front, power up from the front to the back. Also referred to as a jibe broach or a round down.

leeward douse / leeward drop / leeward takedown — a spinnaker douse where the sail is brought down on the boat's leeward side. The foredeck gets control of the spinnaker—by either its foot or lazy guy. The halyard is blown as the foot or lazy guy is used to pull the spinnaker under the jib and onto the deck or down the forward hatch. This is also referred to as a lazy guy takedown. There are also more specific types of leeward drops for specific circumstances, including the float drop and stretch & blow.

leeward gate — two marks, theoretically set perpendicular to the wind, that are located at the end of a windward-leeward racecourse's downwind leg. *Sailing Instructions* typically allow competitors to round to either port or starboard after they pass between the two marks from the correct direction. The distance between the marks is approximately 8 to 10 times the boat length of the longest boats racing.

leeward mark — a mark at the end of a windward-leeward racecourse's downwind leg, or the end of the second of two reaching legs on a triangle or Olympic racecourse. Also called the bottom mark or lee mark.

leeward rail — the rail on a boat's downwind side. The low rail.

leeway — a boat's (usually unwanted) lateral movement to leeward due to the effects of the wind and current. Drift or sideslip.

left — directions such as left and right, as they relate to marks of a gate or other objects, are sometimes relative to windward on the course—towards where the wind is coming from; sometimes they are relative to your current perspective. For example, if a boat is sailing on a downwind course on approach to the leeward gate, the mark to the boat's starboard could be the right or left mark, depending on local or team convention. Usually when you refer to sides of the course and always when discussing wind shifts, left and right are relative to windward. For example, if the wind has been coming from 25 degrees and is now coming from 15 degrees, the wind has shifted 10 degrees left, without regard to the boat's heading or point of sail.

lefty — a colloquialism for a wind shift to the left or counter-clockwise—the numbers for the true wind compass direction decrease. See also: back.

leg — 1) A racecourse element. A leg's beginning and end are both denoted by a mark. You usually refer to a leg by using the travel direction relative to the wind needed to reach the next mark or by using the point of sail used to reach the next mark. For example, you are on a windward leg when you are heading towards the windward or weather mark. You are on a leeward leg when you are heading to the leeward mark or gate. A leg can be less than a mile between marks for a 'round the buoy race, or as long as 12,000 miles between ports of a distance race. 2) The distance covered on one tack or one jibe.

leg out — jargon for accelerating away from or in front of a competitor or fleet.

lenticular cloud — a cloud type with elements that resemble smooth lenses or almonds, and that are more or less isolated. These clouds are caused by a wave wind pattern created by mountains or another orographic cause, such as sloping terrain. They also indicate down-stream turbulence on the barrier's leeward side. Viewed from the ground, the clouds appear stationary as the air rushes through them.

letterbox douse — a spinnaker takedown used during heavy weather or when you are sailing hot angles with a large asymmetrical kite. The spinnaker is hidden behind the main. The lazy guy on a symmetrical kite or the lazy sheet on an a-sail is run over the boom from the leeward side, under the main's loose foot, and down the companionway. The trimmer trims hard to get the spinnaker's foot closer to the boom. When the douse is called, the pit blows the halyard halfway down and the floater hauls in on the line down the companionway. The trimmer eases the sheet as the kite is pulled in, and when the kite is under control, the pit blows the halyard and the foredeck spikes off the tack shackle with a fid. Remember to disconnect the spin gear and halyard and to re-run them as soon as possible. This is also referred to as an envelope drop or a mail slot drop. These names come from the analogy of dropping a letter or envelope into a mailbox or letterbox's slot. Also known as a Whitbread douse or simply an over-the-boom douse.

Leukemia Cup — the various regattas held throughout the United States to raise money to find cures for blood cancers and to raise blood-cancer awareness. First held at a single yacht club in 1988, The Leukemia Cup Regatta is now sailed at 38 locations each season. Top fund-raisers from each regatta are qualified to compete in the Leukemia Cup Challenge at the end of the year. For more information, browse to http://www.leukemia-lymphoma.org/regatta.

leverage — the distance between boats relative to the direction perpendicular to the rhumb line. Also refers to the advantage one boat earns by getting to a favorable wind shift or wind speed variation earlier, or sailing in it longer than her opponent. For example, if two close competitors are sailing upwind and the winds shift left, the boat farther left relative to the rhumb line gains. If the winds shift right, the boat farther right gains. Every boat length of separation increases the probability for gain or loss and magnifies the amount of gain or loss. Gains are realized only when a leveraged boat consolidates with her opponents. Until then, the gains are only theoretical. Compare to: gauge and height.

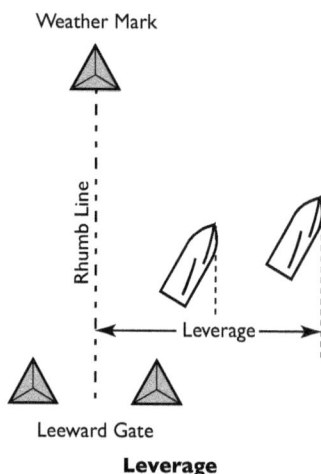

Weather Mark

Rhumb Line

Leverage

Leeward Gate

Leverage

LHYA — Lake Huron Yachting Association. For more information, browse to http://www.lhya.org.

lifelines — wire rope that runs horizontally around a boat's outside edge, often in pairs. The wire rope attaches to the bow and stern pulpits, and runs through stanchions, forming a security perimeter. Lifelines, in combination with stanchions and pulpits, keep crew and objects from going overboard, or at least slow their exit. Some believe the term "rail" refers to the lifelines, but it is actually shorthand for the toe rail—the edge around a boat's deck. Life rails are metal tubes (instead of wire) that run horizontally around a boat's perimeter. Lifelines and life rails are generally referred to as guardrails.

lift (sail theory) — laminar, attached airflow over a sail's leeward side has to travel a greater distance than air that flows over the windward side. Since airflow over the leeward side has to travel farther, it has to travel faster in order to reach the leech (i.e., trailing edge) at the same time as the air that flows over the windward side. The faster-flowing air on the leeward surface has a lower pressure than the slower-moving air on the sail's windward surface. This pressure difference generates lift and pulls the boat to leeward and forward. This is known as Bernoulli's Principle or the Longer Path Explanation. Water that flows over either side of a keel at differing rates also creates lift. The net effect of lift working against lateral resistance and drag is what drives a boat forward.

lift (wind) — a shift in true wind direction more aft on a boat's sail plan, which makes the apparent wind lighter and more aft. Upwind, a lift allows a helmsman to head up or alter course to windward and point closer to the direct course to the windward mark. Downwind, a lift causes a helmsman to head up and point away from a direct course to the leeward mark. Upwind, sail on lifts and tack on headers so that you point as close as possible to the windward mark. Downwind, sail on headers and jibe on lifts so that you sail tighter and faster down the rhumb line. A lift usually arrives in a puff that moves laterally across a boat's course aft of the prevailing wind direction; e.g., more than 45 degrees aft of a close-hauled sailing course. The opposite of a header.

lifted jibe — a jibe (i.e., downwind tack) that is affected by a lift, which causes you to head up and point away from the direct course to the leeward mark, or to jibe.

lifted puff — a short-duration increase in true wind speed with a shift in true wind direction more aft than the prevailing wind direction; e.g., more than 45 degrees aft of a close-hauled sailing course. See also: lift (wind). Compare to: headed puff.

lifted tack — a tack that is affected by a lift, which allows a boat to sail a course more directly towards a windward mark than she could otherwise.

lifting keel — a keel that is retractable, usually with the aid of a winch due to ballast weight. Daggerboards built like bulb keels are often referred to as "lifting keels," as they are retractable into the boat to reduce the draft, and to allow for loading a boat onto a trailer.

light — 1) A mild or low force, as in a light wind. 2) Many aids-to-navigation, such as buoys and lighthouses, show fixed or blinking lights to indicate their location or to identify them. 3) A sail that is eased too much and is luffing, or 4) A boat that is sailing too close to the wind. See also: luffing. Compare to: fat and heavy.

light air — wind velocity between one and three knots (one to three-and-a-half miles per hour). Force 1 on the Beaufort wind scale. Finding pressure is the priority when racing in light air because puffs move slowly down the course and a slight increase in pressure can have a significant effect on boat speed.

light sails — a collective term for the spinnakers, daisies, and other lightweight sails set on a run or reach.

lightweight sheets — a special set of sheets used in very light air. Constructed of lightweight, high-strength, low-stretch line such as Kevlar, they minimize the weight a sail has to carry. Sometimes referred to as light sheets.

line — a rope or cord used to control sail shape, to position spars, and to do myriad other things onboard a boat.

line honors — the first boat to cross a finish line. After handicapping adjustments are applied, the first boat to cross the finish line may not be the race's winner. See also: barn door.

line sight — to position your boat past either end of a start line and then to align the two marks that define the start line with an immovable object on shore. When the boat is between the start line marks, the relationship of the object on shore to either of the start line marks helps to determine the boat's distance to the start line. Also called establishing a range, ranging, sighting the line, or transits. See also: mid-line sag.

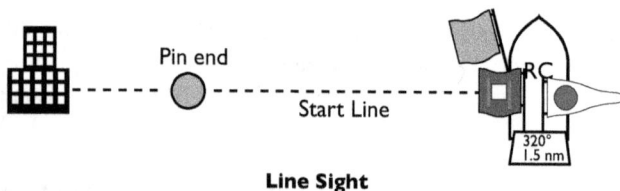

Line Sight

LMPHRF — Lake Michigan Performance Handicap Racing Fleet. For more information, browse to http://www.lmphrf.org.

LMSRF — Lake Michigan Sail Racing Federation. For more information, browse to http://www.lmsrf.org.

LMYA — Lake Michigan Yachting Association. For more information, browse to http://www.lmya.net.

LMYRA — Lake Murray Yacht Racing Association. For more information, browse to http://www.columbiasailingclub.org/lmyra.

local knowledge — knowledge and familiarity with local waters and conditions. This familiarity goes well beyond that available from charts and other publications. Often shared freely, but gained only through experience.

lock it up — a colloquialism that describes turning a helm quickly to its stop so that you can make a sharp turn. For example, to miss colliding with a mark after being frozen out of a rounding.

log — 1) A record of positions, courses, or activities. 2) A device to measure the rate of a boat's motion through the water—a speedometer. Another term for the speedometer on a boat is knotmeter. A slang term for speedometer is funmeter.

long eyes — slang for binoculars.

longitude — a reference to a position on the Earth's surface. Lines of longitude are imaginary lines that run due north and south around the Earth through the Poles; they are perpendicular to the Equator. Longitude is expressed as so many degrees east or west of the Prime Meridian, the line of longitude that passes through the Royal Observatory in Greenwich, England, and that is the zero-degree line. Degrees of longitude can be further subdivided into minutes and seconds: with 60 minutes per degree and 60 seconds per minute. A degree of longitude varies in size from approximately 60 nautical miles at the Equator to zero at the poles. A position is expressed as degrees, minutes, and seconds; or degrees and decimal minutes. Also known as a meridian. Compare to: latitude.

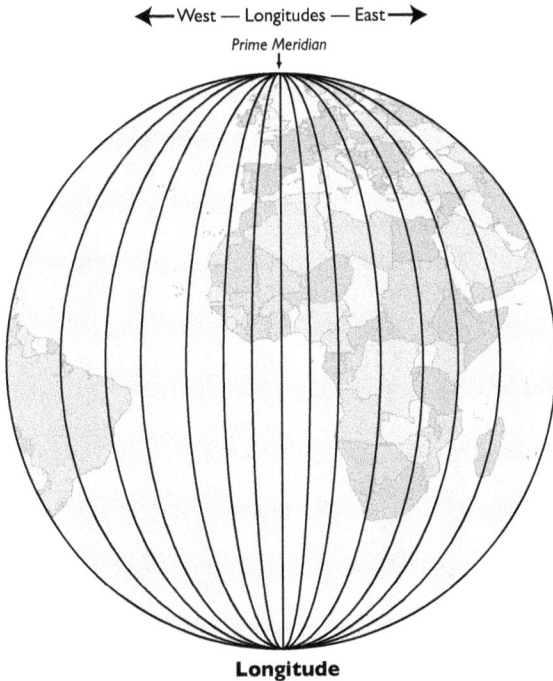

Longitude

loose cover — a tactical maneuver where a windward boat is in a position that limits a leeward boat's maneuverability without impeding her wind. See also: hip and tight cover. Compare to: blanket.

loose footed — describes a mainsail that is attached to a boom at its tack and clew but whose foot (i.e., bottom edge) is not attached. The opposite of club footed. See also: Velcro clew strap.

loose-luffed — a sail that is attached at its head and tack but that has its luff free flying and unsupported by a stay. On some sails, such as a staysail, a wire or Spectra line in the luff allows it to be tensioned enough to resist sagging to leeward in strong winds. See also: spinnaker and staysail.

Loos gauge — a device used to measure tension in wire rope or solid rod used as a boat's standing rigging. Loos gauges are sized to the particular wire rope or solid rod diameter used. A product of Loos & Co. For more information, browse to http://www.loosnaples.com.

LORC — Lake Ontario Racing Council. For more information, browse to http://www.lorc.org.

low — an area of comparatively low pressure, it has winds that spiral upward and inward in a counter-clockwise direction in the Northern Hemisphere and clockwise in the Southern Hemisphere. A cyclone.

low clouds — stratiform or cumuliform clouds with bases below 6,500 feet (2 km) above the ground. Stratiform clouds include stratus and stratocumulus. Cumuliform clouds include cumulus and cumulonimbus. The referenced altitude applies in the middle latitudes or temperate zone. In the Polar Regions, these clouds are found at lower altitudes. In the tropics, the defining altitudes for cloud types are generally higher. The main low clouds are cumulonimbus, cumulus, stratocumulus, and stratus.

Low Point (scoring) System — a methodology used to select the winner of a race or of a series of races. In a Low Point System, a boat's score is her finishing place without regard to how many competitors were entered in the race or finished later. The boat with the fewest cumulative points at the end of a race or series of races is the winner. This is one of two scoring systems defined by the *Racing Rules of Sailing* and is the one predominantly used, unless the applicable *Notice of Race* or *Sailing Instructions* identifies another scoring system. The alternative defined scoring method is the Bonus Point System. See also: Cox-Sprague Scoring System and High Point System.

low-pressure system — an air region where the barometric pressure is lower than that of the air that surrounds it; has winds that converge and ascend; and rotates the same direction as the Earth. This is counterclockwise in the Northern Hemisphere and clockwise in the Southern Hemisphere. It is the opposite of a high-pressure system or an anti-cyclone. Winds are relatively lighter near the outer edge of a low-pressure system and speed up as they move towards the center, though there may be a lull at the center. Also called a depression. Known as a cyclone to British and Commonwealth sailors.

Low Pressure Center Wind Flow

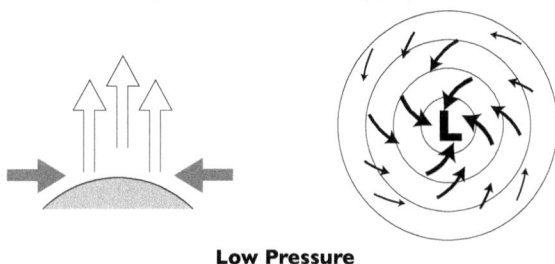

Low Pressure

LP / LPG — initialisms for "Luff Perpendicular" or "Longest Perpendicular of Jibs." The perpendicular distance from a sail's luff to its clew. For more information, browse to http://www.orc.org/rules/IMS 2009 - v1.04.pdf.

LSYA — Lake Superior Yacht Association. For more information, browse to http://www.lsya.org.

luff — 1) A sail's forward edge or leading edge. On a jib or genoa, the luff is attached to a headstay or forestay. On a mainsail, the luff is attached to a mast. See also: loose-luffed. 2) A maneuver used just prior to a start to slow a boat and maintain position. Or, more generally, a term used to describe a substantial course change to windward toward a windward opponent to force her towards head-to-wind. See also: luffing rights.

luff break — describes when a spinnaker's leading edge collapses or curls in. A properly trimmed symmetrical spinnaker shows a slight break approximately one-third of the way down from the head. If the break is lower, the pole is too high and should be lowered; if the break is higher, the pole is too low and should be raised. If the sail breaks excessively, it needs to be trimmed, the pole moved forward, or a lower course steered. Also known as a reverse curl.

luff douse — a spinnaker douse where the sail is brought down on a boat's leeward side. The foredeck crew gets control of the sail by its luff, and, optionally, someone else gets control of the sail by its foot. The spinnaker pole is rotated forward and lowered. Then, the halyard is blown as the foredeck pulls the spinnaker down by its luff and the foot is used to pull the spinnaker under the jib and onto the deck or down the forward hatch. There are other types of leeward drops for specific circumstances, including the float drop and stretch & blow.

luff extension — a length of luff tape/boltrope added to a sail's head to lengthen its hoist. For example, a #4 jib's luff may not go all the way to the top of the headstay, but if a luff extension is added, you can raise the halyard to its full hoist position. Also known as a pennant.

luff flake — a sail that is flaked so its luff is gathered directly over its tack. You accomplish this by either first taking a cheater flake at the tack or by making wider folds towards the tack and narrower folds towards the clew. This allows the luff to enter a pre-feeder or luff groove at a shallow angle and to feed more easily. Bow crew prefer luff-flaked sails because they are easier to hoist, but sails with battens that are luff flaked are harder to stow. See also: cheater flake. Compare to: leech flake and sail maker's flake.

luff grommets — the metal eyelets along a storm jib or heavy weather jib's luff. Used with lashings or hanks in addition to boltrope in a luff groove, they secure the sail to the headstay or forestay.

luff groove — a vertical slot in a mast or a headstay's aft face. It accommodates and provides continuous support for the luff of a sail that uses boltrope. A sail is secured at the luff by sliding its luff tape/boltrope into a sail feed and up the luff groove. Optionally, a pre-feeder is positioned before the sail feed to remove wrinkles and minor twists in the sail, so its luff tape/boltrope will slide smoothly into the sail feed. Also called a spar cove. See also: head foil.

luffing — 1) Deviating from course towards the wind, such as to head up to force an overlapped windward boat to windward. 2) A sail flapping in the wind. A sail luffs when it has too steep an angle of attack; i.e., is too far out relative to the wind. If a sail is too far out, it will wave like a flag and is said to be "luffing." Luffing reduces boat speed because it increases drag and decreases a sail's performance. A properly trimmed sail will not flutter. Sometimes referred to as ragging. See also: forereaching.

"… the motions of our sail; the play of its pulse so like our own lives, so thin and yet so full of life, so noiseless when it labored hardest, so noisy and impatient when least effective."

Henry David Thoreau (1817-1862)
American essayist, poet, and practical philosopher

luffing match — a tactical maneuver on a downwind leg, where a boat to leeward sails dramatically above her proper course (i.e., luffs) to prevent a competitor from passing her to windward.

luffing rights — a colloquial term. A boat is said to have luffing rights over a boat she overlaps to windward when she has the right to sail above her proper course, even if it forces the boat to windward to change course to keep clear. There is no proper course before a start signal, so a leeward boat can luff head-to-wind as long as she gives the windward boat room to keep clear. After the start signal, the leeward boat has luffing rights only if she acquired the overlap from other than astern and within two of her hull lengths. See also: *RRS-2009* rules 11, 16, and 17.

luff perpendicular — a measurement used to describe a headsail's size. It is the dimension of the 90-degree angle from a headsail's luff to its clew, and is expressed as either a distance (e.g., 15 feet) or a percentage of a boat's J dimension (e.g., 150%). The J dimension is the distance measured along the deck from the forestay pin to the mast's forward edge. Headsails with an LP of more than 100% are considered overlapping and are referred to as genoas; otherwise, they are referred to as jibs. Also known by the initials LP and LPG.

luff tape — a reinforcing cord sewn along a sail's luff or foot. Allows the luff or foot to be secured in a grooved head foil, mast, or boom and takes the principal strain when the sail is flying Also called boltrope, the only thing referred to as rope aboard a boat. See also: dual-groove head foil.

luff tie flake — folding a sail's luff into bights or folds in layers parallel to the foot, and then wrapping a sail tie through the sail's head and around its luff. This is a compromise flake done to quickly get a sail off the deck, while enabling it to be hoisted again without too much trouble. See also: run the tapes. Compare to: brick.

lull — a short-duration decrease in true wind speed. Moves the apparent wind direction more forward on a boat's sail plan. Upwind, lulls affect a boat more frequently, but for a shorter duration than downwind, because the boat and the lull move in opposite directions. Downwind, lulls are less frequent but affect a boat for a longer duration than upwind, because the lull and boat move in the same general direction. Also called a hole. See also: velocity header.

LYRA — Lake Yacht Racing Association. For more information, browse to http://www.lyrawaters.org.

M

mackerel sky — a sky covered with cirrocumulus or altocumulus clouds composed of ice crystals, with small vertical extent and in shapes that resemble mackerel scales.

Mac Race — Chicago Yacht Club's Race to Mackinac. An annual 333-mile race from Chicago's lake front to Mackinac Island in Lake Huron. Billed as the longest annual freshwater race in the world. For more information, browse to http://www.chicagoyachtclub.org. See also: Port Huron Mac and Super Mac.

macramé — as in "making macramé" or "holding a macramé class." Slang that describes the twisting, tangling, or crossing of sheets, halyards, or other control lines. Similar terms used include "getting your knitting in a tangle" or "making pasta." See also: frizzle line.

made! — a verbal confirmation that a task, such as the afterguy being set in a spinnaker pole's jaw, a sail being hoisted to its full height, or a line being made fast to a cleat, has been completed.

maelstrom — an extremely violent storm, usually a hurricane.

mainsail — (pronounced "mainsul.") A large sail set aft of the mast and above the boom. Usually the biggest working sail; often simply called the main. This sail provides both driving force and balance to a boat.

mainsheet — a line that controls the tension in a mainsail's leech when sailing upwind and that controls the position of a boom's aft end when sailing downwind. Usually connected to the boom.

main trimmer — the crew member whose core responsibilities include working with the sheet and other control lines that set a mainsail's shape for maximum performance. This crew member also controls the traveler and oversees the control of the backstay, boom vang, cunningham, and outhaul. With a short crew, the main trimmer may also act as tactician.

make fast — to attach or secure a line.

making trees — slang for going faster than and catching up to or passing a competitor. "Making trees" comes from watching the trees on shore in relation to another boat. If more and more trees appear in front of the observed boat, then she is slipping back and the observing boat is going faster in relation to the shore. The observing boat is "making trees." Conversely, if more trees appear behind the observed boat, then the observing boat is probably slipping behind and the observed boat is "making trees" on the observing boat. Some say "making land" instead. In areas where the waterfront is packed with tall buildings, this phenomenon is known as "making condos."

mammatus — clouds with hanging protuberances, like pouches, on their under surface. Typical of turbulent conditions.

mares' tails — long, well-defined wisps of cirrus clouds that resemble a horse's tail. According to folklore, mackerel scales and mares' tails make lofty ships carry low sails. The appearance of these clouds foretells an approaching storm, so sails get lowered to protect boats from the expected high winds. See also: cirrus.

marina — a man-made or natural docking or mooring facility for boats. Provides protection from wind, current, and waves, and offers marine services. Also known as a boat basin. See also: harbor, pier, and wharf.

mark — a buoy that denotes the beginning or end of a leg, start or finish line, or other racecourse element; any object the applicable *Sailing Instructions* require a boat to leave on a specified side; or a race committee boat surrounded by navigable water from which the starting or finishing line extends. Marks can be movable inflatable spheres, cylinders, or tetrahedrons (i.e., drop-in buoys) or metal and stationary; i.e., government or permanent marks. The inflatable kind is usually some fluorescent color: orange, yellow, white, or pink. The fixed variety come in all colors: usually red, green, or some combination of yellow and black. Marks on the course are sometimes referred to as rounding marks or turning marks to distinguish them from start or end marks. They are also referred to by their position on the course, such as jibe mark or reaching mark, weather mark or windward mark, or leeward mark or bottom mark. A mark is also referred to as a pin. Inflatable marks are sometimes referred to as pillows.

mark boat — a small motorboat used to set, change, and retrieve inflatable marks (i.e., drop-in buoys) on the racecourse. Also known as a crash boat or mark-set boat. Compare to: committee boat.

mark racing — inshore racing around buoys that define a multi-leg racecourse. See also: buoy racing.

mark-room — the space a boat needs to sail to a mark in the present wind, current, and wave conditions while maneuvering almost immediately in a competent, orderly, and safe manner, and then room to sail her proper course around that mark. However, mark-room does not include room to tack unless the boat is overlapped to windward and on the inside of a boat required to give mark-room. *RRS-2009* rule 18 and, implicitly, rule 14 cover mark-room. See also: double rights.

Marlboro country — a jocular term for the bow because you have to be tough to work up there, or because of the cowboy who works up there.

marshmallow — an inexperienced, inept, or timid skipper who is assumed will be slow over the start line and will cause little interference.

martin breaker — a device used in conjunction with a lanyard to remotely release a trigger-release shackle. See also: plug fid.

mast — 1) A large, vertical spar that supports one or more sails. Backstay, forestay, headstay, hounds, shrouds, and spreader are all components used to support a mast. Also known colloquially as a pole or stick. See also: bare poles. 2) The crew member whose core responsibility is to work with the pit and bow crew to hoist and drop sails. The mast crew may also assist with the spinnaker pole during jibes.

mast abeam rule — a no-longer-used rule that turned off a leeward boat's luffing rights when a windward boat's helm was forward of a line that crossed through the leeward boat's mast and was perpendicular to its centerline. See also: luffing rights.

mast bend — describes how much a mast's middle is bowed forward from a straight line between its masthead and heel or deck partners. Mast bend is what primarily adjusts draft depth in a mainsail's upper two-thirds. Both shroud tension and backstay tension control mast bend. A mast is referred to as inverted when its middle is bowed aft. See also: baby stay and chicken stay.

masthead fly — a wind vane mounted on a masthead. Apparent wind angle is shown by the relationship of the wind vane's head or tail to stationary tabs placed aft of the vane's pivot point and at an approximately 30-degree angle to either side of the boat's centerline. Some masthead flys are connected to the boat's electronic instruments. British and Commonwealth sailors call it a wind hawk. See also: chicken, paddles, and Windex.

masthead rig — a rigging configuration with headstay and backstay attached to the mast along the same horizontal plane. Compare to: fractional rig.

masthead sail — a sail that is hoisted to and flown from the masthead.

mast jack — a device used to pre-tension a rig and tune a mast. An alternative to the more conventional turnbuckle method. Typically a hydraulic ram mounted upside down inside the mast.

mast partners — a structure that reinforces the deck opening through which a keel-stepped mast passes. See also: partners.

mast rails — the stainless steel tubing that forms a safety rail for a crew member working at the mast. One mast-rail design uses vertical supports and waist-high horizontal rails on a single plane, in an L-shape or semi-circle. Other configurations are also possible. Also called mast pulpits or sissy bars.

mast step — the point, socket, or box where a mast's foot, butt, heel, or bottom is secured. A keel-stepped mast transfers its compression forces directly to the keel, usually by passing through a deck opening called the partners and by being secured directly above the keel. A deck-stepped mast has its bottom secured to the deck and either uses another structural member to transmit compression forces down to the keel or is secured in a strong and convenient place that spreads the compressive loads of the mast over a wide area. The fore/aft mast butt position in combination with the shrouds affects rake and pre-bend. With a keel-stepped mast, the partners are a very low pivot point relative to the total mast height. Therefore, very small mast butt movements fore and aft have dramatic implications on rake and lateral tilt. See also: partners.

match race grading — as the match race grade progresses from 5 to 1, the requirements get more stringent.

match racing — a style of race with only two competitors on the course at a time. The opponents battle one-on-one. Match racing is conducted under a modified set of rules as listed under *Racing Rules of Sailing* Appendix C. See also: America's Cup. Compare to: fleet racing and team racing.

maxi — a boat designed to the maximum rating allowed under either the International Measurement System (IMS) or the International Offshore Rule (IOR). See also: box-rule.

MAYRA — Mid Atlantic Yacht Racing Association. For more information, browse to http://www.mayra.org.

MBSA — Massachusetts Bay Sailing Association. For more information, browse to http://www.massbaysailing.org.

MBYCA — Massachusetts Boating & Yacht Clubs Association. For more information, browse to http://mbyca.org.

MCYA — Mississippi Coast Yachting Association. For more information, browse to http://www.mcya.info.

meat hook — a colloquial term for a broken and bent-up strand within a wire rope. It catches, cuts, or stabs clothing or body parts. Sometimes referred to as a fishhook.

median wind — the wind that flows from the midway point between the extremes of oscillating shifts, or the direction from which the wind blows most often.

Mercator chart — a map on which the meridians of longitude and parallels of latitude cross at right angles and all the parallels have the same length as the one at the Equator. Because a Mercator chart is a projection of the globe onto a flat map, the representation of the Earth becomes increasingly distorted towards the poles. Almost all coastal navigation charts are Mercator charts because of their faithful representation of direction. Named for the 16th century Flemish cartographer and mathematician, Gerhardus Mercator. Also known as a Mercator Projection.

meridian — one of the imaginary lines that run due north and south around the Earth through the poles and that denote longitude. A meridian runs perpendicular to the Equator. Compare to: parallel.

mesohigh — a small area of high pressure within a squally frontal cell. Caused by the downdrafts of cold air within the squall-line cumulonimbus.

mesoscale — 1) A size scale that refers to weather systems smaller than synoptic-scale systems but larger than microscale or storm-scale systems. Horizontal dimensions generally range from a half-mile to a hundred miles or more. 2) On a time scale, a weather event that lasts from several minutes to several hours.

messenger — a light line used to haul a heavier working line. Also referred to as a mouse line.

Mexican — a spinnaker douse wherein a boat does a no-pole jibe, but the spinnaker is left flying on the new windward side, where it collapses against the jib (i.e., it is backwinded) as it is pulled down. West Coast and Southern Hemisphere sailors sometimes call this a Kiwi. Generally referred to as a jibe takedown. Legend has it that Buddy Melges coined the term during the 1992 America's Cup. San Diego's prevailing winds were so consistent that every time the boats rounded the leeward mark and executed this takedown, they were pointed towards Mexico.

MexORC — Mexican Ocean Racing Circuit. For more information, browse to http://www.mexorc.com.

MHC — Mohawk Hudson Council. For more information, browse to http://www.rcyc.net/public/council.

MHRA — Multi-Hull Racing Association. For more information, browse to http://www.catamaranracing.org.

microburst — a strong downdraft that induces an outburst of damaging winds on or near the Earth's surface. The outflow at the surface is normally less than 2.5 miles (4 kilometers) in diameter, with peak winds that last only two to five minutes. See also: downburst.

microscale — the smallest scale of weather phenomena. Ranges in size from a few inches to a few miles. Larger phenomena are classified as mesoscale. Microscale also refers to small-scale weather phenomena that have life spans of less than a few minutes, affect very small areas, and are strongly influenced by local temperature and terrain conditions.

mid-bow — a crew member whose core responsibility is to be an extra hand as needed. A mid-bow may be asked to help repack spinnakers and organize and stow sails below decks. On deck, this crew member works with the foredeck, mast, and pit crew to help hoist and drop sails and may assist with the spinnaker pole during jibes. A mid-bow is selected as much for his or her strength and agility as for his or her sailing ability. Also known as a caddy, floater, runner, sewer, sewer rat, squirrel, and sweeper.

middle clouds — clouds with bases between 6,500 and 23,000 feet (2-7 km) above the ground in the middle latitudes or temperate zone. Mainly composed of water droplets, but may also contain some ice crystals at higher altitudes or lower temperatures. Altocumulus, altostratus, and nimbostratus are the main middle cloud types.

middle latitudes — the latitude belt roughly between 35 and 65 degrees north or south. Also referred to as the temperate region or temperate zone. The Great Lakes all fall within the middle latitudes.

mid layer — a middle clothing layer used as an insulator to keep heat in and cold out. Accomplished by creating a still or dead air layer between fibers. Popular insulating materials include wool, which naturally wicks away moisture, and fleece, a synthetic material that maintains its insulating ability even when wet and that spreads the moisture out so the material dries quickly. Also referred to as an insulating layer. Is usually put on over a base or wicking layer.

midline sag — a phenomenon where competitors near a start line's middle believe, because of their distance and angle to the references at either end of the line, that they are closer to the line than they actually are. Seen from above, boats appear to form a concave shape to leeward. A competitor that uses a line sight or attempts a dip start (where allowed) can take advantage of this phenomenon.

millibar (mb) — a barometric pressure measurement unit. Atmospheric pressure usually ranges between 950.0 and 1,050.0 millibars reduced to sea level (1 millibar equals 0.0295301 inches of mercury).

mine! — an indication from a tailer or grinder who has temporarily taken control of a sheet or other control line, such as when asked to add wraps to or take wraps off a winch, that he or she has control of the line. Compare to: yours!

Mini Transat — a biennial race that is held in odd years for 21-foot boats that are sailed single-handed. This 4,200-nautical-mile race is sailed in two legs: from La Rochelle, France, to Funchal, Portugal, and then on to Salvador de Bahia, Brazil. For more information, browse to http://www.transat650.org.

MORC – Midget Ocean Racing Fleet. A time-on-distance single-number handicap measurement system for offshore race boats under 30 feet in overall length. For more information, browse to http://www.ussailing.org/offshore/hcapsys.asp.

MOCRA — Multihull Offshore Cruising & Racing Association. For more information, browse to http://www.mocra-sailing.co.uk.

moderate breeze — a wind velocity between 11 and 16 knots (12 to 18 miles per hour). Force 4 on the Beaufort wind scale. When racing in moderate air, taking advantage of wind shifts is a priority because puffs blow through so quickly that getting into a beneficial wind shift will do more to get a boat to the next mark sooner than will looking for more pressure. See also: heavy air.

MOM — an acronym for "Man Overboard Module," a Survival Technologies Group trademark. A canister that contains inflatable and lighted devices, including an inflatable horseshoe-shaped buoyant device, an inflatable locator pylon, and a self-opening sea anchor. The contents of a MOM help locate and retrieve a crew member who has fallen overboard. The canister is typically mounted on the stern rail and its contents are deployed when someone pulls the pin on the canister's top. Note: the force of gravity deploys the canister's contents, so if a boat is on her ear, the canister's contents will have to be manually withdrawn.

mommy boat — a derogatory term for a coach or support boat.

Monel — Special Metals Corporation's trademark for the stainless metal alloy often used in marine applications, such as mousing wire.

monkey nuts — slang for a roller-type sail pre-feeder. Also called monkey balls.

moor — to attach a boat to a mooring or to dock it.

mooring — a location where a boat can tie up. Often a chain or steel cable connected to a heavy weight on the sea floor or a pin anchored into the seabed.

mooring buoy — a floating marker that indicates a mooring.

mooring line — a rope or line that secures a boat to a mooring or dock.

MORF — Midwest Open Racing Fleet. For more information, browse to http://www.racemorf.org.

motor-sailing — sailing with the engine running and in gear.

mouse — to secure a screw or shackle with twine or safety wire to prevent it from opening accidentally.

MSA — 1) Manitoba Sailing Association. For more information, browse to http://www.sailmanitoba.com. 2) Midwest Sailing Association. For more information, browse to http://www.midwestsailing.com.

MSSA — Mount Sinai Sailing Association. For more information, browse to http://www.mssa.org.

mushrooms — 1) Slang for the crew members sent below to relax on the leeward cushions near the mast when the winds are really light. This offers many advantages: wind drag is reduced, the slot is not clogged, and their weight is concentrated closer to the boat's center of gravity. Low centered weight also helps reduce pitching in leftover waves and swell. Being sent below is not always fun for the crew, but they can get out of the sun, have some food, and catch up on some reading. Also known as being bilge brothers or putting dogs in the doghouse. 2) What crew members who are not part of the afterguard consider themselves because they are kept in the dark until the last second.

Mylar — DuPont Teijin Films' trademarked name for the polyester film used in sail construction because of its high strength and light weight.

N

---

nanny goat — a term of affection for a female member of the Island Goat Sailing Society, whose members have sailed in the Chicago to Mackinac race 25 times or more. See also: Grand Ram and old goat.

national authority — an organization acting as the governing body for the sport of yacht racing in a particular country or region. See also: prescriptions.

nautical mile — a unit of distance equal to one minute of latitude on the Earth's surface at the latitude in question (that varies from approximately 1,843 meters at the Equator to 1,861.6 meters at the poles). Internationally standardized as 1,852 meters or 6,076.12 feet, but commonly taken as 6,080 feet. A nautical mile is equal to 1.151 statute miles and is the unit of geographical distance used on "salt-water" charts. Speed measurement is done in knots, where one knot equals one nautical mile per hour.

navaids — slang for aids-to-navigation: charted objects available to assist in determining position or a safe course, or to warn of danger. Electronic devices used for navigation are known as electronic navaids.

> "To insure safety at sea, the best that science can devise and that naval organization can provide must be regarded only as an aid, and never as a substitute for good seamanship, self-reliance, and sense of ultimate responsibility, which are the first requisites in a seaman and naval officer."
>
> *Admiral Chester W. Nimitz (1885-1966)*
> *Commander of the U.S. Pacific Fleet*
> *during World War II*

navigation — the (black) art and science of specifying the proper course and direction a boat should travel from one location to another.

navigator — the crew member whose core responsibilities include specifying the proper course and direction a boat should take to get from one location to another, and who is in charge of all the electronic instruments and navigational charts onboard. The navigator is also responsible for gathering information on locations, routes, conditions, boat performance, and meteorological input, often starting months before major events.

naviguesser — a term of endearment for the navigator. An alternative is navigician.

nav station — shorthand for navigation station. The table a navigator uses to review charts and to plot courses. The typical location of the GPS/chart plotter and communications equipment (i.e., electronics aids-to-navigation) below decks. Navigatorium and office are other slang terms used.

NBSA — New Brunswick Sailing Association. For more information, browse to http://www.nbsailing.nb.ca.

NBYA — Narragansett Bay Yachting Association. For more information, browse to http://www.nbya.org.

Newport-Bermuda — a 635-nautical-mile biennial race run in even years from Newport, R.I., to Bermuda. Sponsored by The Cruising Club of America and Royal Bermuda Yacht Club. Also called the Thrash to the Onion Patch. For more information, browse to http://www.bermudarace.com.

new wind — wind from a new direction or of a different strength than the current wind.

nimbostratus — mid-level clouds composed mainly of water droplets, but may contain some ice crystals at higher altitudes or lower temperatures. Nimbostratus clouds are formed by the downward thickening of altostratus, are characterized by their gray color, and are normally associated with steady rain. Nimbostratus clouds are generally associated with fall and winter conditions, but can occur during any season. The "stratus" suffix suggests that the cloud is flat and stable, while the "nimbo" prefix suggests that the cloud contains rain.

NJYRA — North Jersey Yacht Racing Association. For more information, browse to http://www.njyra.org.

nm — an abbreviation for nautical mile.

non-skid — a surface preparation applied to decks to provide traction under both wet and dry conditions. Non-skid comes as paint or sheets applied to hard surfaces, or as patterns the manufacturer molds into the fiberglass decking.

NOOD Regatta — National Offshore One-Design Regatta. A series of three-day regattas held throughout the United States and Canada for one-design models. Started by *Sailing World* magazine in 1988. The overall winner from each region competes in the champion-of-champions regatta for the national title. For more information, browse to http://www.sailingworld.com/nood_regatta.jsp.

NOR — an initialism for *"Notice of Race."*

North Atlantic High — a large subtropical semi-permanent center of high atmospheric pressure located over the Atlantic Ocean at the Horse latitudes (i.e., sub-tropic latitudes between 30 and 35 degrees North). When this weather system is located in the Western Atlantic it is referred to as the Bermuda High. When it is located in the Eastern Atlantic it is referred to as the Azores High.

North Pacific High — a semi-permanent center of high atmospheric pressure located over the North Pacific Ocean between 30 and 40 degrees North latitude and between 140 and 150 degrees West longitude. The North Pacific High has a major influence on boats competing in any of the trans-pacific races, including Transpac, Pacific Cup and Vic-Maui. See also: slot cars.

Notice of Race — information about a particular event, including its date, time, and location. The *NOR* also contains information on eligibility requirements and entrance fee schedules, and resolves conflicts between ISAF, Class, and One-design rules.

NRO — an initialism for "national race officer." A US Sailing designated position. See also: race officer.

NSA — Northeast Sailing Association. For more information, browse to http://www.ussailing.net/nsa.

NSYA — Nova Scotia Yachting Association. For more information, browse to http://www.nsya.ns.ca.

#10 jib — a small pennant hoisted half way up the head foil by a topping lift and then secured to the base of the mast by a spare line. Prevents the head foil from flapping in the wind and making considerable noise. A head foil can also be silenced by wrapping a jib halyard around it a few times, securing the halyard's shackle to a tack ring, and tensioning the halyard. Also referred to as an anti-flapper, a silencer, and many other colloquialisms.

nun — a red, even-numbered buoy that marks a channel's right (i.e., starboard) side as a boat returns to port—within the United States and other territories using the region B lateral buoyage system. In territories where the region A lateral buoyage system is used, red buoys are on the left (i.e., port) side of a channel when entering a harbor. The nautical memory aid, "red-right-return," is only applicable in region B. Nuns are usually paired with cans.

O

---

obstruction — any object that a boat would have to substantially change course to avoid, if she were within one of her hull-lengths from it and sailing directly towards it. Generally, something at least one-third of a hull-length in size. Smaller objects would not require a substantial course change. Whether something can be classified an obstruction is important only when applying racing rules or arguing protests. But if it is in your way, do something to avoid it.

occluded front — a complex front formed when an advancing cold air mass overtakes a receding cold air mass and, in the process, forces up above the surface the warm air that previously separated the two masses. Also known as an occlusion. The type of frontal boundary the two masses create depends on how they meet. See also: cold front and warm front.

Oceanic Pole of Inaccessibility — in the ocean, the point that is farthest from any land. It lies in the South Pacific Ocean at approximately 48°52.6'S by 123°23.6'W, a point approximately 1,670 miles (2,688 km) from the nearest land: Ducie Island, in the Pitcairn Islands, to the north; Maher Island, Antarctica, to the south; and Motu Nui, off Rapa Nui in the Easter Island Group, to the northeast. Also known as Point Nemo.

Ockam — a brand name of advanced racing instrumentation systems. For more information, browse to http://www.ockam.com.

OCS — an initialism for "on the course side." The scoring abbreviation used to indicate that, at a boat's starting signal, some part of her hull, crew, or equipment was on the course side of the start line and she either failed to re-start properly or violated *RRS-2009* rule 30.1. The boat has the maximum points allowed assessed against her when the race is scored using a Low Point System. The maximum points allowed may be different for an individual race than for a race that is part of a series longer than a regatta. See *RRS-2009* Appendix A. The applicable *Notice of Race* or *Sailing Instructions* may also modify the number of points assessed. Replaced the PMS ruling.

offset mark — a mark set 6 to 10 boat lengths from a primary mark in the same direction that the primary mark is to be rounded. An offset mark is set between 80 and 90 degrees to the wind direction and must be rounded in the same fashion as the primary mark. Most often used at weather marks, but may be used at leeward marks. For example, an offset mark is used to keep boats in the process of hoisting spinnakers and turning downwind away from those approaching the windward mark on a beat. Known as a spacer mark or spreader mark to British and Commonwealth sailors.

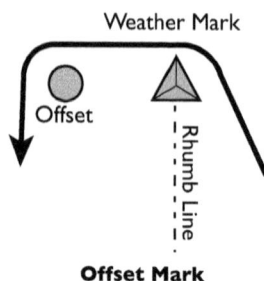

Weather Mark

Offset

Rhumb Line

Offset Mark

offshore breeze / offshore wind — wind that blows from the land and out towards the water. The wind always veers and increases in speed as it moves out over the water, without regard to the angle of the wind to the coastline. See also: land breeze.

offshore race — a race that is conducted on a large body of water and that lasts an extended period of time—from a few hours to several days or more. Offshore races can begin near one port and finish near another (i.e., a port-to-port race) or can return to the starting port after covering considerably more miles than a buoy race. Also referred to as a distance race. Offshore race strategy evolves as a race progresses. Early in the race, the strategic priorities are to find the most favorable weather pattern, to get to the weather pattern before the competition, and to be better placed within that weather pattern. Of course, as competitors approach the finish mark of an offshore race, tactics shift more towards buoy race strategy, where the priorities are to stay between any opponents and the next mark or wind shift, and to consolidate any leverage gained.

off the wind — away from the direction from which the wind blows. Usually with the wind from abeam or aft of abeam.

old goat — a term of affection for members of the Island Goat Sailing Society, whose members have sailed in the Chicago to Mackinac race 25 times or more. Officially known as an island goat.

Olympic course – the former name for a six-legged windward-leeward triangle course. The course is comprised of a windward leg followed by two reaching legs, a windward leg, a leeward leg and a finish to windward. This course is now referred to as a windward-leeward-triangle course.

one-design — any boat built to certain pre-defined standards or rules so that she is substantially like all others in the same class. Only those changes specifically listed in the class rules are allowed. All others are prohibited. One-design boats compete boat-for-boat without any time-allowance handicap ratings. With the elimination of boat design variables and time adjustments, skill, tactics, and crew maneuver execution have the greatest impact on a boat's performance. Theoretically, if crews of equal ability sail the boats, then all boats should cross the finish line at the same time. Compare to: box-rule and open-class.

one-legged beat — a major wind shift that skews the course so much that you can nearly fetch the windward mark.

One-Turn Penalty — a self-imposed penalty for violating *RRS-2009* rule 31. A competitor performs a One-Turn Penalty, by promptly making a turn in one direction, including one tack and one jibe, in exoneration for the rule violation instead of retiring from a race. Often referred to as "doing turns" or a "360." Failure to do "turns" may result in a witness lodging a protest and the infringing competitor being disqualified. Ring around the rosie is slang for doing penalty turns. See also: *RRS-2009* rule 44.2.

on her bottom — in the water, as opposed to on a truck or trailer. A boat delivered on her bottom is sailed or motored to her destination.

on her feet — as in the phrase, "keeping a boat on her feet," means to keep a boat level—not heeled over.

Onion Patch — 1) A reference to Bermuda, owing to the island's agricultural history and its most famous crop. 2) A series of three races surrounding and including the Newport-Bermuda race. The series starts with New York Yacht Club's Annual Regatta and concludes with the Anniversary Regatta of Royal Bermuda Yacht Club. For more information, browse to http://www.onionpatchseries.com. Compare to: Potato Patch.

onshore breeze / onshore wind — a wind that blows off the water towards shore. Caused by a sea breeze or gradient wind direction. Any changes to wind speed or direction occur over the land. Compare to: offshore wind.

on the hard — slang for a boat that is in dry dock and on boat stands or in a cradle or trailer.

ooching — *RRS-2009* rule 42.2 (c) defines ooching as "sudden forward body movement, stopped abruptly." This is a prohibited action. Rule 42.3 lists specific exceptions.

open — when referring to the top third of a sail's leech, means that it is twisted more to leeward than the sail's bottom two-thirds. When referring to the distance between a jib's leech and a mainsail's luff, means that the gap or slot is wide.

open-class — similar to one-design and box-rule, where boats are built to certain pre-defined standards or rules with minimums and maximums, but with some latitude for design and outfitting. In an open class, any changes are allowed except those specifically prohibited in the class rules. No handicap is applied. Compare to: one-design and PHRF.

optimum sailing angle — as far as a boat's course relative to the wind, the angle that provides the greatest progress towards or away from the wind. See also: polar diagram and VMG.

ORC — Offshore Racing Congress. The organization that administers both the ORC Club Rule and the ORC International Rule. For more information, browse to http://www.orc.org.

ORMA — Ocean Racing Multihull Association. For more information, browse to http://www.multicoques-orma.com/en.

ORR — Offshore Racing Rule. A measurement-based handicap rating system for offshore cruising and racing boats. The rating is based on a boat's hull, her rig and weight measurements, her sail inventory, and the results of a velocity prediction program (VPP), a complex computer program that estimates a specific boat's performance over a range of wind speeds and sailing angles. The Offshore Racing Association (ORA), an alliance of the Chicago Yacht Club, the Cruising Club of America, and the Transpacific Yacht Club, administers the ORR. For more information, browse to http://www.offshorerace.org. See also: IRC and PHRF.

OS — Ontario Sailing. For more information, browse to http://www.ontariosailing.ca.

oscillating (wind) shift — winds that shift in direction, first to one side, then to the other of a mean direction, and back again. Because a boat sails in a wind shift longer when going downwind, an oscillating shift upwind may be a persistent shift downwind.

outer distance mark — the term used by British and Commonwealth sailors for the mark at the start or finish line's end opposite that marked by the principal race committee boat; the pin end. See also: inner distance mark.

outer limit mark — a colored band that indicates one of three limits while a boat is racing, depending on where the mark is located. At a masthead, the mark's lower edge is the limit that a sail's head may be hoisted to. At a gooseneck, the mark's upper edge is the limit that a sail's tack may be pulled down to. At a boom's aft end, the mark's forward edge is the limit that a sail's clew may be pulled out to. The band is in a contrasting color to the spar on which it is placed. Also known as the black band.

outgrabber — a snatch block that is connected to the aft end of a boom and that is used in a manner similar to a barber hauler to adjust a spinnaker's sheeting angle farther outboard. The snatch block is a flying block placed on a spinnaker sheet between the clew and the aft sheet block. It is manually adjusted by means of a control line led through turning blocks or fairleads along a boom's underside to its aft end. See also: *RRS-2009* rule 50.3. Compare to: twinger.

outhaul — a control line used to pull a sail's foot out along a spar. One of the control lines used to adjust a mainsail's draft depth. As a broad rule of thumb, a mainsail wants to be flatter when close-hauled and fuller for sailing off the wind.

outside — the opposite side of a competitor than the intended mark. As regards sails, the one behind another—from the crew's perspective.

outside jibe — describes when an asymmetrical spinnaker's clew passes forward of its luff during a jibe, and follows an approximately 270-degree arc. Compare to: inside jibe. The deciding factor between doing an inside versus an outside jibe may be the a-sail's size. On a large boat, such as an SC70 with an extremely large a-sail, there may not be enough room to execute an inside jibe. An outside jibe is the only option. See also: gybulator.

outside set / inside douse — to hoist a new sail outside or to leeward of the working sail, and then to douse the inside or windward sail as a way to maintain speed and respond to wind shifts and wind velocity changes. See also: dual-groove head foil, jib peel, and spinnaker peel.

over-bend wrinkles — over-bending the mast usually causes wrinkles in the mainsail. These wrinkles extend from mid-mast to farther aft than mid-boom and rob the boat of valuable power. Also called inversion wrinkles. See also: speed wrinkles.

over early — when at a boat's starting signal, some part of her hull, crew, or equipment was on the course side of the start line. An improper or premature start. See also: OCS.

overlap — the situation where any portion of one boat's hull or equipment (in their normal position) is forward of a line perpendicular to the aftermost point of another boat's hull or equipment (in their normal position). The two boats are considered overlapped. Also, two boats not otherwise overlapped are considered overlapped when a third boat between them overlaps both. This term applies only to boats on the same tack unless *RRS-2009* rule 18 (concerning rounding and passing marks) applies, or if both boats are sailing more than ninety degrees from the true wind. See also: clear ahead and clear astern.

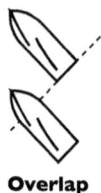

Overlap

overpowered — a boat that is heeling excessively because she has too much sail up or because the sails are too full for the current conditions. See also: de-power and reefing.

over-square — as it relates to a spinnaker pole, means that the pole is set at an angle shallower than perpendicular to the wind; the outboard end is pointed somewhat into the wind. Also known as over-trimming the pole. Situations when the pole is purposely over-square include when the apparent wind is fewer than 120 degrees off the bow, and when you want to direct the sail's force more forward.

overstand — to sail past the layline on the final approach to an upwind mark, which requires a boat to sail at a wider angle than her close-hauled course to reach the mark. Or, to sail past the layline on the final approach to a downwind mark, which requires a boat to sail a narrower angle than she normally would to reach back to the mark. This is also known as overlaying. See also: layline.

over-the-boom douse — a spinnaker takedown used during heavy weather or when sailing hot angles with a large asymmetrical kite. The lazy guy on a symmetrical kite or the lazy sheet on an a-sail is run over the boom from the leeward side, under the main's loose foot, and down the companionway. When the douse is called, the halyard is blown halfway down and the line down the companionway is hauled in. This is also referred to as an envelope drop, a letterbox douse, a mail slot drop, or a Whitbread douse.

overwrap — a line fouled around a winch in such a way that the wraps are no longer clockwise concentric circles around the drum in a single layer.

OVSA — Ohio Valley Sailing Association. For more information, browse to http://www.ussailing.net/OVSA.

P

Pacific Cup — a biennial 2,070-nautical-mile transpacific boat race from the Golden Gate Bridge in San Francisco to Kaneohe, Oahu, in Hawaii. Held in even-numbered years since 1980. For more information, browse to http://www.pacificcup.org. See also: North Pacific High and Potato Patch.

pack — as it refers to a spinnaker, to place it twist-free within its turtle, with its corners on top and accessible. This allows the spinnaker to be quickly and easily connected to the appropriate running rigging. It can then be hoisted and will fill properly without fouling or wrapping. See also: run the tapes, spinnaker bands / spinnaker stops and tee it up.

paddles — slang for the stationary tabs of a masthead fly. Along with a wind vane, show apparent wind angle. See also: chicken and Windex.

padeye — a fixed loop or other deck hardware to which fittings such as blocks or shackles are attached. May also be used as a fairlead. A folding D ring bolted through the deck is also used for the same purpose.

palm — a leather, fingerless glove with extra material in the palm. Used as hand protection when working with needles, such during sail repairs. Also called a sailor's palm.

parallel — one of the imaginary lines around the Earth. It is parallel to the Equator and denotes latitude. Compare to: meridian.

parked-up — slang for being stopped dead in the water in a no-wind area. See also: becalmed, drifter, ghost and zephyr.

parrel beads — the beads that are strung on a wire loop and attached to a sail's tack or luff. Used as a way both to secure the luff around a roller-furled sail and to enable it to move around or up and down. The spinnaker tacker from ATN serves the same purpose.

partners — the structures that reinforce the deck opening through which a keel-stepped mast passes. Wooden or rubber chocks or wedges keep the mast firmly secured within the partners, after the mast has the desired rake and pre-bend. Also referred to as a mast ring. A rubber or canvas boot or collar encloses the partners and makes them weather tight.

patrol boat – a boat used to chase spectators and Rodneys off a racecourse.

pay out — to ease a line.

PBO — a composite fiber rigging weighing one-fourth as much as rod rigging, at one-and-a-half times the strength and three times the fatigue life, though it is more susceptible to degradation from light and humidity than rod rigging. Used to save weight aloft. PBO stands for polybenzoxazole [poly (p-phenylene-2, 6-benzobisoxazole)].

pedestal — 1) A columnar support for the wheel or helm in a cockpit. The pedestal may also function as a binnacle. 2) A winch drive mechanism's columnar support. See also: grinding pedestal.

peeling — hoisting a new sail outside (i.e., to leeward of) or inside (i.e., to windward of) the working sail and then dousing the working sail as a way to maintain speed and respond to wind shifts and wind velocity changes. See also: jib peel and spinnaker peel.

peeling ring — a three-segment ring with a trigger-release snap shackle permanently attached to each of two segments. Used in spinnaker peels. An afterguy and spinnaker sheet gets connected to the third segment after being run through a spinnaker pole's jaw. One snap shackle gets connected to a spinnaker's tack. The tack of a new spinnaker can be connected to the unused snap shackle. The old chute is spiked off with a fid once the new one is hoisted and drawing. A device generally referred to as a peeling strop. Tylaska refers to these as asymmetrical tack rings.

peeling strop — the general term for a device used during a headsail or spinnaker peel. See also: changing sheet, handcuffs, peeling, and peeling ring.

PEIYA — Prince Edward Island Yachting Association. For more information, browse to http://www.peisailing.com.

pelican clip / pelican hook — a quick-release hook that is used on lifelines. Allows the railing to be opened and closed so that passengers and crew can more easily get on or off. A pelican hook is attached to a section of lifeline, and then engaged with an eyelet on a stanchion. The side-opening hook design allows the lifeline to be taut when the hook is closed, and the tension helps to hold the hook closed. A spring-loaded pin is retracted to open the hook. The name comes from the hook's resemblance to a pelican's beak.

penalty turn — a maneuver performed in exoneration for violating specific rules of *RRS-2009* instead of retiring from a race and to avoid being disqualified. There is a One-Turn Penalty, done by promptly making a turn in one direction, including one tack and one jibe, for violating rule 31 and touching a mark. Infringements of any rule in *RRS-2009* Part 2—When Boats Meet require a Two-Turns Penalty, done by promptly making two turns in the same direction, including two tacks and two jibes. Often referred to as "doing turns" or a "360" or "720." Failure to do "turns" may result in a witness lodging a protest and the infringing competitor being disqualified. Ring around the rosie is slang for doing penalty turns. See also: *RRS-2009* rule 44.2.

pennant — 1) A wire or line added to the shackle on top of a mooring buoy, or added to the head or tack of a sail, to lengthen its hoist. For example, a #4 jib's luff may not go all the way to the top of the headstay, but if you add a head pennant (i.e., a luff extension), the halyard can be raised to its full hoist position. A #4 may have, and a storm jib will have, a pennant added to its tack to raise its foot a few feet off the deck so waves that wash over the deck can drain away. Sometimes spelled pendant but pronounced without the "d." 2) A triangular-shaped flag. Also called a streamer.

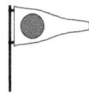

Pennant

permanent backstay — the standing rigging that runs from a boat's masthead to her stern and that counteracts headstay/forestay forces. With traditional masthead rigs without running backstays, and on larger fractional rigs, the permanent backstay controls both mast bend and headstay sag. Typically referred to as the backstay. See also: running backstay and topmast backstay.

permanent marks – permanently placed private marks. Compare to: drop-in buoys.

permanent (wind) shift — winds that shift in only one direction over a period of time. For maximum advantage, sail into a permanent shift upwind. To gain a more favorable sailing angle after a jibe, sail away from a permanent shift (assuming steady wind speed) when going downwind.

persistent (wind) shift — winds that consistently shift in only one direction before they return to a mean direction. For maximum advantage, sail into a persistent shift upwind. To gain a more favorable sailing angle after a jibe, sail away from a persistent shift (assuming steady wind speed) when going downwind. Because a boat sails in a wind shift longer when going downwind, an oscillating shift upwind may be a persistent shift downwind.

PFD — an initialism for "personal flotation device." A life jacket or life vest designed to float the wearer in an upright position and, in most cases, roll a person from a face-down to a face-up position if the wearer accidentally enters the water. Available in several sizes, types, and styles.

PHRF — an acronym for "Performance Handicap Racing Fleet," a registered trademark of US Sailing. A PHRF rating is a locally administered handicapping system that is based on a boat's performance potential, her demonstrated performance, and other subjective factors in varying combinations, depending on which organization issues the rating. Sailboat race organizers in the United States use PHRF handicapping as a way to quantify the performance of dissimilar boats and thereby allow them to compete against one another in the same event. The boat with the higher rating—the slower boat—is handicapped in a particular race by the number of seconds equal to her rating minus the faster boat's rating, times either the number of miles in the race or the elapsed time of the race. For example, boat A has a PHRF rating of 52 and boat B has a rating of 47. The race is 8 miles long. Boat A has a 40-second (52–47 times 8) handicap. If boat A crosses the finish line fewer than 40 seconds after boat B, boat A wins. See also: time-on-distance correction and time-on-time correction. Compare to: IRC, ORR, and Portsmouth.

piano — a term used variously for the pit crew member, for the location where this crew member works, and for the clutch banks or stopper banks that hold halyards and control lines. Keyboard is also a term used. See also: pit and stopper bank.

PICYA — Pacific Inter-Club Yacht Association. For more information, browse to http://www.picya.org.

pier — a man-made structure that extends over water and is perpendicular to shore. Has piles or pillars for support, allowing water to flow under it. Constructed for foot or vehicle traffic. Sometimes designed to allow for boats to dock. Compare to: dock and wharf.

pilot berth — a single bunk located outboard of a settee in the main saloon. There may be only one, or there may be one on each side of the cabin.

pin — 1) To be in a controlling position that prevents an opponent from tacking or jibing to reach a mark, such as by tacking into position on the opponent's windward hip. Compare to: shut the door. 2) Another term for a mark.

pinch / pinching — sailing to windward slightly above an optimum course, causing a boat's speed and power to diminish greatly. The opposite of footing. Also known as feathering or forereaching. Stealing and starving are antiquated slang terms.

pin end — Slang for the start line's end opposite that marked by the principal race committee boat. It is almost always the start line's left end when you are facing towards the weather mark. Or, slang for the finish line's end opposite that marked by the principal race committee boat. Known as the outer distance mark to British and Commonwealth sailors.

pin top sail — slang for a triangular sail. Also known as pin-headed. Compare to: fat head main.

pipe berth — a collapsible narrow bunk that is made from metal or carbon pipes, covered with cloth or padding, and hinged to the inside of a hull or bulkhead in a boat's quarters. Can be angled to compensate for a boat's heel. Also called a pipe cot. See also: quarter berth.

pit — 1) The crew member whose core responsibilities include controlling the halyards that hoist sails, and controlling other lines such as the boom vang, topping lift, and outhaul. The pit crew also organizes the boat's interior and retrieves and stows sails. 2) The area where the pit crew works, such as at a coachroof's aft end or the base of a mast. Sometimes referred to as the keyboard or piano.

pitching — a boat's fore and aft rotation around her transverse axis as her bow is lifted by a passing wave crest and then plunges into following wave trough.

pitchpoling — describes when a boat tumbles end-over-end. Usually happens when a boat is surfing down the face of a wave, loses control, and buries her bow at the bottom of the wave. The force of the wind combined with the boat's forward momentum causes her to flip. Often a catastrophic event. See also: down the mine.

PIYA — Pacific International Yachting Association. For more information, browse to http://www.ussailing.net/piya.

planing hull — a hull shape designed to develop positive dynamic pressure so that its draft decreases with increasing speed. Given enough driving force, a planing hull can achieve higher speeds than a similarly sized displacement hull, as a planning hull is not limited by waterline length. See also: hull speed. Compare to: displacement hull.

PLB — an initialism for "personal locator beacon." A portable transmitter that sends out a personalized emergency distress signal when a rescue is needed. It uses a radio signal and a unique digital code to alert Cospas-Sarsat satellites to a person's position. The digital code is used to locate pre-registered information about the PLB's possessor, such as name, and contact information.

plug fid — a device used in conjunction with a lanyard to remotely release a trigger-release shackle. Most useful at night or in heavy weather—times when it is too dangerous to go to the end of the spinnaker pole to release a spinnaker. Also called a martin breaker.

plug it in — slang for connecting a sail for hoisting. Same as to "tee it up."

plumb bow — a bow with a nearly vertical forward edge. A plumb or near-plumb bow design maximizes length at the waterline (LWL), increasing upwind speed potential for a given length overall (LOA). A plumb bow is typically more buoyant than a raked bow, which helps to keep the bow from burying in a wave. It is also considered visually appealing. Also known as a destroyer bow, a straight bow, a straight stem or a vertical bow. See also: hull speed and knuckle.

P measurement — the length from a boom's upper edge to the bottom of the black band at the masthead—the distance between the lower limit mark and the upper limit mark. A mainsail's luff length from tack to head.

PMS — an initialism for "premature start." An antiquated ruling that, at a boat's starting signal, some part of her hull, crew, or equipment was on the course side of the start line and the boat did not exonerate. See also: OCS.

podium finish — to finish a race or race series in first, second, or third place and earn the privilege of standing on the podium to receive a medal or trophy.

pointing — sailing as close to the wind as possible without losing speed. If a boat is pointed too high, she begins to pinch or luff and loses speed. The opposite of falling off or footing.

pointing ability — how close to the wind a boat can sail in her current configuration without losing speed.

point mode — trimming sails and flattening a boat to make the most progress to windward in moderate to heavy air and smooth water. Height mode can be achieved only after the boat attains full speed by trading speed for pointing ability. Also known as height mode. See also: feather and scallop. Compare to: foot mode.

Point Nemo — in the ocean, the point that is farthest from any land. It lies in the South Pacific Ocean at approximately 48°52.6'S by 123°23.6'W, a point approximately 1,670 miles (2,688 km) from the nearest land: Ducie Island, in the Pitcairn Islands, to the north; Maher Island, Antarctica, to the south; and

Motu Nui, off Rapa Nui in the Easter Island Group, to the northeast. Named after Captain Nemo, the fictional hero of Jules Verne's *Twenty Thousand Leagues Under the Sea* (1869). Also known as the Oceanic Pole of Inaccessibility.

point of sail — refers to a boat's direction of travel in relation to the wind. The points of sail include beam reach, broad reach, close-hauled, close reach, in irons, and running.

pointy end — a jocular term for the bow.

polar air mass — an air mass that originates over the cold northern portions of North America, Eurasia, and the oceans.

polar diagram — a graphical chart that plots target performance data for a specific boat. Includes theoretical boat speed and heeling angle for every true wind speed and true wind angle combination, along with the associated upwind and downwind VMGs; i.e., velocity made good against the wind direction. Also known as a boat performance table and polars. See also: isochrone.

pole in — to trim the afterguy and bring the spinnaker and pole windward, so the pole is oriented perpendicular to the wind. See also: squaring the pole.

p.o.m.e. — a derogatory phrase a New Zealander uses in reference to someone from the United Kingdom. Stands for "prisoner of mother England."

pooped — 1) To have a wave break over a boat's stern. Comes from the French word " la poupe," which means "stern," and from what you say after a breaking wave hits. See also: following seas. 2) The way you feel after a hard day racing.

poop stance — the crouch a helmsman assumes just before cresting a big wave or as a boat is about to broach: the feet are spread wide, the knees are bent, and the weight is shifted back.

poor man's twin — flying two jibs simultaneously, one in each slot of a dual-grooved head foil (e.g., Tuff Luff) or with their hanks interleaved. One jib is sheeted to the boom's aft end; a spinnaker or whisker pole holds out the other. Used for better performance downwind when a boat is too shorthanded to use a spinnaker. An illegal racing configuration. Also referred to as a butterfly. Compare to: double-headed.

pop it! — a colloquial command to trip the spinnaker pole during a jibe maneuver. See also: trip! / trip it!

port — 1) A sailboat's left-hand side when you are facing the bow, or forward. Everything to the left of the boat's centerline is to port. 2) A window in the cabin top or hull, or 3) A commercial harbor.

Port Huron Mac — Bayview Yacht Club's Race to Mackinac Island. An annual race from Port Huron, Michigan, to Mackinac Island, Michigan. The race is conducted over the 252-mile Thunder Bay Course or the 298-mile Cove Island Course. Billed as the world's longest consecutively run offshore freshwater yacht race. For more information, browse to http://www.byc.com/mack.

port pole — an off-the-wind course with the wind coming from port, the boom on the starboard side, and the spinnaker pole extended to the port side. A boat carrying a port pole is on port tack.

Portsmouth yardstick — a time-on-time handicapping system, based on a boat's demonstrated performance, for centerboard boats, multihulls, keelboats, and offshore classes. This is a system that race organizers use to allow dissimilar boats to compete against one another in the same event. Also known as a Portsmouth Rating or Portsmouth Yardstick Scheme. US Sailing is the ruling authority in the United States. In the United Kingdom, the Royal Yachting Association administers ratings. For more information, browse to http://www.rya.org.uk. See also: time-on-time correction. Compare to: IRC, ORR, and PHRF.

port / starboard rule — a colloquial term for *RRS-2009* rule 10.

port tack — sailing with the wind coming from the port side. Also, when sailing by-the-lee, with the boom on the starboard side.

port tack layline — the invisible line that leads up to a windward mark and along which you can sail an optimum close-hauled course on port tack and clear the mark on the desired side. Also, the line down to a leeward mark and along which you sail fastest to the mark on port tack.

port-to-port racing — a race that begins in or near one port and finishes in or near another. The race is conducted on a large body of water and lasts an extended period of time—from a few hours to several days or more. Also referred to as distance racing or offshore racing. See also: Chicago Mac, Fastnet, Sydney-Hobart, and Transpac. Compare to: buoy racing.

postponement – there are three types of postponements: indefinite postponement, races postponed – further signals ashore, and races postponed to another day. When racing is postponed indefinitely the race committee displays the AP flag and sounds two signals. When racing is postponed and there are further signals ashore the race committee displays the AP flag over the H flag and sounds two signals. When races are postponed to another day the race committee displays the AP flag over the A flag and sounds two signals.

Potato Patch — the Potato Patch shoal on the North side of the entrance to San Francisco Bay; part of the Four Fathom Bank. So named because, back in the 1800s, boats carrying potatoes from farms around Bolinas Lagoon to markets in San Francisco would occasionally run aground on this sand bar and spill their cargo. Compare to: Onion Patch

power reaching — sailing with the apparent wind angle between 70 and 120 degrees, depending upon the boat and sails being used. A maximum speed point of sail between close reaching and broad reaching, but it can be deeper than beam reaching.

practice sails — good sails are expensive, and many classes limit how many new sails can be purchased per year, so the best suit of sails is reserved for actual races. For practice sessions, a different suit of sails—often former racing sails—is used. See also: sail inventory. Compare to: delivery sails and racing sails.

pre-bend — the forward curvature of a mast's vertical plane when there is no backstay tension or other loads on the rig, other than from the shrouds—the middle of the mast is more forward than a line drawn from masthead to mast heel. The benefits of pre-bend include matching a mast's bend to a mainsail's luff curve and preventing mast inversion. When the pre-bend and luff curve are matched, the mast/sail combination works more efficiently. Also bent masts are more stable than straight ones. Mast pre-bend is induced by adjusting the mast butt/step location, the chock thickness at the partners, forestay length, and shroud tension. A smooth curve from deck opening to masthead is preferred. See also: mast jack and turnbuckle.

pre-feeder — a device used to remove wrinkles and minor twists in a sail, so its luff tape/boltrope will slide smoothly into a luff groove's sail feed opening on a mast or head foil. This allows for hoisting the sail more easily and quickly, and prevents damage to the sail. One pre-feeder type is a semi-circular ring with an opening slightly larger than luff tape. On either side of the opening are large rollers. Another type consists of a pair of smooth prongs that radiate aft, downwards, and outwards

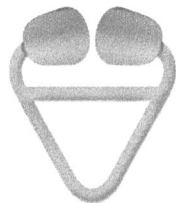

Pre-feeder

from either side of the sail feed. The purpose of each design is to accommodate the severe angles of the incoming luff tape and to redirect it towards the feeder. The roller types are also known as monkey balls or monkey nuts.

pre-feed the guy — to pull a spinnaker's tack forward to the spinnaker pole's outboard end prior to hoisting the sail, so it will fill more quickly as it is set. Often done on the approach to a windward mark, or between the windward and offset marks.

preparatory flag / prep flag — the flag raised one minute after the class flag, to indicate four minutes to a start, then lowered one minute before the start. Often the code flag for the letter "P" is used. Also known as a Blue Peter. The applicable *Sailing Instructions* may modify the sequence timing.

prepare to jibe! — an expression used to alert the crew that the helmsman is about to begin a jibe.

prescriptions — additions or modifications to the *Racing Rules of Sailing*; are made by a national authority and apply to racing within the national authority's country or region. See also: *RRS-2009* rule 86.

press down — to turn away from the direction from which the wind blows. For example, when sailing downwind, heading up in the lulls to maintain speed and pressing down in the puffs for better positioning. See also: head down, scallop, and soak it.

pressure — the wind force against a sail; wind strength or velocity. A spinnaker trimmer uses the term to describe the force present in the sheet being trimmed. Crew sitting on the rail use the term to refer to changes in wind speed, such as when calling, "building pressure."

pressure gradient — the difference in atmospheric pressure between two points. Wind is the air movement from the higher-pressure area to the lower-pressure area.

pressure gradient wind — steady horizontal air motion along curved parallel isobars or contours in an unchanging pressure or contour field, assuming there is no friction, divergence, or convergence. Pressure gradient wind blows parallel to the isobars shown on weather charts and at speeds inversely proportional to the distance between the isobars. Tightly spaced isobars indicate strong winds. Widely spaced isobars indicate weaker winds. Also referred to as gradient wind. Wind on deck will always be backed and slower than at the masthead. How much depends upon surface friction and the stability of the air.

prevailing winds — the most frequently observed wind direction over a given period of time.

preventer — a line that runs forward from a boom to aid in controlling its movement during an accidental jibe. Some call this device a boom guy or a lazy guy. See also: human preventer.

primary winch — the largest-diameter or most powerful winch on a boat. Usually located on either side of the cockpit on the coamings, it is used to handle the heaviest loads, such as jib sheets and spinnaker guys.

privileged vessel — an outdated moniker for the vessel that has the right and duty to maintain course under the applicable Navigation Rules, when boats meet or cross, or when one boat is overtaking another. The current term for this vessel is the stand-on vessel.

PRO — an initialism for "principal race officer." The most senior race officer at a particular event or venue, and the person who oversees all the other race officers. Has the final decision in all safety matters, including whether it is safe to start or complete a race. Approves the *Sailing Instructions*. Conducts or assigns someone to conduct the competitors' meeting. Assumes direction and responsibility for race committee personnel, equipment, and assignments. Chooses and sets the racecourse. Makes sure the race committee complies with the *SIs* and the *Racing Rules*. Makes or approves all race committee decisions. Serves as the liaison between regatta organizers, competitors, and the protest committee.

prod — slang for a bowsprit.

prognostic chart — a forecast prediction chart that may include pressure, fronts, precipitation, temperature, and other meteorological elements. Also known as a prog.

program – shorthand for sailing program. All of the activities surrounding a boat racing campaign, including boat preparation and maintenance, practice and racing.

proper course — the fastest course a boat would sail if no other boats were around. This may not necessarily be a straight line because of puffs, lifts, and waves. Referred to in specific rules of *RRS-2009*. This term is typically used only when applying racing rules or arguing protests. Also known as the racing line.

prop walk — the sideward force created by a spinning propeller. Most pronounced when a boat is moving astern. For example, a right-handed prop (i.e., clockwise turning when viewed from astern) will walk the stern to port when powering astern. A left-handed or counter-clockwise turning prop will walk the stern to starboard.

protest committee — the judges who hear protests and requests for redress. Members of the protest committee are appointed by the entity that puts on the related event or by the race committee for the event. Protests are allegations made by a boat, race committee, or protest committee under *RRS-2009* rule 61.2 and that allege a boat has violated a rule. A request for redress under *RRS-2009* rule 62.1 is based on a claim or possibility that one or more stated actions has, through no fault of the boat, made her score in a race or series significantly worse.

protest flag — a solid red flag displayed immediately by a boat that claims to have been fouled. Also called the Bravo flag.

protesterone — the hormone responsible for a propensity to file protests. See also: flag 'em.

provision – to plan, acquire and stow any needed food and beverage items aboard a boat. Collectively, the items are provisions. See also: snacktician.

PRYCA — Potomac River Yacht Clubs Association. For more information, browse to http://www.potomacriveryachtclubs.org.

puff — a short-duration increase in true wind speed. Moves the apparent wind direction more aft on a boat's sail plan. Puffs come from the prevailing wind direction, so distinguish puffs by looking to weather for a concentration of ripples across the water. The water will usually be darker where it is disturbed. Also look for the ripple direction to see whether the puff is a lift or a header. A lifted puff comes from aft of the prevailing wind direction; e.g., more than 45 degrees aft of a close-hauled sailing course. A headed puff comes from forward of the prevailing wind direction; e.g., fewer than 45 degrees aft of a close-hauled sailing course. Upwind, puffs affect a boat more frequently than they do downwind, but they are of a shorter duration because the boat and the puff move in opposite directions. Downwind, puffs are less frequent than upwind, but they affect a boat for a longer duration because the puff and boat move in the same general direction. Also known as a gust cell. See also: cat's paw, directional puff, header, lift, and velocity lift.

pull down patch — a patch, located in a spinnaker's center, that a light line attaches to. The line is used during a spinnaker takedown. Prohibited in some classes. Also known as a belly button, the recovery point, a retriever patch, or a takedown patch.

pull strings — slang for the various activities of trimming sails and adjusting control lines.

pumping — *RRS-2009* rule 42.2 (a) defines pumping as "repeated fanning of any sail either by pulling in and releasing the sail or by vertical or athwartship body movement." This is a prohibited action. Rule 42.3 lists specific exceptions.

pump-out station — a shore-side location where you can legally empty a boat's holding tank. The tank actually gets vacuumed out, not pumped out.

purchase — obtaining a mechanical advantage for increasing applied force when lifting or pulling, such as with a block & tackle.

pursuit race — where the slowest boats are given a sufficient head start and then the faster boats set off in pursuit. The time delay between class starts depends upon the time-on-distance handicap rating for each class. Theoretically, if boats of different classes are sailed by crews of equal ability, then all boats should cross the finish line at the same time. The applicable *Sailing Instructions* indicate the starting times for each class. As also known as a reverse handicap race.

putting dogs in the doghouse — slang for the crew members sent below when the winds are really light, to relax on the leeward cushions near the mast. This offers many advantages: wind drag is reduced, the slot is not clogged, and their weight is concentrated closer to the boat's center of gravity. Low centered weight also helps reduce pitching in leftover waves and swell. Being sent below is not always fun for the crew, but they can get out of the sun, have some food, and catch up on some reading. Also known as being bilge buddies or mushrooms.

Q

quadrant — a circular plate that is at the rudderpost and receives the steering cables from the helm.

quarter — one side of a boat aft of the beam and to the stern. A boat has two quarters: port and starboard. Note: the two forward sides are the bows.

quarter berth — a bunk or small cabin located in a boat's quarter.

quartering sea —waves on a boat's quarter.

quartering winds — winds from a boat's quarter.

Quattro winch — a winch with two drum diameters, one above the other. The wide-diameter lower drum is used to trim spinnaker sheets quickly, whereas the smaller-diameter upper drum is used when more power and self-tailing ability is needed for halyards or other control lines. Manufactured by Harken. Sometimes referred to as quads.

quay — a man-made structure that is at the water's edge and parallel to shore. Designed to allow for boats to moor alongside. Compare to: dock, marina, pier, and wharf.

Queen's Cup — an annual yacht race across Lake Michigan from Milwaukee, Wisconsin, to Muskegon, Michigan. Is conducted by the South Shore Yacht Club. The trophy, a Victorian silverwork cup, dates back to 1853 and passed through various hands before settling in Milwaukee. For more information, browse to http://www.ssyc.org.

quick-stop method — a procedure executed to quickly recover someone who has gone overboard. For more information, browse to http://www.ussailing.org/safety/ISAF/appd.htm.

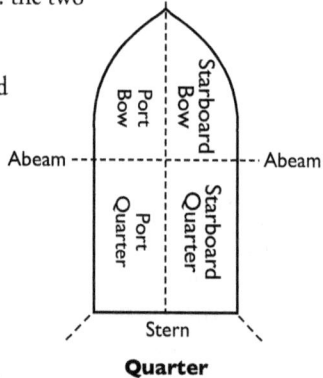

R

---

rabbit start — an informal race start that uses only the participating boats and no marks. One boat serves as the rabbit, while all others keep downwind. The rabbit crosses all the other boats on port tack. The line sailed by the rabbit is the start line, with the rabbit's stern being the windward end of the line. The rabbit enters the race once all other competitors have crossed the start line. The rabbit's stern is always the favored end.

race committee — the various people who organize, manage, and conduct a race or regatta. The race committee's goal is to provide safe and fair racing to all competitors.

race committee boat — a boat that contains the race officials who manage a race. The race committee boat displays placards or flags that indicate the selected course and a placard that indicates the direction and bearing to the first mark. The RC boat may also display other flags that indicate modifications to the races or rules listed in the *Sailing Instructions*. In addition, attention, start, warning, and sequence sounds and flags originate from the race committee boat. Also referred to as the committee boat, RC boat or signal boat. Compare to: mark boat.

race officer — a person knowledgeable about race management rules and procedures. US Sailing designates three race officer levels: club, regional, and national. Each is expected to properly run races for the types of boats, competitors, racing formats, and events run at his or her level. Each is also expected to understand the *Racing Rules of Sailing* as they relate to administering and conducting races at his or her level. A person who can manage the "on-the-water" race and regatta operations.

racer chasers — yacht racing groupies.

racing — *RRS-2009* designates that "a boat is racing from her preparatory signal until she finishes and clears the finishing line and marks, or retires, or until the race committee signals a general recall, postponement, or abandonment."

racing line — the fastest course a boat would sail if no other boats were around. Known as proper course when applying the *Racing Rules of Sailing*.

***Racing Rules of Sailing* (RRS)** — as published by the International Sailing Federation (ISAF), and as adopted by each national authority, the rules that govern the way all yacht races are conducted. *Notices of Race* (*NOR*) and *Sailing Instructions* (SI) issued by the organization that sponsors a race may modify the *Racing Rules of Sailing* for the covered race. The ISAF issues new rules every four years. The most recent edition is the *Racing Rules of Sailing for 2009-2012* (*RRS-2009*). Also known as the ISAF Rule Book.

racing sails — high-end mainsails, headsails, and other sails assembled from panels built of high-strength polyester, aramid (Kevlar), or carbon fibers sandwiched within plastic film such as Mylar. Also, a boat's best inventory of spinnakers and staysails. Good sails are expensive, and many classes limit how many new sails can be purchased per year, so the best suit of sails is reserved for actual races. Compare to: delivery sails and practice sails.

radiation fog — the fog created when radiational cooling at the Earth's surface lowers the air temperature near the ground to or below its dew point; i.e., the temperature when it becomes completely saturated with moisture. Formation is best when there is a shallow, relatively moist air layer beneath a drier layer, clear skies, and light surface winds. This primarily occurs during the night or early morning. See also: ground fog.

RAF — an initialism for "retired after finishing." The scoring abbreviation used to indicate that a boat completed a race and then retired for some reason. The boat has the maximum points allowed assessed against her when the race is scored using a Low Point System. The maximum allowed points may be equal to the total number of registered entrants, or it could be the number of entrants plus one or more points. The maximum points allowed may be different for an individual race than for a race that is part of a series longer than a regatta. See *RRS-2009* Appendix A. The applicable *Notice of Race* or *Sailing Instructions* may also modify the number of points assessed.

rafted / rafting — a mooring procedure for two or more boats that are tied up side-by-side at a dock, on a mooring ball, or at anchor.

ragging — a sail flapping in the wind. Typically referred to as luffing.

rail — any railing or plank that is around a hull's perimeter and that offers protection to crew or equipment. Examples are grab rail, life rail, rub rail, and toe rail. Often, when crew are instructed to sit on the rail, they are being asked to sit across the toe rail—the edge around a boat's deck—and hike out.

rail meat — slang for any crew whose primary job is to hike out to counteract excessive heeling or to induce healing. A kinder job description is stability technician.

rail tail — a pseudo-medical malady that describes the pain felt in the back of the legs or buttocks as a result of sitting on a thin, hard toe rail and hiking out for several hours.

rake — the amount that a mast is inclined aft of plumb. Masts are usually designed for one to two degrees of rake. Too much rake increases weather helm because the sailplan's center of effort is moved aft. Straightening the mast decreases weather helm.

rash guard — a base clothing layer that is worn next to the skin and that provides chafe protection. Also, because it moves moisture away and allows it to pass through the fabric and evaporate, a base clothing layer is also referred to as a wicking layer. British and Commonwealth sailors use the term rasher.

ratchet block — a drag-inducing block with an internal mechanism that allows the sheave to rotate in only one direction, snubbing a line and reducing a line's load. The ratchet mechanism can be completely engaged or disengaged, or (with newer models) set to engage at a pre-set line tension. A specialized ratchet block from Oxen is also self-cleating. Pull the line once to cleat it. Pull it again to release it.

RBVIYC — Royal British Virgin Islands Yacht Club. For more information, browse to http://www.rbviyc.org.

RDG — an initialism for "redress given." The scoring abbreviation used to indicate that as a result of a jury hearing a request for redress, a boat's score has been changed.

reacher — a special spinnaker used when reaching—the point of sail on which a boat sails across the wind. On a beam reach, the wind is abeam—about 90 degrees from the boat's course. On a close reach, the wind is between about 45 and 90 degrees—also called sailing shy. On a broad reach, the wind is on the quarter, greater than 90 to about 150 degrees. The other spinnaker type is a runner—used when running downwind. A reaching spinnaker or shy kite is cut flatter than a running spinnaker.

reaching — sailing with the true wind coming from between 45 and 150 degrees off the bow. If a boat is heading towards 12:00 and the winds are from 1:30 to 2:45 or 9:15 to 10:30, the boat is on a close reach. If the winds are from approximately 3:00 or 9:00, the boat is on a beam reach. A boat is broad reaching when the wind is from 3:15 to 5:00 or 7:00 to 8:45. Higher than close reaching is close-hauled. Lower than broad reaching is a run. See also: beam reach, broad reach, close-hauled, and power reaching.

reaching hook — a clip set abeam a mast at the rail. Used to hold a spinnaker sheet acting as an afterguy outboard and to provide a better angle for controlling the spinnaker pole's position—especially when it is close to the headstay while reaching. Needed only on a small boat that controls the chute with just two sheets and no twingers. Also referred to as a guy hook or spinnaker brace hook.

reaching leg — a racecourse leg you sail on a reach without the need to tack or jibe to reach the next mark.

reaching mark — the turning point between the two downwind reaching legs of a racecourse. For example, on a triangle or Olympic course, a mark set at a 90-degree angle to the rhumb line and half way between the windward mark and leeward mark. Also referred to as a jibe mark.

reaching sheet — a sheet rove through a snatch block. Positioned at the rail, it is used to move a jib or genoa's sheeting angle outboard. This produces a more efficient sail shape and opens the slot between the jib and main when you are reaching or running. Compare to: barber hauler and inhauler.

reaching strut — a short spar used to hold a spinnaker guy outside the lifelines. It keeps the guy off the shrouds and provides a better angle for controlling a spinnaker pole's position—especially when it is close to the headstay while reaching. A reaching strut is attached to the mast and set perpendicular and abeam just above the lifelines. Also called a jockey pole.

ready about! — an expression used to alert the crew that the helmsman is about to begin a tack.

recalls — there are two kinds: individual recalls and general recalls. An individual recall is when the line sighter on the race committee boat identifies one or more individual competitors as being on the start line's course side at the race's official start (OCS). The race committee displays the X flag and sounds a signal—to avoid confusion, it is probably a different sound than is used as the start signal. The X flag remains on display until all identified boats have properly restarted. If the applicable *Sailing Instructions* allow, the race committee may also notify those competitors who were over early by hailing them or alerting them over the radio. However, competitors are expected to know whether they started correctly. See also: *RRS-2009* rule 29.1. A general recall occurs when the race committee cannot determine which competitors violated the starting sequence rules or when there is an error in the starting sequence. The race committee initiates a general recall by displaying the First Substitute flag and then firing two sounds. See also: *RRS-2009* rule 29.2. For penalties that are applied for rule violations at the start, see also: Black Flag Rule, I Flag Rule, and Z Flag Rule.

reef cringles — the reinforced grommets or thimbles in a sail. Designed to prevent chafe by or to the reefing lines that pass through the sail.

reefing — reducing a hoisted sail's area to improve a boat's stability and to reduce the risk of injuring crew, capsizing, broaching, or damaging sails in a strong wind. For example, the first reef may reduce a main's sail area by 25 percent, and the second reef may reduce it by 50 percent.

reefing hook — a metal bracket that forms a U shape and is attached at the gooseneck. The upper arms of the U are bent to resemble upside-down Js and are bent slightly aft. Reefing rings on the mainsail go over the end of one or both Js when reefing and become the new tack.

reefing line — the line used to reef a sail. The reefing line passes through reef cringles, which become the reefed sail's new tack and clew. See also: reefing rings.

reefing rings — one or more metal rings attached to a mainsail's luff at one or more points above the tack. On some sails, each ring is attached via nylon webbing to only one side of the sail. On others, two rings are connected together with nylon webbing and the webbing passes through a reef cringle or grommet. Reefing rings are used in conjunction with reefing hooks to form a new tack when reefing a main.

reef points — the lines attached to a mainsail used to tie any extra sailcloth out of the way after a sail has been reefed.

reeve / rove — to pass a line or cord's end through a hole or aperture such as an eye, block, or sheave; to Lead. To withdraw the line is to unreeve it.

regatta — a race series where points are awarded based on a boat's finish in each race. The winner is the boat with the best, usually lowest, cumulative score. See also: Bonus Point (scoring) System, Cox-Sprague Scoring System, High Point (scoring) System, and Low Point (scoring) System.

relative bearing — an angle in relation to a boat's centerline, expressed in degrees; e.g., 30 degrees to port.

release! — a command given to a jibsheet trimmer or tailer to rapidly ease and then unwind a working jib sheet from its winch drum during a tack (or jibe, if using a jib) to allow a headsail to transfer to the opposite side. There are several steps involved in a smooth, effective release: i) Remove the jib sheet from any self-tailer or cam cleat. ii) Take a few wraps off the drum while holding the remaining wraps with one hand and the sheet's tail with your other hand. iii) Hold at least one foot of sheet between your off-winch hand and the winch, with your thumb on the off-winch hand pointing away from the winch. iv) Upon the release command, ease the sheet by removing your on-winch hand from the wraps and moving your hand holding the tail towards the winch. v) Pull up on the sheet and unwind it from the winch in a counter-clockwise direction, ensuring that there are no kinks in the sheet as it runs. A sail is released when its luff just begins to flutter.

RET — an initialism for "retired." This scoring abbreviation is used to indicate that a boat began a race and then retired for some reason. The boat has the maximum points allowed assessed against her when the race is scored using a Low Point System. The maximum points allowed may be different for an individual race than for a race that is part of a series longer than a regatta. See *RRS-2009* Appendix A. The applicable *Notice of Race* or *Sailing Instructions* may also modify the number of points assessed.

retire — to choose to drop out of a race either before or after finishing. Common reasons for retiring include crew injury, colliding with something, gear failure, or being protested. You typically notify the race committee when retiring from a race. See also: RAF and RET.

retriever patch — a patch, located in a spinnaker's center, that a light line attaches to. The line is used during a spinnaker takedown. Prohibited in some classes. Also known as a belly button, a pull down patch, the recovery point, or a takedown patch.

reverse curl — describes when a spinnaker's leading edge collapses or curls in. A properly trimmed symmetrical spinnaker's leading edge shows a slight reverse curl approximately one-third of the way down from the head. If the reverse curl is lower, the pole is too high and should be lowered. If the reverse curl is higher than this, the pole is too low and should be raised. If the sail reverse curls excessively, it needs to be trimmed, the pole moved forward, or a lower course steered. Also known as a break or luff break. Compare to: leech break.

reverse Mexican — a windward spinnaker drop that is followed by a jibe. Compare to: Kiwi or Mexican douse.

reverse pump — a maneuver used to accelerate in a puff without becoming overpowered. Just before a puff arrives—because someone is calling every one, right?—the crew hikes hard to flatten the boat and the helm foots off slightly. The main is eased as the puff hits. As the boat accelerates, she is brought back to course and the main is trimmed.

reverse transom — a flat surface whose upper edge is canted forward (i.e., an inward rake) across the aft end of a boat. Compare to: sugar scoop stern and transom stern.

RHKYC — Royal Hong Kong Yacht Club. For more information, browse to http://www.rhkyc.org.hk.

rhumb line — the straight-line course between two marks. A line that passes through all meridians at the same angle. When drawn on a Mercator chart, the rhumb line is a straight line. However a Mercator chart is a distortion of a round globe on a flat surface, so a rhumb line course is longer than a great circle route.

ridge — as it relates to weather, an elongated, relatively high barometric pressure zone that is associated with an area of maximum anti-cyclonic circulation. The opposite of a trough.

riding sail — describes two different styles of sail that help maintain a boat's direction into or nearly into the wind during heavy weather or while at anchor. One style is a flat-cut sail with no belly; this is rigged from the backstay and tacked off to one rail at the shrouds. The other style is shaped like a wedge; this is rigged from a boom's aft end and tacked to each quarter. Also called an anchor sail, backing sail, or stability sail. A riding sail is often used in combination with a sea anchor while at sea in storm conditions.

rig — 1) Shorthand for the standing rigging—the composite fiber, wire, or rod support lines for the mast, including shrouds, backstay, and headstay. 2) To put the spars, sheets, guys, and related equipment in position to make a boat ready for sailing.

right — directions such as right and left, as they relate to marks of a gate or other objects, are sometimes relative to windward on the course—towards where the wind is coming from; sometimes they are relative to your current perspective. For example, if a boat is sailing on a downwind course on approach to the leeward gate, the mark to the boat's port could be the right or left mark, depending on local or team convention. Usually when referring to sides of the course and always when discussing wind shifts, right or left are relative to windward. For example, if the wind has been coming from 15 degrees and is now coming from 25 degrees, the wind has shifted 10 degrees right, without regard to the boat's heading or point of sail.

righting moment -- the amount of force available to keep a sailboat upright when the wind is trying to push her over; i.e., self-righting ability. In keelboats, righting moment is provided by the weight and depth of the keel, but can also come from crew weight to weather. Water ballast can also be used to improve righting moment.

right-of-way — no boat ever has unlimited "right of way." Every boat is responsible for collision avoidance at all times. When two boats are on intersecting courses or when one boat is overtaking another, one is the "stand-on" vessel—and has the right and duty to maintain course—so the other, the "give-way" vessel, may alter course to keep clear. For more details, see *International Regulations for Preventing Collisions at Sea* rules 16 and 17, *Inland Navigation Rules* rules 16 and 17, and *RRS-2009* Part 2—When Boats Meet.

righty — a colloquialism for a wind shift to the right or clockwise—the true wind compass direction numbers increase. See also: veer.

ring around the rosie — slang for performing one or more penalty turns.

ring ding — slang for a device used to secure a clevis pin. More properly called a cotter ring or safety ring.

roach — sailcloth that extends aft of a straight line between a mainsail's head and clew. The more roach a mainsail has, the more drive it provides on a reach or run. Generally, battens are required to support roach. See also: fat head main.

rocking — *RRS-2009* rule 42.2 (b) defines rocking as "repeated rolling of the boat, induced by body movement, repeated adjustment of the sails, or steering." This is a prohibited action. Rule 42.3 lists specific exceptions.

rodeo — a way to prevent a lazy spinnaker sheet from getting tangled. Accomplished by standing behind the shroud, pulling the lazy sheet tight, and then snapping it forward in a circular motion to wrap it over the spinnaker pole's jaw-end. Once it is wrapped around the jaw end, the section of lazy sheet forward of the beam is wrapped around the working guy.

rodney — a disparaging term for a rude and clueless powerboat owner. Based on Rodney Dangerfield's antics in the movie *Caddyshack*.

roll — a boat's repeated inclination, first to one side and then to the other along her longitudinal axis. Happens in response to any combination of wind pressure on her sails, wave action against her hull, or unbalanced crew or cargo weight.

rolled — slang for being passed by a competitor to windward and then being gassed by her.

rolling starts — in a multi-division race, describes using the preceding class or section's starting signal as the warning signal for the succeeding class or section. Rolling start use may be expressly stated in the applicable *Sailing Instructions*, or may be implied by the listed starting times or sequences.

rollout — slang for broaching. See also: jibe broach, leeward broach, or round down.

roll tack — a method for completing a tack quickly and with minimum speed or position loss during light air. With everybody sitting on the low side to induce heel, the helm calls and begins the tack as everyone hikes out harder to help the boat turn with minimum rudder movement. As the boat arrives at head-to-wind, the whole crew moves in unison quickly and smoothly to the other rail, and then hikes hard to help the boat complete the turn and to get the sails to snap to the other side of the boat. The force of the sails tacking and immediately filling with air gives the boat a surge forward. The rocking motion also propels the boat through the water. Finally, as the boat settles in on the new tack, everyone hikes as needed to maintain proper heel angle.

room — *RRS-2009* generally defines room as the space a boat needs to sail to a mark in the present wind, current, and wave conditions while maneuvering almost immediately in a competent, orderly, and safe manner. See also: mark-room.

rope — a generic term for line or cordage before it comes aboard a boat. Once aboard, rope is generally referred to as line, or specifically by its use: halyard, guy, sheet, etc. Boltrope in a sail's luff or foot is the only thing properly referred to as rope aboard a boat.

RORC — Royal Ocean Racing Club. For more information, browse to http://www.rorc.org.

round — to sail around a mark in the specified direction, as in "round to port." While *RRS-2009* does not define a mark rounding, a boat is considered to round a mark when she passes it onto the course's next leg.

round-an-end rule — *RRS-2009* 30.1 states, "If flag I has been displayed, and any part of a boat's hull, crew, or equipment is on the course side of the start line or one of its extensions during the last minute before her starting signal, she shall thereafter sail from the course side across an extension to the pre-start side before starting." Dipping the line is inadequate. If a boat is on the course side for any reason during the last minute of a start sequence, such as being over early, to start properly, she must sail around either end of the line before restarting. Also referred to as the I flag rule.

round down — a downwind, leeward broach, where the bow turns away from the wind and the boat heels considerably. This is the most dangerous type of broach. There is usually a violent, uncontrolled jibe and, unless the spinnaker pole is immediately put on the headstay, it will bury in the water and place extreme loads on the mast. The combination of these two forces offers a high probability of dismasting the boat. To recover, the mainsheet, boom vang, runners, spinnaker sheet, and afterguy should all be eased. A good rule of thumb to remember is to "ease the wet side." Once the boat is brought back under control, the sails can be trimmed back in again. Just as the boat is de-powered from back to front, she should be powered up from front to back. Also referred to as a jibe broach. See also: broach.

round head — slang for a symmetrical spinnaker, a loose-luffed sail that is flown forward of the headstay, whose leading edge can be moved to correspond to the wind, and that is vertically symmetrical.

rounding mark — a buoy that denotes a leg's end and that the applicable *Sailing Instructions* require a boat to leave on a specified side as she passes onto the next leg. See also: mark. Compare to: scoring gate.

round-robin – a match and team racing format in which each competitor or team races against every other competitor or team. The winner is determined by total point accumulation.

round up — a windward broach, where the bow turns into the wind and the boat heels considerably. Is potentially a catastrophic event and is only slightly less dangerous than a round down. To recover, the mainsheet, boom vang, and spinnaker sheet should all be eased. The guy should be kept trimmed, because easing it allows the kite to remain full, which could worsen the situation and prevent recovery. A good rule of thumb to remember is to "ease the wet side." Once the boat is brought back under control, the sails can be trimmed back in again. Just as the boat is de-powered from back to front, she should be powered up from front to back. See also: broach.

RRO — an initialism for "regional race officer." A US Sailing designated position. See also: race officer.

RRS-2009 — an abbreviation for the "Racing Rules of Sailing for 2009-2012" as published by the ISAF.

rub rail — an applied or thickened structural member at the rail. Runs horizontally around a boat's hull at the outer-most edge, at the top of the topsides or gunwales, and protects the hull against damage from rubbing against a pier or another boat. Also known as a rubbing strake or rub strake.

rudder — a vertically oriented fin that is at or under a boat's stern at the centerline, or two vertically oriented fins set equidistant from the centerline. Is used in steering. Colloquially referred to as the blade, especially on smaller boats. See also: helm.

rules — several sets of rules govern the way a particular race or series of races is conducted. On the international level, there are the *Racing Rules of Sailing*, the *Equipment Rules of Sailing*, the various *ISAF regulations*, and the *IRC rating rules*. On the national level, the applicable rules include the national authority's prescriptions to the *Racing Rules of Sailing*, ORR rules, and any class or handicapping rules. Finally, on the local level, there are the *Notice of Race*, *Sailing Instructions*, and any local rules.

rules of the road — slang for the *International Regulations for Preventing Collisions at Sea* and the *Inland Navigation Rules*. These rules outline each boat's responsibilities if there could be a collision between two or more boats, along with other navigational and operation regulations. The *Inland Navigation Rules* differ slightly from those for international waters. No boat ever has unlimited "right of way," because every boat is responsible for collision avoidance at all times. See also: *COLREGS* and *Racing Rules of Sailing Part 2—When Boats Meet*.

run / running — 1) The point of sail away from the direction from which the apparent wind blows. If a boat is headed towards the 12:00 position, the wind is coming from anywhere between the 5:00 and 7:00 positions. Her jib is eased all the way out and set opposite the boom (See also: wing and wing) or she is flying an asymmetrical or symmetrical spinnaker. Her boom is set all the way out to the leeward shrouds. The apparent wind speed, the speed of the wind that flows over the boat, is lower than the true wind speed, because the boat is sailing away from the wind. Boat speed and wind speed cancel each other out. See also: reaching sheet. 2) To allow a line to feed freely is to let it run. See also: blow.

runner — 1) Shorthand for a running backstay. 2) The crew member whose core responsibility is to help as needed. A runner may be asked to help repack spinnakers and organize and stow sails below decks. On deck, this crew member works with the foredeck, mast, and pit crew to help hoist and drop sails and may assist with the spinnaker pole during jibes. A runner is selected as much for his or her strength and agility as for his or her sailing ability. Also known as a caddy, floater, mid-bow, sewer, sewer rat, squirrel, and sweeper. 3) Shorthand for a spinnaker designed for use when running.

running backstay — a device adjusted to prevent a mast from over-bending or pumping. It is attached between each quarter and a point on the mast near the forestay attachment point or at a point on the mast near the uppermost spreaders. Often referred to by the shorthand runner. Typically only the runner to weather is trimmed. The leeward runner is left eased. Running backstays are part of the running rigging and are usually present only on boats without swept-back spreaders. Also known as a preventative backstay. See also: checkstay, safe, and topmast backstay.

running rigging — the movable lines used to hoist sails, control their shape and position, and control spars. Examples are downhauls, guys, halyards, outhauls, and sheets.

running spinnaker change — to set a second spinnaker before dousing the first as a way to maintain speed and respond to wind shifts and wind velocity changes. The new spinnaker is hoisted either outside (behind, from the crew's perspective) or inside (in front of) the working sail. As the new sail is trimmed in, the old sail is doused. Also referred to as skinning, a spinnaker peel, or a straight-line change. See also: inside set and outside set.

run the tapes — to inspect each edge of a sail to ensure that it is twist-free. Usually done by tracing each edge of the sail with your fingers just prior to hoisting or packing it.

runway — the start line. Running out of runway means the timing of your starting tactics is off and unless an alternative tactic is executed immediately the boat will end up past the start line's end before the starting gun.

RYA — Royal Yachting Association. For more information, browse to http://www.rya.org.uk.

S

---

sacrificial anode — a less noble metal used to protect structural metals, such as through-hull fittings, propellers, and shafts, from the electrochemical degradation of galvanic corrosion. When two different types of metal are in contact and subject to a corrosive environment, such as immersion in saltwater, galvanic corrosion occurs and the least noble metal is sacrificed. For example, zinc is less noble—less corrosion resistant—than the brass used in propellers or through-hulls, so the zinc corrodes while the brass remains intact. If the zinc completely corrodes, the brass begins to corrode. In freshwater, magnesium is the preferred anode. It is recommended that anodes be replaced when they have corroded to 50% of their original size. No matter what metal is actually used for an anode, it is generically referred to as a zinc.

safe! — the verbal confirmation that a windward running backstay (i.e., runner) is properly tensioned, so the leeward runner can be eased and the main let out to leeward.

sail — an assembly of natural or synthetic textiles fashioned into a shape designed to catch or convert wind into motive force. An airfoil or air dam. See also: blooper, code 0, genoa, jib, mainsail, spinnaker, staysail, and storm trysail.

SAIL — Sailing Association of Intermountain Lakes. For more information, browse to http://www.rmsail.org.

sail area/displacement ratio (SA/D) — a comparison of how much sail a boat carries relative to her weight. It is a power-to-weight ratio. The calculation for SA/D is as follows: sail area in square feet divided by displacement in cubic feet—raised to the two-thirds power. The higher the number, the better a boat will perform in light air.

sailboard — a banner or signboard that displays a boat's sail number. The number's size, its colors, and the background material's color are specified in the *Notice of Race* for each race that requires a sailboard. A typical specification is as follows: "Each character shall be at least ten (10) inches high and made of contrasting marine-grade reflective material mounted on a black background." The applicable *Sailing Instructions* for each race that requires a sailboard usually specifies where aboard the boat the sailboard is to be displayed and when. Sometimes referred to as a reflective sailboard or sail number board.

sail button — a tag that is attached to a sail and that signifies that the sail meets the specifications of the issuing fleet or class, such as one-design.

sail cover — a protective cover used to preserve a sail when it is flaked or furled and left exposed to weather.

saildrive — an engine, transmission, and propeller drive system connected in a single package. The engine connects directly to the drive unit that contains the transmission, and extends down from the bottom of the hull. A saildrive eliminates a traditional inboard motor's extended propeller shaft, cutlass bearing, and stuffing box.

sail feed — the opening that is in a mast or boom's spar cove or luff groove and into which a sail's boltrope or slides are inserted. See also: pre-feeder.

sailing angle — the angle of a boat's course relative to the wind. The angle gets progressively larger as a boat goes from a beat to a reach to a run. See also: point of sail.

Sailing Instructions — a list of the rules and procedures applicable to a particular race or race series, such as a regatta. These include the courses, signals, and starting sequences the Race Committee will use, as well as the race schedule, restrictions, scoring procedures, and any other pertinent information. *Sailing Instructions* can be modified only by the specific procedure detailed in the initial version or as the *Racing Rules* allow.

sail inventory — 1) The sails that are onboard at any one time. The number of sails carried aboard may be limited by class rules, *Sailing Instructions* or rating rules. 2) The entire complement of sails for a particular boat—wherever they are located. All the sails aboard a boat are also called its suit of sails or wardrobe.

sail loft — the business of making and repairing sales, and the location where these activities are done.

sailmaker's flake — to prepare a sail for long-term storage by forming it into even bights or folds in layers parallel to its foot, like an accordion. Unlike a flake used for rapid hoisting, this flake is done in a way that leaves the head and body of the sail centered between the tack and clew. See also: brick. Compare to: leech flake and luff flake.

sailmaker's weight (sm-oz) — weight in ounces for a piece of fabric that measures 28.5" x 36", or approximately 80% of a square yard.

sail number — the unique number assigned to a particular boat for identification purposes and shown on her mainsail, spinnaker, and overlapping headsails. The boat's manufacturer may issue a number related to her hull serial number. Various organizations, such as the United States Sailing Association (US Sailing), the Canadian Yachting Association (CYA), or the America's Cup Class technical director, also issue sail numbers.

sailor's palm — a leather, fingerless glove with extra material in the palm. Used as hand protection when working with needles, such as when repairing a sail. Also called a palm.

sail plan — the sail configuration currently deployed.

sail ring — a ring that is sewn into a mainsail's tack and that is captured by a mainsail's tack fitting at the gooseneck, or the ring that is sewn into a headsail's tack and that is captured by a shackle or hook on a bow horn. The ring sewn into a sail's tack is also referred to as a tack ring.

sail slugs — small metal or plastic fittings that are sewn to a sail's luff and that fit into a spar cove or luff groove. Used to attach a sail to a spar. Sometimes referred to as sail slides or track slides.

sail tie — nylon webbing in various lengths, often with a loop sewn into one end. Used to secure a flaked mainsail to a boom, to secure a jib flaked on deck after a douse, and for a million other uses. Also known as a gasket.

sail twist — the amount that a sail's leech sags farther to leeward near its head than near its clew. See also: closed and open.

saloon — pronounced as if it were spelled salon. The main part of a cabin below deck. Bunks and settees for crew may be located along the saloon's walls or bulkheads. A nav station is typically located in the saloon.

salopettes — an exterior protection clothing layer made from waterproof, breathable material that keeps sealed against the weather with waterproof zippers and seams. Configured similar to bib overalls with pants and integrated chest and back panels held up by shoulder straps, or as a one-piece unit without sleeves. Salopettes keep clothing dry but provide little insulation. Warmth is controlled with insulating layers worn under the salopettes.

samurai douse — slang for cutting a halyard to douse a sail. Presumably done because the halyard is fouled and cannot quickly be freed. Unlikely to be done more than once during a buoy race.

Santa Ana wind — an offshore wind that drains air from the Western high-desert areas to Southern California coastal regions. This wind warms as it descends into the lower altitudes towards sea level.

sausage — a tubular headsail storage bag that allows the appropriate running rigging to be quickly and easily connected without having to open the bag. This allows the sail to be ready for rapid deployment without being exposed to wind and weather. This also allows for the sail to be quickly disconnected and removed from the deck, if a last-minute sail change is called for. Just before the sail is hoisted, the Velcro or zipper that holds the bag closed is opened and the sail is hoisted without fouling. The nicer styles of headsail storage bags have two zippers: a short one at the tack end and a long one that runs a majority of the bag's length. The long zipper can be pulled apart without damage if its pull is at either end. Once its sail is hoisted, a sausage is prepared for storage by running both zipper pulls back to their starting ends and reconnecting them. The bag is rolled from the clew end to the end of its long zipper. This roll is stuffed into and zipped up inside the short zipper end. This compact package is easily stored or tossed to the bow when needed. Also called a sausage bag or turtle. See also: flake, pack, run the tapes, and z-fold.

SAYRA — South Atlantic Yacht Racing Association. For more information, browse to http://www.sayra-sailing.com.

scallop — when sailing upwind, to repeatedly sail above an optimum close-hauled course to make distance to windward and then foot to build speed and to keep the sails full and drawing. When sailing downwind, to head up in the lulls to maintain speed and down in the puffs for better positioning. See also: soak it and wally.

SCAR pins — retaining devices that are used to prevent turnbuckles from accidental loosening, but that can be quickly removed for rig tuning. SCAR pins consist of a cotter pin or post attached to and held in place by a Velcro strap that gets wrapped around the turnbuckle's body. Works on both open body and slotted tubular turnbuckles. Also known by many other names, including high-speed pins, quick pins, smart pins, and wrap pins.

sched — (pronounced "sked" or "skeg.") Short for scheduled radio contact. To check in, report position and update weather information. Also referred to as the liar's club.

Scopolamine patch — a prescription antiemetic medication used to treat and prevent motion sickness, nausea, and vomiting. It is most commonly administered as a patch applied to the skin and marketed under the brand name Transderm-Scop, a registered trademark of Novartis Consumer Health. See also: Bonine and Dramamine.

scoring gate — a set of marks between which a competitor must pass in or from a stated direction. More likely positioning marks rather than turning marks. The marks may be defined by buoys, geographic points, GPS coordinates, or any other means. The distance between the marks may be from a few hundred feet to several hundred miles or more, depending upon the type of race being conducted. Boats earn points by passing through the scoring gate, but passing through some scoring gates may be optional. The afterguard must decide whether a boat can earn more points by taking line honors than by diverting to a scoring gate. In a High Point System, the points earned at a scoring gate, or scoring waypoint, may be some fraction of the points earned at the finish. Also known as a middle gate. Compare to: exclusion zone.

scoring system — the methodology used to select the winner of a race or series of races. For example, in a High Point System, a finisher receives one point for each later finisher. The boat with the most points at the end of a race or series of races is the winner. In a Low Point System, a boat's score is her finishing place without regard to how many competitors were entered in the race or finished later. The boat with the fewest points at the end of a race or series of races is the winner. In a Bonus Point System, a finisher receives an increasing number of points, based on a non-linear scale, for each earlier finisher. The boat with the fewest points at the end of a race or series of races is the winner. See also: Cox-Sprague Scoring System.

SCP — an initialism for "(took a) scoring penalty." The scoring abbreviation used to indicate that a boat has been assessed a scoring penalty under *RRS-2009* rule 44.3 and that her score has been adjusted. The adjustment may be different for an individual race than for a race that is part of a series longer than a regatta. See *RRS-2009* Appendix A. The applicable *Notice of Race* or *Sailing Instructions* may also modify the number of points assessed.

screecher — a large headsail that is flown from a bowsprit. Is used for downwind reaches or when there is too much wind for a spinnaker. A screecher looks like a cross between a jib and an asymmetrical spinnaker—often on a furler.

screw — slang for a boat's propeller.

screw shackle — a metal U-shaped connector that attaches to other fittings by the use of a threaded pin (i.e., clevis pin) inserted through the U's arms. Used on the end of a line, such as the main halyard, when it is more important to keep the line secured than to be able to remove it quickly. For even greater security, use a stainless steel or Monel seizing wire to secure the pin to the shackle's frame—known as mousing.

scrutineering — checking that a boat complies with all applicable requirements.

scull / sculling — *RRS-2009* rule 42.2 (d) defines sculling as "repeated movement of the helm that is either forceful or that propels the boat forward or prevents her from moving astern." This is a prohibited action. Rule 42.3 lists specific exceptions.

scupper — in a cockpit, coaming, or toe rail, a channel that allows water to drain out and overboard.

SCYA — Southern California Yachting Association. For more information, browse to http://www.scya.org.

sea anchor — a device deployed off a boat's bow and designed to hold her bow into the wind and waves, and to practically halt her progress. Its use allows the crew to spend minimal time tending to a boat's movement. Compare to: drogue.

sea breeze — a daily coastal air circulation that flows onshore, from the sea to the land near the surface. A sea breeze is caused by the temperature differential between relatively warmer land and a cooler adjacent body of water. The warmer, unstable air rising over the land draws air in from the water. The rising air is then re-circulated out to sea by a higher-level gradient wind that blows offshore. The flow of a sea breeze may penetrate as far as 10 miles inshore and may draw from an equal distance offshore. Predominant during the day, sea breezes reach their maximum during early to mid-afternoon. They flow in the opposite direction of a land breeze. A sea breeze is an onshore breeze, but not all onshore breezes are sea breezes. See also: lake breeze.

seacock — a valve used to shut off plumbing pipes that connect to a through hull, such as a sink drain or head flush-water inlet.

sea gasket coil — the standard nautical method for coiling a line for storage. To coil line into a sea gasket coil, start with an arm's-length clockwise loop of line in your left hand and add additional arm's length clockwise loops of line to the existing loop. If you are coiling laid line such as anchor rode or dock line, add a quarter-turn clockwise twist to each loop with your wrist; doing so will remove kinks. Avoid twisting braided line such as sheets and guys, as this induces kinks. Once most of the line has been coiled, make four counter-clockwise turns around the coil near the top, starting towards the middle and working up. Then, fold a bight (i.e., a loop) into the line and pass it through the coil, above the turns. Next, open the bight, pull it back over the coil's top and down to the turns, and then pull on the bitter end (i.e., the free end of the line) to tighten. To hang the line, push another bight through above the first, twist the bight twice, pass the bitter end through the twisted bight, and then pull. The line can then be hung from a bar using a clove hitch.

sea lawyer — a disingenuous term for a person who tries to reinterpret rules and regulations to his or her personal advantage.

seamanlike rounding — rounding a mark as close and as safely as possible in the present wind, current, and wave conditions and by a crew with average experience. Compare to: tactical rounding.

sea room — navigable water sufficient for safe maneuvering. Waves steepen as water depth decreases, and coastlines can create unpredictable wind patterns, so during storms it may be more advisable to avoid harbors and instead seek sea room.

secure — to make fast or tight. To attach.

seiche — like water that sloshes in a bathtub, a seiche (pronounced "saysh") is a wave caused by prolonged strong winds or other atmospheric or seismic forces that push water toward one side of a lake, bay, or other enclosed or semi-enclosed body of water. This causes the water level to rise on that side and to drop on the opposite side. Gravity acts against the rising water, which causes the wave to oscillate until friction counteracts the wave force.

self-tailer — at the top of a winch, a clamping device that grips the tail of the line wrapped on the winch to prevent the line from accidentally loosening.

send it! — a command to raise or hoist a sail.

separation — 1) Describes fluid particles that detach from a smooth, laminar flow over a foil's surface contour, such as air over a sail or water over a keel or rudder, due to friction, turbulent flow, or angle of attack. See also: stall. 2) The distance between two particular competitors, perpendicular to a course's rhumb line. See also: leverage.

set — a reference for the compass direction towards which current flows.

settee — a berth or couch in a saloon or main cabin.

sewer — 1) Slang for a racing boat's below-decks space that offers sparse accommodations, because it is often hot, dark, and wet. 2) The crew member whose core responsibility is to be an extra hand as needed. A sewer may be asked to help repack spinnakers and organize and stow sails below decks. On deck, this crew member works with the foredeck, mast, and pit crew to help hoist and drop sails and may assist with the spinnaker pole during jibes. A sewer is selected as much for his or her strength and agility as for his or her sailing ability. This crew member is also known as a caddy, mid-bow, runner, sewer rat, squirrel and sweeper.

shackle — 1) A metal U-shaped connector that attaches to other fittings with the use of a threaded pin, a pin inserted through the U's arms and secured with a ring ding, or by means of a closeable latch. See also: screw shackle and snap shackle. 2) A unit of measure for anchor rode on a large ship, with one shackle equal to 15 fathoms or 90 feet.

shake out — to remove a reef.

shear — the frequent rate of speed or direction change over a short duration. Directional shear is a frequent change in direction within a short distance; it can occur vertically or horizontally. Wind shear refers to the frequent change in wind speed within a short distance. It too can occur vertically or horizontally. Horizontal wind shear is the rate of change on a horizontal plane. Vertical wind shear is the rate of wind change with respect to altitude. The typically experienced wind shear on a boat is the increase in the wind's velocity at increasing heights, due to the friction of the water. There can be 15-25% more wind at the masthead than at deck level.

sheave — a grooved wheel inside a block, masthead fitting, or other means of connection. Is used to change a line's direction. Pronounced "shiv."

sheave box — a fitting that contains a sheave. Is used at the point on a spar where an internal halyard or other control line exits.

sheet — 1) A control line that is attached to a sail's clew and is used to adjust the sail's shape and angle to the wind for optimum performance. A sheet is identified by its sail; e.g., jibsheet, mainsheet, or spin sheet. 2) To adjust a sail's trim, as in to sheet in (i.e., pull the sail in) or to sheet out (i.e., let the sail out). To sheet a sail home is to trim it until the sail is set properly.

sheeting angle — the angle of a sail's cord in relation to the boat's centerline, or the angle of a sail's sheet in relation to its luff. See also: angle of attack, barber hauler, inhauler, jib lead car, outgrabber, twinger, and twist.

shell — an exterior protection clothing layer made from waterproof or water-resistant, breathable material. Used to prevent most water from infiltrating. Generally referred to as foulies. Also referred to as oilskins or waterproofs.

shift — a change in wind direction. For example, if the wind has been coming from 15 degrees and is now coming from 25 degrees, the wind has shifted 10 degrees right. If the wind has been coming from 15 degrees and is now coming from 5 degrees, the wind has shifted 10 degrees left. See also: oscillating shift and persistent shift.

shift line — the new layline after a wind shift.

shock cord — an elastic line that is useful in limited rigging or stowage situations.

shore crew — the personnel who support a participant in an event, but who are neither sailing in the event nor part of the race committee. Shore crew are typically technical experts, such as sailmakers, riggers, fitness trainers, and cooks.

shrimping — slang for letting a spinnaker fall into the water during a douse and then dragging it in the water like a trawling shrimp net. Also known as tea-bagging.

shrink-wrap — a polyethylene sheet that contracts when heated. Often draped over a boat as a preparation for long-term storage or over-the-road transportation.

shrouds — parts of the standing rigging that helps to support a mast laterally. Shrouds use composite fiber, or stainless steel wire or rod that run from hull-mounted chain plates on the beams via spreaders to the mast, supporting it side-to-side; i.e., athwartships. D1s (diagonal 1s) run from the chain plate on deck to the lowest spreader's base. D2s are an intermediate set that run from the lowest spreader's tip to the next highest spreader's base. D3s are the next highest set, if the rig has more than two spreaders. The Caps (also called V1s or vertical 1s) run from the chain plate on deck to the masthead, through each of the spreader tips. The Caps and D1s are adjusted with turnbuckles just above the chain plates. On some boats, the D2s run all the way to the deck so you can adjust them without climbing the rig. On other boats, you have to climb to the spreaders to adjust the D2s and higher. Boats usually have one or more shrouds on each side of the mast. Shrouds go to different heights on the mast to prevent the mast from bowing under the load of the wind and sails. Some call them sidestays. See also: continuous rigging, discontinuous rigging, mast jack, and pre-bend.

shut the door — to tactically block a competitor at a start, mark rounding, or finish in such a way as to prevent the competitor from continuing on its intended course, while the attacking boat continues on her intended course. For example, luffing a barging boat to force her to tack away.

shy kite — a reaching spinnaker. Cut flatter than a running spinnaker. See also: reacher.

shy reaching — a point of sail where the wind is forward of abeam—the true wind angle (TWA) is fewer than 90 degrees—but greater than the 45-degree TWA of close-hauled. A boat on a shy reach will have her jib slightly eased and her boom up to a quarter of the way to leeward of the boat's centerline. Also known as close reaching or fine reaching. Compare to: power reaching.

sight lines — the reference lines that are drawn on deck and that show at a minimum 30-, 45-, 60-, and 90-degree angles from the boat's centerline. Sight lines are used to estimate laylines or tack angles, and during other maneuvers. Also called tacking lines. Compare to: transit.

signal boat — a boat that displays placards or flags that indicate the selected course and a placard that indicates the direction and bearing to the first mark. The signal boat may also display other flags that indicate modifications to the races or rules listed in the *Sailing Instructions*. In addition, attention, start, warning, and sequence sounds and flags may originate from the signal boat. Also referred to as the committee boat. Compare to: mark boat.

silencer — a small pennant hoisted half way up a head foil by a topping lift, and secured to the base of the mast by a spare line. Prevents a head foil from flapping in the wind and making considerable noise. A head foil can also be silenced by wrapping a jib halyard around it a few times, securing the halyard's shackle to a tack ring, and tensioning the halyard. Also referred to as a #10 jib, an anti-flapper, and many other colloquialisms.

single-handed — sailing alone. No other crew aboard.

SIs — an initialism for "*Sailing Instructions*."

sked — short for scheduled radio contact. See also: sched.

skinning — setting a second spinnaker or headsail before dousing the first as a way to maintain speed and respond to wind shifts and wind velocity changes. The new sail is hoisted either outside (behind, from the crew's perspective) or inside (in front of) the working sail. As the new sail is trimmed in, the old sail is doused. Also referred to as a peel, a running change, or a straight-line change. See also: inside set, jib peel, outside set, and spinnaker peel.

skinny — references a sail that is eased too much and is luffing, or a boat that is sailing too close to the wind. Also known as sailing light. See also: luffing. Compare to: fat and heavy.

skipper — the crew member who is in charge of a boat's crew and responsible for the boat and her crew's safety.

skippers' meeting — a meeting that the race committee conducts for race participants before a race or regatta begins. Also called a competitors' meeting.

skirt — 1) Jargon that describes the act of pulling a jib's foot inboard over the top of the lifelines after the jib has been sheeted in with its foot hung up outside of the upper lifeline. See also: diving the clew. 2) Sometimes used to refer to a sail's foot.

sky — to pull the shackle at the end of a halyard up to its sheave on the mast. This gets a loose halyard out of the way and prevents it from getting tangled in another line. Done accidentally when the shackle-end of a halyard is let go before it is securely attached to something. Someone has to ascend the mast to retrieve the skied line. See also: frizzle line.

slam-dunk — to tack and tightly cover a competitor that is ducking or that has just been crossed on the opposite tack. Done to gain a controlling position to windward.

sled — slang for an ultra-light displacement boat (ULDB), an open-cockpit racing boat. Its hull shape is designed to develop positive dynamic pressure, so that its draft decreases with increasing speed. Given enough driving force, a sled can achieve higher speeds than a similarly sized conventional boat, as it is less limited by waterline length. Called a sled because it is long, narrow, and specifically designed to slide downhill on mountains of blue water. The Santa Cruz line of boats is a good example. Older sleds that were modified with such upgrades as a taller, carbon mast and larger sails are referred to as turbosleds. See also: turbo-ing.

slip — the water area between two piers or docks where a boat can be secured. Slips are often bounded on either side by a finger pier, with the third side formed by the main pier. A slip may accommodate two boats side-by-side or only one boat. Also called a stall.

slip queen — a dismissive term for a boat that rarely leaves her slip or mooring.

sloop — a sailboat with a single mast that is stepped approximately one-third of the way aft from the bow and fitted with a single headstay or forestay. A sloop usually deploys only one headsail at a time. The vast majority of racing monohull yachts are Bermuda-rigged sloops.

slot — the opening between a jib's leech and a mainsail's luff. Wind that passes through this opening increases the pressure differential across the mainsail, which helps to move the boat forward. See also: closed, open, and speed bubble.

slot cars — legendary navigator Stan Honey's term for the way Transpac competitors follow the 1,020 millibar isobars as they skirt the North Pacific High on their way to Hawaii.

small hours — the late-night and early-morning hours when most non-sailors are warmly tucked in their bed. Also called stupid o'clock.

SMS – Sportsboat Measurement System. A measurement-based handicap system for sportboats racing in Australia. Each boat's handicap is based on measurement of her hull, displacement, and sails to formulate a time-on-time rating. This rating is applied to the boat's elapsed time to obtain her corrected time for the race. For more information, browse to http://www.yachtingvictoria.com.au.

SMSA — 1) South Maryland Sailing Association. For more information, browse to http://www.smsa.com. 2) Southern Massachusetts Sailing Association. For more information, browse to http://www.smsailing.org.

snacktician — slang for the crew member primarily responsible for food preparation.

snailboat — a disparaging term for a sailboat.

snap hook — a hook with a spring-loaded gate that prevents the hook from accidentally coming undone.

snap shackle — a metal U-shaped connector that attaches to other fittings by means of a closeable latch. The latch is opened by retracting a spring-loaded pin, or by operating a trigger mechanism. Used on the end of a sheet or halyard that is frequently removed. For added security, tape or Velcro is placed around the closeable latch. There are various specialty snap shackles, such as Tylaska's J-locks and press locks.

snatch block — a block in a frame that can be opened on one side, which allows the block to be placed on a line that is already rove. An example is a twinger that can be added to a spinnaker sheet already rigged and in use.

snout line — a line connected to and that controls an asymmetrical spinnaker's tack. See also: tack line.

snub — to wrap a line on a winch or cleat to hold it under tension.

soak / soak it — to turn downwind more directly at a leeward mark without collapsing your spinnaker. See also: press down and scallop.

soft shackle — a device used to attach a line to another fitting. Made from a self-tightening loop of high-strength synthetic line such as Dyneema. One brand is Softies, a trademark of Colligo Marine LLC. Liros XTR is another brand. A soft shackle is a modern version of a traditional topsail halyard toggle.

SOG — an initialism for "speed over ground;" speed relative to the sea or lake bottom.

SOLAS — an acronym for "Safety of life at Sea" conference. A part of the International Maritime Organization, which establishes standards for maritime safety. For more information, browse to http://www.imo.org.

Solent (the) — the crescent-shaped English Channel sea-way that separates the Isle of Wight from mainland England.

SORC — Southern Ocean Racing Conference. The organization behind the annual 408-nautical-mile Fort Lauderdale to Charleston Race and the annual 160-nautical-mile Fort Lauderdale to Key West Race. SORC also manages the 811-nautical-mile biennial Pineapple Cup – Montego Bay Race. For more information, browse to http://www.fortlauderdalecharlestonrace.org, http://www.keywestrace.org, http://www.montegobayrace.com, and http://www.sorcsailing.org. See also: feeder race.

SPA – initialism for "spinnaker sail area." A calculation used to obtain a rating certificate.

spar — a pole-like structure that supports a sail. Examples are bowsprit, boom, mast, and spinnaker pole.

Spectra — a brand name for Dyneema, a synthetic fiber reportedly 15 times stronger than steel by weight, and up to 40% stronger than Kevlar. It is also said to be highly resistant to corrosive chemicals and abrasion, and to have extremely low moisture absorption. Royal DSM N.V., a multinational chemicals company headquartered in Heerlen, the Netherlands, commercialized Dyneema.

speed bubble — a jocular term for the bubble that forms near a mainsail's luff; this is caused by wind that deflects off the leech of an overlapping genoa's windward side when the slot is too closed.

speed bump — a facetious term for a dinghy, kayak, or other small boat that is between a racing boat and its destination.

speedo — slang for a boatspeed indicator or knot meter. See also: log.

speed wrinkles — acceptable diagonal wrinkles in the mainsail from mid-mast to about mid-boom. Over-bending the mast usually causes wrinkles that extend farther aft on the main. They are called over-bend wrinkles and rob the boat of valuable power.

spike — a tapered tool used to open trigger-release snap shackles, such as Tylaska, Wichard, or Gibb brands. Also called a fid or tripping fid. See also: plug fid.

spin gear — shorthand for a spinnaker sheet and spinnaker guy, as a unit. For example, a foredeck crew's request to ease the starboard spin gear is a request to ease both the spinnaker sheet and spinnaker guy on the starboard side.

spinnaker — a loose-luffed sail tacked forward of the forestay/headstay. Its tack can be moved to correspond to the wind, so laminar airflow can be maintained at a wider range of wind angles than is possible with stationary tack headsails. The sail is designed for sailing off the wind, from a reaching course to a downwind course; i.e., with the wind 60-180 degrees off the bow. Spinnakers are constructed of very lightweight fabric, usually nylon, and are often brightly colored. Spinnakers may be optimized for a particular range of wind angles, as either a reaching or a running spinnaker, by their panel and seam shape. A spinnaker is often called a chute, because it resembles a parachute in both construction and appearance. The edge of a symmetrical spinnaker presented into the wind—the leading edge—is referred to as the luff. The trailing edge is the leech. When the symmetrical spinnaker is jibed, the new leading edge is the luff. Typically, a spinnaker is packed in its own bag, called a turtle, with its three corners on top for ready access. Spinnakers are sometimes referred to by the slang term spi, and a symmetrical spinnaker is also referred to as a round head. See also: afterguy, asymmetrical spinnaker, downhaul, leech break, luff break spinnaker sheets, spin gear and topping lift. See also: kite.

spinnaker bands / spinnaker stops — the thread, rubber bands, or yarn used for tying a spinnaker's cloth in such a way that enables fully hoisting it and pre-feeding its tack to the pole end in strong winds without the spinnaker filling prematurely. Accomplished by gathering the spinnaker material from each leech towards the sail's middle and, optionally, depending on the expected wind speed, gathering or rolling the foot up towards the center, forming each corner into a long tube. Each tube is then secured with cotton thread, rubber bands, or wool yarn ties approximately every two to three feet. An alternative method is to fold the spinnaker in half by matching the clews and leeches, tightly rolling the spinnaker from the fold, and then stopping or banding the single tube. As a spinnaker is hoisted, firmly trimming the sheet breaks a few stops or bands. The wind breaks the rest. Stopping or banding a kite is also called wooling, just as a kite that has been stopped or banded is said to be wooled. See also: frog legged.

spinnaker bucket — a fixed bin from which a spinnaker is launched and also in which it is stored after a douse.

spinnaker design profiles — spinnakers are designed to accommodate varying wind speed ranges, just like jibs, and are designed to work best in specific apparent wind angle ranges. In broad terms, spinnakers are either designed as reaching sails or running sails. Reaching sails have a narrower profile than runners, with the angle between the leech tapes at the head around 85 to 95 degrees. In addition, reachers are flatter in the center than runners. Running sails are typically described as having broader shoulders, with the angle between the leach tapes at the head around 110 degrees. Spinnakers designated as AP— all-purpose—are usually cut as runners.

spinnaker guy — a control line used to adjust a spinnaker's angle of attack to the wind and, therefore, its effectiveness. The spinnaker guy, often referred to simply as the guy, is used to rotate a spinnaker pole's outboard end fore or aft as needed (and with it the spinnaker's tack). A spinnaker guy is adjusted in unison with the downhaul, spinnaker sheet and topping lift to form the spinnaker into the most efficient shape and to position the spinnaker at the most effective angle to the wind. It is run from a symmetrical spinnaker's windward clew (or an asymmetrical spinnaker's tack when flown from a spinnaker pole), through the spinnaker pole's jaw, then aft, optionally through one or more blocks, to a cockpit winch. Also referred to as an afterguy, brace, spin guy, or working guy. See also: spin gear.

spinnaker net — a device used to prevent a spinnaker from wrapping around the headstay, and is designed to do so without interfering with the spinnaker's wind or the pole's downhaul. A spinnaker net is hoisted like a jib to fill the upper half of a foretriangle. One design consists of a light mesh about the size of a small headsail, with either boltrope or hanks on the luff, a small-diameter line (to stiffen the leech), and several strips of nylon webbing sewn horizontally onto the mesh (to give it some rigidity). It sets on a spare jib halyard and its clew is tied off at the mast base. Another design uses line to form a triangle attached at the stemhead and mast base, with its apex hoisted on a halyard. More line, tied at either end to the legs of the triangle, is used as horizontal members spaced a few feet apart. A spinnaker net is used in light, sloppy, or shifty winds, when sailing deep; i.e., 140+ degrees AWA. Also used when you might outrun the apparent wind when surfing down big waves. A #3 jib set on a boat's centerline can be used for the same purpose, if class rules allow. Also called a foretriangle dam.

spinnaker peel — to set a second spinnaker before dousing the first as a way to maintain speed and respond to wind shifts and wind velocity changes. The new spinnaker is hoisted either outside (behind, from the crew's perspective) or inside (in front of) the working sail. As the new sail is trimmed in, the old sail is doused. Also referred to as a running spinnaker change, skinning, or a straight-line change. See also: inside set and outside set.

spinnaker pole — a spar that extends perpendicular from a mast and that is used to spread a spinnaker's foot to windward and to position the sail at the most effective angle to the wind. A spinnaker pole's inboard end is connected to a spinnaker pole car or mast ring, which allows the pole to be raised or lowered. A topping lift holds up its outboard end and a downhaul—or what some refer to as a foreguy—holds down its outboard end. The pole's inboard end pivots at the mast. An afterguy that opposes the forces of the spinnaker positions the spinnaker pole's outboard end fore and aft as needed. Also occasionally referred to as a spinnaker boom. See also: dip pole jibe and end-for-end jibe.

spinnaker pole car — a device that allows a spinnaker pole's inboard end to be raised or lowered to match wind and sailing conditions. The car travels on a vertically oriented track attached to the mast's forward face. Either a pin stop or purchase system is used to control the car's height. Also referred to as a mast car or pole slide.

spinnaker pole jaw — the U-shaped receptacle that is at a spinnaker pole's outboard end and that accepts an afterguy. The afterguy is held in place by means of a spring-loaded, manually retractable pin or piston across the jaw's opening. A trip line retracts the pin and locks it open. A trigger in the jaw's bottom unlocks the pin and allows it to close when it is depressed by the insertion of the afterguy or by other means. Also referred to as a beak, end fitting, terminal, or throat.

spinnaker sheet — a control line that is attached to a clew and used to adjust a spinnaker's shape. A spinnaker sheet is adjusted in unison with the afterguy, downhaul, and topping lift to form the spinnaker into the most efficient shape and to position the spinnaker at the most effective angle to the wind. Often referred to by the shorthand spin sheet. See also: lightweight sheets.

spinnaker size indications — spinnakers are sometimes referred to by a number (e.g., #1, #2, #3) to indicate their relative sail area as opposed to their specific size; a lower number indicates a larger sail area. Thus, a #1 is the largest reaching spinnaker on the boat, and is larger than a #3, etc. On a boat with an extensive wardrobe of sails, the various sizes of symmetrical spinnakers may be referred to as S1, S2, S3, etc., and the various sizes of asymmetrical spinnakers may be referred to as A1, A2, A3, etc. Odd-numbered sails are reaching sails. Even-numbered sails are runners.

spinnaker staysail — a staysail designed to be set under (i.e., to weather of) a spinnaker, tacked either at mid-bow or at the weather rail, depending on sailing angle. Its head is hoisted on a jib or spinnaker halyard and its sheet run through a snatch block on the leeward rail or through the leeward jib lead car. A racing staysail is often stored in a bag with a single sheet attached to its clew. Its luff is fed through the bag to a shackle that gets attached to a padeye, D-ring or perforated toe rail and the staysail is launched directly from the bag. See also: daisy sail and windseeker.

spinnaker trimmer — a crew member whose core responsibility is to control the sheets and other control lines that set a spinnaker's shape for maximum performance.

spinnaker weight indications — spinnakers are commonly referred to by a weight, such as .5oz, 0.75oz, or 1.5oz. These refer to the generic weights for the unfinished cloth used in sail making. Since spinnaker weight terminology is confusing and the material often weighs significantly more than the designated weight, it is best to think of spinnaker fabric weights as metaphors for light, medium, or heavy, not literally as .5oz, .75oz, or 1.5oz. The actual cloth weight can be stated per sailmaker's yard in ounces (sm-oz) or grams per square meter (gsm) of the material used to construct the sail. A sailmaker's yard is 28.5" by 36", or approximately 80% of a square yard. What is referred to as 0.5oz actually weighs 0.82-0.9 sm-oz or 35-38 gsm. A 0.75oz actually weighs 0.95-1.05 sm-oz or 41-45 gsm. A 1.5oz actually weighs 1.48-1.79 sm-oz or 64-77 gsm.

splash — slang for putting a boat in the water—usually after winter storage or after extensive work.

split tacks — to take the opposite tack when sailing to windward with another boat.

spool shackle — a device used to retain a line attached to another fitting. With one version from Tylaska Marine Hardware, an eye splice loop is passed through a spool around another fitting and then over the ends of the spool. With another version from Equiplite Pty Ltd, a loop of line is passed laterally through a double-ringed spool. A control line is eye spliced around one of the rings. The line through the spool is fed through another fitting and over the remaining ring of the spool. The loop is held in place by a wrap of Velcro.

sportboat / sportsboat — a light-displacement monohull keelboat designed for maximum speed. Usually with a high sail area to displacement ratio (SA/D), and capable of attaining hull speed in moderate breeze. A sportboat typically has a length overall (LOA) of 35 feet or less and is self-righting. A sportboat also typically has a maximum beam width of under 10 feet so it can be put on a trailer and transported without a special permit. Compare to: sled.

spray suit — an exterior protection upper-body clothing layer with soft neoprene neck, wrist, and waist seals. Gives greater protection than conventional foul weather gear. Also known as a bowman's smock or smock.

spreader — a horizontal support that extends laterally from a mast and that is used to change the angle of a shroud.

spreader boot — a rubber boot placed over a spreader's outboard end. Prevents sails from chafing on the spreader tip.

spreader patch — an extra cloth patch sewn onto a sail where it could chafe from rubbing against rigging, fittings, stanchions, or spreader tips.

spreaders, swept-back — horizontal supports that extend laterally and 15-30 degrees aft of abeam from a mast. Swept-back spreaders help prevent the mast from pumping and help keep the headstay tensioned, which eliminates the need for running backstays. See also: pre-bend.

spring line — 1) A line used to prevent a boat from moving fore or aft while docked. A bow spring line runs from a deck cleat near the stern to a dock cleat near the bow. A stern spring line runs from a deck cleat forward of the beam to a dock cleat near the stern. Midships spring lines run from an amidships deck cleat to dock cleats near the bow or stern. 2) A line used as a pivot while docking or leaving a dock.

sprit — shorthand for bowsprit.

squall — the sudden onset of strong winds with speeds that increase to at least 16 knots (18 miles per hour) and sustained at 22 or more knots (25 miles per hour) for at least one minute. The intensity and duration of a squall are longer than those of a gust. Squalls can be of short duration, such as 20-30 minutes. The strongest winds are at the leading edge, which extends about two miles out in front and typically diverges but sometimes converges. A hand-bearing compass is used to track a squall's center to determine whether the boat will pass in front of, behind, or through it. Squalls are also referred to by their appearance or composition. A wind squall exhibits more wind than rain; a rain squall has more rain than wind; a black squall is a squall accompanied by dark, ominous clouds and generally by heavy rain; and a white squall is a sudden squall that is so violent that air and water are white with rain and spray blown up from the sea's surface, but that lacks the usual dark, ominous squall clouds.

squall line — active thunderstorms in a narrow band or line that is not associated with a cold front. A squall line may form from an outflow boundary or the leading edge of a mesohigh and can extend for several hundred miles.

square knot — a temporary knot used to join together two similar-sized lines that are not subject to strain. Also called a reef knot.

square the pole — to use the afterguy to rotate a spinnaker pole horizontally so it is oriented perpendicular to the wind. See also: over-square and under-square.

square top main — a mainsail with an over-sized roach. The sail is designed with much more sailcloth aft of a straight line between the head and clew than a typical sail that comes to a point—known as a pin top. The head is also squared off. This greatly increased roach makes the sail more elliptical and more efficient, and puts more sail area where the wind is both stronger and more consistent. The result is more sail power both upwind and downwind. With this design of sail, the upper end of the leech automatically compensates for gusts because of its tendency to twist off in a gust. A permanent backstay interferes with the over-dimensioned roach when tacking or jibing. In order to swing the boom across, either the sail is reefed before the maneuver and the reef shaken out after, or top-mast backstays are used. Also known as a fat head main. See also: Chinese jibe and flicker.

squirrel — a crew member whose core responsibility is to help as needed. A squirrel may be asked, for example, to help repack spinnakers and to organize and stow sails. This crew member is also known by several other terms, some with more positive connotation than others, including caddy, floater, mid-bow, runner, sewer, and sewer rat, and sweeper.

SSB — Single Sideband Radio. A two-way radio that operates in the amateur radio bands and can communicate with other SSB radios at great distances— up to thousands of miles, depending upon atmospheric conditions. A Single Sideband Radio can also transmit and receive data, such as weather maps, forecast data, and e-mail. See also: GRIB.

SSCA — Saskatchewan Sailing Clubs Association. For more information, browse to http://www.sasksail.com.

SSS — an initialism for IRC's "stability & safety screen." A value that represents the seaworthiness of a particular boat, based on her hull and rig dimensions, self-righting ability, and various design ratios. Some races require that a boat meet a minimum qualifying SSS value to enter.

stable — as it relates to air, describes air that is colder than the surrounding air and that sinks or stays in place if already near the land or water's surface.

stack — the art, science, and drudgery of moving to a more strategic location anything that is not bolted down above or below decks. Moving the stack counteracts or induces heel, or affects fore-aft trim. The items moved can include sails, gear bags, spare parts, food stores, tools, and crew. If the wind speed is light, everything may be moved forward; in heavy air, items are moved to the high side and aft. Note: *RRS-2009* rule 51 prohibits moving dead weight or ballast as a means of adjusting trim or stability, and sails not currently deployed are considered ballast. The applicable *Sailing Instructions* may modify rule 51. See also: putting dogs in the doghouse and water ballast.

stake boat – a boat located beyond the extended rhumb line to a mark. A flag is flown high above the water on the stake boat to help competitors locate the mark.

stall — the condition that arises when an airfoil (i.e., a sail) or hydrofoil (i.e., a rudder or keel) is turned too far off the wind or water flow, and the flow separates from at least one side of the foil—there is no longer attached flow. A stall also arises when a foil is turned directly into the flow and there is no longer a pressure differential across the two sides of the foil. In either case, the foil no longer provides lift. A telltale is said to be stalled when it hangs limp, or, on a mainsail, when it curls around to leeward. See also: angle of attack.

stanchion — a vertical support for the lifelines that run horizontally around a boat's edge.

standing part — the part of a line that is made fast, such as to the becket of a block & tackle, as distinct from the bitter end. Some consider the standing part to be the inactive, middle part of a line.

standing rigging — composite fiber, or stainless steel wire or rod support lines for a mast, including shrouds, backstay, and headstay. Rig is shorthand for the standing rigging.

stand-on vessel — when two boats are on intersecting courses or when one boat is overtaking another, one is the stand-on vessel—and has the right and duty to maintain course—so the other, the give-way vessel, may alter course to keep clear. In general, a boat that is on starboard tack or that is being overtaken is the stand-on vessel. For more details, see *International Regulations for Preventing Collisions at Sea* rules 16 and 17, *Inland Navigation Rules* rules 16 and 17, and *RRS-2009 Part 2—When Boats Meet*.

starboard — the right-hand side of a boat when you face the bow, or forward. Everything to the right of a boat's centerline is to starboard.

starboard! — a notice, shouted to a competitor on port tack, from a boat that wants to assert her rights as a starboard-tack boat.

starboard end — a start line's end that is to starboard when you are looking from the pre-start side of the line towards a weather mark. It is typically the start line's end marked by the principal race committee boat. Also referred to as the weather end, though the starboard end of a start line is not necessarily the weather end, especially if the line is set square to the wind, though people refer to it as such.

starboard pole — an off-the-wind course with the wind coming from starboard, the boom on the port side, and the spinnaker pole extended to the starboard side. A boat carrying a starboard pole is on starboard tack.

starboard tack — a course with the wind coming from starboard, or when sailing by-the-lee, with the boom on the port side.

starboard tack layline — an invisible line that leads up to a windward mark along which you can sail an optimum close-hauled course on starboard tack and clear the mark on the desired side. Or, the line down to a leeward mark, along which you sail fastest to the mark on starboard tack.

star dock — a multi-sided, closed-center dock or pier with finger docks that radiate out from the main dock. A star dock is used to accommodate several boats in a cluster. Each boat is secured to an anchored structure, but the structure is not connected to shore. You need a dinghy or water taxi to reach a star dock. A star dock is a cross between a mooring can or buoy and a slip.

start — according to *RRS-2009*, "a boat starts when, having been entirely on the pre-start side of the start line at or after her starting signal, and having complied with rule 30.1 if it applies, any part of her hull, crew or equipment crosses the start line in the direction of the first mark." See also: OCS and recalls.

start line — an invisible line usually designated as between a pole with an orange flag on the Race Committee boat and a colored buoy that marks the line's pin end. For a windward/leeward course, the start line is theoretically set perpendicular to the wind. For a distance race, the line is set perpendicular to the rhumb line. Several factors influence start line length: the number of competitors in the largest fleet, maximum boat length, manoeuvrability of the boats racing, wind velocity, wave height, and current drift and set. A start line may be set 0.1 nm or more leeward of the leeward mark to keep starters away from earlier section boats that may already be rounding the leeward mark. See also: box, favored end, and inner distance mark.

> "Whoever is first in the field and awaits the coming of the enemy will be fresh for the fight; whoever is second in the field and has to hasten to battle will arrive exhausted."
>
> Sun Tzu (6th- to 5th-century B.C.)
> Chinese general in The Art of War, Ch. 6

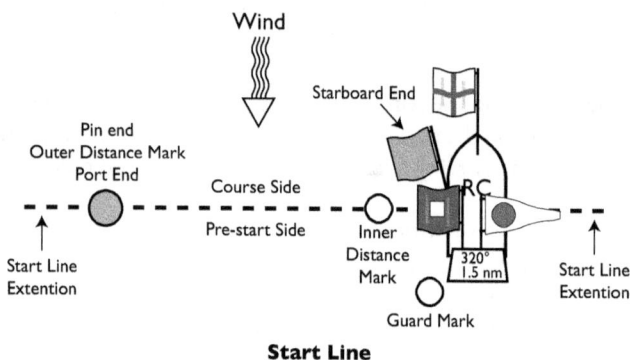

Start Line

start line bias — whether and how much a start line's angle differs from being perpendicular to the wind. See also: favored end.

statute mile — a unit of distance equal to 5,280 feet, 1,760 yards, or 1.609344 kilometers. Also known as a land mile. The unit of measure for distance traveled on U.S. waters of the Great Lakes.

stay — a generic term for an individual part of the standing rigging, such as forestay, backstay, cap shroud, diagonal or sidestay.

staysail — (pronounced "staysul.") A sail designed to be set under (i.e., to weather of) a genoa or spinnaker and tacked either at mid-bow or at the weather rail, depending on sailing angle. A staysail is hoisted on a jib halyard, spinnaker halyard, or topping lift, either on an inner-stay or loose-luffed. Its sheet is run through a snatch block on the leeward rail or through the leeward jib lead car. See also: daisy sail and windseeker.

steering groove — describes how sensitive boat performance is to movement of the helm. The amount you are able to steer to either side of a boat's current optimal sailing angle without negatively affecting velocity made good (VMG). Depending on the conditions and sail shape, the groove upwind can be as narrow as one or two degrees, or as wide as five degrees. Downwind, the groove can be as wide as 25 degrees. Flatter headsails and spinnakers create a narrower steering groove. Draft more forward creates a wider, more forgiving steering groove. A headsail with a rounder entry from more headstay sag makes the steering groove wider, but at the expense of pointing ability. The steering groove is wider, and a boat has more "feel," when heeled over. Also called the envelope, groove, or steering envelope.

stem — the forward-most point on a boat's hull. This traditional nautical term is not often used by itself, though it is used as the root of other terms.

stemhead — the forward-most point on the deck, directly above the stem.

stemhead fitting — a heavy-duty bracket that is at the bow or stem and that is used as a forestay, headstay, and anchor roller attachment point. Also, the location of a tack ring or tack shackles for headsails.

stern — the back end of the boat. The after-most laterally oriented vertical surface.

stern ballast — slang for a helmsman. Transom ballast is another term used.

stern fitting — a heavy-duty bracket at the stern; is used as a backstay attachment point.

stern line — a dock or mooring line that runs from a stern to a dock, float, pier, or pile.

stern pulpit — the stainless steel tubing that forms a safety rail around a boat's stern, including vertical supports and usually double horizontal rails. On a boat that uses lifelines, the lifelines usually connect to each forward end of the stern pulpit as part of a continuous safety perimeter. Also called the stern rail or taffrail. In Britain, the safety rail around the stern is referred to as a pushpit, as it is opposite the pulpit.

stick — slang for a mast.

sticky back — slang for adhesive-backed tape used to repair sails. Nylon repair tape is for spinnakers and drifters. Dacron and Kevlar/Mylar repair tape is for temporary repairs on a main, jib, or genoa, but sewing the patch in place can make the repair permanent.

stinkpot — a disparaging term for a powerboat.

STIX — an acronym for IRC's "STability IndeX." A number that represents the seaworthiness of a particular boat, including her ability to remain upright or to return to her normal upright position after being knocked down. Some races require that a boat meet a minimum qualifying STIX value to enter. See also: angle of vanishing stability and inclining.

stopper bank — clutch cleats grouped together on each side of a coachroof. Also occasionally called a keyboard or piano.

stopper knot — a knot that is in a line's end and that prevents it from running through a grommet or block; e.g., a figure 8 knot.

stops — rubber bands or yarn used to bind a spinnaker's cloth in such a way that enables fully hoisting it and pre-feeding its tack to the pole end in strong winds without the spinnaker filling prematurely. See also: spinnaker bands / spinnaker stops.

storm jib — a small, strongly built sail used as a headsail in storm conditions. Often made from orange-colored material or with orange highlights. A storm jib can be hanked onto a headstay, its luff can be inserted into a headstay's luff groove, or it can be hanked onto an inner stay. If a storm jib is constructed with boltrope and the sail also has luff grommets, the grommets are used to lash the luff to the forestay as a backup, in case the luff groove fails. If a storm jib lacks grommets, they can be added. The preferred location for a storm jib is on an inner stay, if available. A halyard run to a mid-bow padeye can also be used as a temporary inner stay. Using a mid-bow location moves the center of effort farther aft and keeps crew off the bow. A storm jib also has a high clew to keep the sail clear of waves that wash over the deck. British and Commonwealth sailors use the term spitfire.

storm surge — a great dome of water, often 50 miles wide, that comes sweeping across a coastline near where the eye of a hurricane will make landfall. This abnormal rise of the sea is primarily due to the storm's wind.

storm trysail — a small, strongly built sail used in place of a mainsail in storm conditions. Often made from orange-colored material or with orange highlights. The sail is either rigged to the boom and mainsheet, or is free flown. With either setup, the head is hoisted on the mail halyard, and the trysail's tack is attached to the tack ring at the gooseneck (or, if it has a long tack pennant, to a point at the mast base). If the trysail is rigged to the boom, the mainsail is removed from the boom and stored below. Both the outhaul and a reef line are connected to the clew, along with a Velcro clew safety strap, and the mainsheet is used to position the trysail. If the trysail is free flown, the boom's aft end is lowered to the deck and secured, and sheets are run from each quarter to the trysail's clew, typically from the spinnaker sheet turning blocks.

stow — to store properly.

strapped in — a reference to a spinnaker that is so over-trimmed that it is stretched tight around a headstay or along the side of a boat.

strategic advantage — a course, position, or maneuver that is beneficial to one or more competitors due to its more advantageous wind or current, or due to the absence of interference.

strategy – the course you would sail around a racecourse absent other boats to complete the course as fast as possible. Strategy is facts: wind speed, current, etc. Tactics is the practical application of those facts.

stratocumulus — layers or patches of low clouds that consist of rounded masses or rolls with blue sky in between. Stratocumulus can form from cumulus clouds that form into layers and often appear as regularly arranged elements that may be mosaic-like, rounded, or roll-shaped, with relatively flat tops and bases. Stratocumuli are light or dark gray, depending on the size of the water droplets and the amount of sunlight that passes through. Precipitation is rarely associated with these clouds. Stratocumulus can usually be seen after a rainstorm, and their disappearance signals that fair weather is probably approaching.

stratus — low clouds composed of water droplets. Stratus clouds form a low layer that usually covers the entire sky like a blanket and brings gray and dull weather. Stratus clouds occur when a layer of air cooled to below its dew-point temperature condenses into liquid droplets. Light mist and drizzle can sometimes accompany stratus clouds. Although stratus clouds can produce drizzle or snow, they rarely produce heavy precipitation. Clouds that produce heavy precipitation may exist above a stratus layer. Stratus clouds are perhaps the most common of all low clouds. Stratus is the Latin word for layer or blanket and conveys that the cloud is flat and stable.

stream — 1) Shorthand for the Gulf Stream. 2) British and Commonwealth sailors use the word stream to refer to the horizontal movement of water due to the rise and fall of the tide. See also: current.

streamer — 1) Slang for a telltale, the wool or nylon strips that are fastened near a jib's luff, a mainsail's leech, and sometimes other locations. They indicate attached airflow over the part of the sail where the telltales are located. 2) Slang for a pennant or flag.

stretch & blow — a heavy-air spinnaker douse. The spinnaker pole is eased forward to the headstay, and the spinnaker sheet is trimmed on hard. These actions pull the foot tight and make it impossible for the clews to fall into the water—that's the stretch part. The foredeck grabs the sail's foot from underneath the jib, and then the spinnaker halyard is blown— that's the blow part. The kite's upper half floats out over the water. The trimmer eases the spin sheet as the foot is pulled under the jib and onto the deck or down the forward hatch. This is a specific method of float drop.

strip — a colloquial term for douse—to quickly lower a sail. The opposite of hoist. Also known as a drop or takedown.

stripped line — a double-braid line with some portion of its outer cover removed to save weight. A Class II or core-dependent double-braid derives all of its strength from the inner core; the outer cover provides no strength, only wear protection.

stripper line — a line used to temporarily hold a spinnaker's tack during a peel. See also: changing sheet.

strong breeze — wind velocity between 22 and 27 knots (25 to 31 miles per hour). Force 6 on the Beaufort wind scale. See also: heavy air.

Stugeron — a prescription antiemetic medication used to treat and prevent motion sickness, nausea, and vomiting. Stugeron is a registered trademark of Janssen Pharmaceutica Ltd. and is available only outside the United States. Its generic name is Cinnarizine. See also: Bonine, Dramamine, and Transderm-Scop.

stupid o'clock — the late-night and early-morning hours when most non-sailors are warmly tucked into their beds. Also called small hours.

sucker — any tactic or maneuver that tricks another boat into going the way the attacking boat wants her to go. For example, a boat laying a mark foots off just as an opponent passes astern, which leads the opponent to believe that the attacking boat is not laying the mark. This tactic suckers the opponent into sailing past the layline and overstanding.

sugar scoop stern — the aft end of a boat designed or modified such that the hull extends aft beyond the stern; i.e., the after-most laterally oriented vertical surface. The hull extension increases a boat's waterline length and improves her performance. Also known as a French stern, ice cream scoop or scoop stern. A type of reverse transom. Compare to: canoe stern and transom stern.

suit of sails — refers to either a boat's full complement of sails or the sails currently deployed. A boat can have multiple suits in its wardrobe or sail inventory. See also: sail plan.

sundowner — an alcoholic drink consumed after completing the day's racing, usually on deck while watching the sunset.

sun shot — the use of a sextant to measure the sun's angle relative to the horizon. When a sun shot is taken at noon it is known as a noon shot.

Super Mac — the sporadically held 490-mile race from Chicago's lakefront to Mackinac Island, and then down to Port Huron, Michigan. Jointly sponsored by the Chicago Yacht Club and Bayview Yacht Club. For more information, browse to http://www.chicagoyachtclub.org or http://www.byc.com.

surface analysis — a weather map that depicts surface weather conditions plotted from reported data or computer-generated models. Surface analysis maps generally display isobars, fronts, and high- and low-pressure centers.

surfing — like on a surfboard, using wave power to increase boat speed by accelerating down a wave's leeward face in a controlled way. The surf is initiated when a wave picks up the stern and the boat gets pointed straight down the face of the wave. As the surf begins, the boat is steered across the wave to extend the surfing period. Sometimes, a timely pump of the mainsail can help initiate a surf.

survival suit — an extreme-conditions protection layer designed to prolong survival even if the wearer remains immersed in cold water. Made with a waterproof outer shell, watertight zippers and seams, watertight hood, face seal for wind and water protection, detachable mitts, neoprene wrist seals, and attached boots; optionally lined with closed-cell foam for insulation and buoyancy. Some survival suits are inflatable, or have inflatable components. An insulating layer must also be worn for warmth. Also known as an abandonment suit or immersion suit.

swag — the T-shirts, hats, bottle insulators, and myriad other logo/branded and promotional items given away at regattas and other gatherings. Insincere application of a term used in the 1600s for booty or loot—illegally acquired goods. But, really, who would steal this stuff? Australians and New Zealanders also use this term for the contents of their gear bag. Some believe that swag is an acronym for "stuff we all get."

swage — to squeeze a terminal fitting onto a wire under very high pressure, in order to connect the two.

sweating — as it relates to halyards, standing at a mast and quickly pulling a bight of halyard outwards from the mast, as another crew member winches it in—tails it; hoisting a sail. See also: jump.

sweeper — a crew member whose core responsibility is to help as needed. A sweeper may be asked, for example, to help repack spinnakers and to organize and stow sails. Also known as a caddy, floater, mid-bow, runner, sewer, sewer rat, and squirrel.

swell — wind-generated waves produced some distance away, perhaps hundreds or thousands of miles away, or at an earlier time. Swell are waves that have lasted longer or have traveled farther than the winds that produced them. As these waves approach areas of weaker winds, their crest-heights diminish and their wave periods elongate.

Swiftsure – the Swiftsure International Yacht Race comprises six different races over four separate courses, all starting and ending near Victoria Harbour, British Columbia. The longest race and the event's namesake is the Swiftsure Lightship Classic, a 139-nautical-mile loop around Swiftsure bank. For more information, browse to http://www.swiftsure.org.

swing keel — a keel that can be angled to counteract heeling forces. See also: canting keel.

Sydney-to-Hobart — the annual race run every December 26 since 1945. Goes from Sydney Harbor, across the Tasman Sea into Storm Bay, and then up the Derwent River to Hobart. Sometimes referred to by Australians as the Blue Water Classic. For more information, browse to http://rolexsydneyhobart.com.

symmetrical spinnaker — a loose-luffed sail that is vertically symmetrical and that is flown forward of the headstay. Its leading edge can be moved to correspond to the wind. Referred to by the slang terms chute, kite, round head, and spi. Compare to: asymmetrical spinnaker.

synoptic chart — any map or chart that depicts meteorological or atmospheric conditions over a large area at any given time.

synoptic scale — 1) The size of migratory high- and low-pressure systems that are in the lower troposphere and that cover a horizontal area of several hundred miles or more. 2) On a time scale, a weather event that lasts for several days or weeks.

T

---

tabernacle — an on-deck structure that supports the butt, heel, or foot of a mast that does not pass through the deck to the keel. Comprised of two cheeks or sides that support a bolt or pin that is run through the mast base. The bolt acts as a pivot point for raising or lowering the mast. See also: mast step.

tack — 1) On a triangular sail, the bottom forward corner where the luff meets the foot. This is the corner that gets connected to a bow horn, guy, tack shackle, tack ring, or tack line. 2) A boat's course as determined by which side is to windward. If the wind is coming from starboard, the boat is on starboard tack. If the wind is coming from port, the boat is on port tack. When sailing "by the lee"—sailing with the wind coming from behind, and on the same side the mainsail is on—a boat's windward side (and, therefore, the tack she is on) is the side opposite to that on which her mainsail is carried. Unless a boat is head-to-wind, she is always on either port tack or starboard tack. 3) To change tacks by turning a boat so that her bow passes through the eye of the wind, which brings the wind that was once over one side now over the opposite side. The mainsail and headsail (if hoisted) are also brought to the opposite side. A boat is considered on the new tack once she passes head-to-wind. Compare to: jibe.

tacking angle — the angle between port tack and starboard tack courses for a given boat in a given wind. There is typically an inverse relationship between wind speed and tacking angle; tacking angle decreases as wind speed increases. See also: pointing ability.

tacking duel — to repeatedly tack in an attempt to elude a covering boat or to continue to cover an opponent. Usually happens during the last upwind leg between the two lead boats, or between two boats in a battle for overall position in the standings.

tack line — a line connected to and that controls an asymmetrical spinnaker's tack. The line allows for positioning the a-sail's tack to suit wind conditions and for adjusting the spinnaker's luff tension. A tack line is led from an a-sail's tack to a sheave at a bowsprit's end or through a spinnaker pole's jaw, and then back to the cockpit. On boats that use a pole for both a-sail and sym kites, a downhaul may serve double duty as a tackline. Also called a snout line or tack downhaul line.

tack ring — 1) A heavy metal ring that is sewn into a mainsail's tack and that is captured by a mainsail's tack fitting or pin at the gooseneck; or the ring that is sewn into a headsail's tack and that is captured by a shackle or tack fitting on a bow horn. The ring sewn into a sail's tack is also referred to as a sail ring, tack cringle, or tack grommet. 2) The semi-circular bracket that is located at the stemhead and that contains shackles used to capture a headsail's tack or that the shackle on a headsail's tack fastens to. The bracket at the stem is also referred to as a bow horn or stemhead bracket.

tack shackle — a snap shackle that is located on the semi-circular bracket at a stemhead and that is used to fasten a headsail's tack, or the snap shackle that is on a headsail's tack and that is used to fasten it to a stemhead bracket or tack ring.

Tacktick — a brand name of wireless racing instrumentation systems. For more information, browse to http://www.tacktick.com.

tactical rounding — rounding a mark in manner that puts a boat in the most favorable position after the rounding. For example, a mark rounding where a boat stays a couple of boat lengths wide on approach to the mark and cuts close to the mark as she finishes the turn and continues onto the next leg. Done to maintain boat speed and to avoid making a sharp turn. Compare to: seamanlike rounding.

tactical/routing software — software that combines boat-performance characteristics from polar diagrams, wind and current forecast data files from GRIB files, and electronic navigational charts (ENCs) to predict the quickest route between points. Several brands—such as Deckman (from B&G), Expedition (from Expedition Performance Systems Ltd), VNS MAX Pro (from Nobeltec), MaxSea (from MaxSea International), RayTechRNS (from Ray Marine), and SailFast (from SailFast LLC)—are available.

tactician — the crew person whose core responsibilities include positioning the boat on the course where she will gain the most benefit from the effects of wind, tide, sea conditions, and competitors' positions. The tactician is the boat's eyes and ears. Part of the afterguard.

tactics – course you sail around a racecourse to beat other boats. Strategy is facts: wind speed, current, etc. Tactics is the practical application of those facts.

tag line — a light line used to haul a heavier line, or a line used during a spinnaker peel. See also: changing sheet and messenger.

tail — 1) To pull the slack out of a line or to apply tension to a line exiting a winch, to keep it from releasing until it can be cleated. 2) A line's end. 3) A line attached to the end of a wire to make it easier to use. 4) To gather the unused end of a line neatly so that it does not become tangled.

tailer — a crew member who tails a line while another crew member grinds the winch that the line is wrapped around.

takedown — a colloquial term for douse—to quickly lower a sail. The opposite of hoist. Also known as a drop or strip.

taking a stern — to pass behind a competitor on the opposite tack or jibe. Also known as dipping or ducking. Compare to: crossing.

tang — a bracket or fitting that is on a spar and that is used as an attachment point for rigging. See also: hounds.

target boat speed — how fast a given boat should be going for a particular wind strength (i.e., velocity) and angle—the boat's theoretical potential. You compare actual performance achieved versus potential performance to evaluate your trim settings, sail selections, and tactical decisions. See also: polar diagrams, tactical/routing software, and velocity prediction program.

t-bone — when one boat rams another amidships at a right angle. The worst kind of collision.

TCC — an initialism for "time correction coefficient." For a particular boat, the handicap calculated under the IRC rating rule. A boat's TCC is applied to her elapsed time to obtain her corrected time.

team racing — a series of contests between team of competitors. A team is made up of two, three, or four boats. Each boat works in concert with her teammates to triumph over competing teams. Equally matched or one-design boats are used and compete boat-for-boat without any time-allowance handicaps. Races are scored using a Low Point System; i.e., 1 point for first, 2 for second, etc. The team with the lowest cumulative point total at the end of the race or series of races wins. Team racing is conducted under a modified set of racing rules as listed under *Racing Rules of Sailing* Appendix D. See also: Digital N course, knockout, ladder, and round robin.

tee up — slang for preparing a sail for hoisting by connecting its sheets, halyard, or other control lines, as in "tee up the chicken chute!" See also: plug it in.

telltales — the wool or nylon strips that are sewn or fastened on or near a headsail's luff, a mainsail's leech, and sometimes other locations. They indicate attached airflow over the part of the sail where the telltales are located. Also called flickers, streamers, ticklers, ticks, woolies, or yarns. Many words are used to describe the way a telltale is flying—or not flying. A telltale is said to be breaking when its loose end is lifting, twirling, or fluttering. A telltale is said to be stalled when it hangs limp, or, on a mainsail, when it curls around to leeward. When both the leeward and windward telltales in a set are constantly streaming aft, lift and drag are both at their highest point. If you steer just a little higher—so the windward telltale flips about every two to three seconds—the sail will be at its best combination of lift to drag. Here are two trimming tips: move the sail to the breaking telltale—if the windward telltale is breaking, trim in the sail; and sail away from the breaking telltale—if the windward telltale is breaking, bear away slightly.

Jib Telltales

Full Speed
Outside   Both telltales streaming back.

Point
Slightly higher than full speed course. The inside telltales will rise and the outside telltales stream back. At the first sign of speed loss, fall off to full speed mode.
Outside

Pinch / Feather
Higher than point mode. The outside telltales stream while the inside telltales lift & twirl. If you lose speed you are pinching, if not, you are feathering.
Outside

Acceleration
Slightly lower than full speed course. The outside telltales will dance and the windward telltales stream straight back.
Outside

Stall
No airflow over stalled side of sail
Outside

Telltale Indications

temperate zone — the latitude belt roughly between 35 and 65 degrees north or south. Also referred to as the middle latitudes or temperate region. The English Channel and most of the Mediterranean Sea fall within the temperate zone.

tether — a short line that connects a safety harness to a padeye or jackline.

thermal — a rising parcel of air that is less dense and warmer than the surrounding air. Is generally produced when the Earth's surface is heated or when cold air moves over a relatively warmer surface, such as warm water. See also: offshore breeze and onshore breeze.

the room — shorthand for the protest hearing room.

3rd sail — an auxiliary engine.

Thrash to the Onion Patch — a colloquial term for the Newport-Bermuda race.

three-hull-length zone — an area around a mark within a distance of three hull lengths of the boat nearer to it. When the zone is applied at a mark, certain rules apply to allow inside boats to round the mark safely. The three-hull-length zone is only affective for fleet racing. *RRS-2009* changed the definition of the zone at a mark. See also: two-boat-length circle.

through hull — a permanent (and intended) opening that is installed in a hull and that has a fitting attached to a seacock and hose, a transducer, or another device. Through hulls are used to expel wastewater, such as from a sink; to let seawater in, such as for engine cooling; and to allow for the placement of sensors, such as a depth gauge. A seacock is attached directly to the through hull before any hoses are attached, so that water flow can be easily shut off if the hose fails. Soft wood plugs should be available to force into a through hull in case the through hull fails. Transducers should be equipped with caps to place over the hole should the transducer itself need to be removed. Also known as skin fittings. See also: sacrificial anode.

throw-out — if a certain number of races have been completed in a series, a competitor is allowed to exclude the worst one or more individual race scores from the scores used to calculate that competitor's overall score. Individual scores subject to a DNE (i.e., disqualification not excludable) or DGM (i.e., disqualification for gross misconduct and not excludable) must be included in the overall score. The applicable *Sailing Instructions* state whether any scores are thrown out, and if so how many. Also known as a discard.

thwart — a seat or structural member that runs laterally across a cockpit. Often the helm seat aft of the pedestal.

tick – 1) Approximately one degree of compass heading. Typically used as a directive to the helmsman to, for example, "come up a few ticks." 2) Slang for a telltale.

tide — the rising of the ocean surface caused by gravitational forces of the Moon and Sun. Set is the reference for the compass direction towards which the water flows. Drift is the reference for the speed at which the water flows. British and Commonwealth sailors refer to the horizontal movement of water due to the rise and fall of the tide as the stream.

tight cover — a tactical maneuver where a windward boat impedes a leeward boat's wind by keeping the leeward boat in the covering boat's wind shadow. This is done to slow down the leeward boat or to force her to change course, but the covered boat can time her tacks to stay in phase with wind shifts and diminish any lead the covering boat has. Also referred to as close cover or hard cover.

tight reaching — a point of sail where a boat is sailing towards the wind but lower (i.e., farther from the wind) than close-hauled. If a boat is sailing towards the 12:00 position, the wind is coming from between either 1:30 and 2:45 or 9:15 and 10:30. A boat on a tight reach would have her jib eased slightly and her boom up to a quarter of the way leeward of the boat's centerline. Also known as close reaching, fine reaching, or shy reaching. See also: barber hauler, power reaching, and reaching sheet.

tilt gauge — an instrument used to determine a boat's heel angle or fore and aft pitch angle. Also called a clinometer or inclinometer. Lev-o-gage from Sun Company is a popular brand.

timed run — a starting maneuver where a boat heads away from her intended starting point on a broad reach for a pre-determined time, tacks, and then sails close-hauled, arriving at the start line at full speed just as the starting gun is fired. Also known as a Vanderbilt start.

time-on-distance correction — a scoring method that adjusts each competitor's finish time based on their handicap rating and the total race distance. The handicap used is the number of seconds per nautical mile of rhumb line racecourse distance above or below the benchmark—usually the first boat to finish. Boats with a low handicap number owe time to any competitor with a higher handicap. Boats with a high handicap are owed time by any competitor with a lower handicap. See also: IRC, ORR, and PHRF.

time-on-time correction — a scoring method that adjusts each competitor's finish time based on their handicap rating and the total time of the race. The handicap used is the ratio of the potential average speed of each boat to an arbitrary standard boat, and is generally expressed as a multiplier. Boats with a low handicap number owe time to any competitor with a higher handicap. Boats with a high handicap are owed time by any competitor with a lower handicap. See also: IRC, ORR, and PHRF.

TLE — an initialism for "time limit expired." This scoring abbreviation is used to indicate that a boat failed to complete a race within the time allotted. The boat has the maximum points allowed assessed against her when the race is scored using a Low Point System. The maximum allowed points may be equal to the total number of registered entrants, or it could be the number of entrants plus one or more points. The maximum points allowed may be different for an individual race than for a race that is part of a series longer than a regatta. See *RRS-2009* Appendix A. The applicable *Notice of Race* or *Sailing Instructions* may also modify the number of points assessed.

toe rail — a raised edge around a deck's outer perimeter. On old wooden ships, these would be part of the gunwales—pronounced "gunnels" to rhyme with "tunnels."

top mark — a mark at the end of a racecourse's upwind leg. Synonymous with weather mark and windward mark.

top-mast backstay — the lines that are led from a masthead to each quarter, that support a mast, and that counteract headstay forces. Whenever you are tacking or jibing and if you want to maintain mast support, the new weather backstay has to be tensioned before the new leeward backstay is released. With some designs, a backstay can be disconnected from a quarter and re-connected to a hydraulic ram in the stern's center so that it operates more like a traditional permanent backstay. Referred to by many names, including masthead runners, preventer backstays, and split rope backstays. Compare to: running backstay.

topper — slang for a topping lift when it is attached to a spinnaker pole.

topping lift — a control line used to hold up a spar or boom's outboard end, such as on a spinnaker pole. A topping lift is adjusted in unison with the afterguy, downhaul, and spinnaker sheet to form the spinnaker into the most efficient shape and to position the spinnaker at the most effective angle to the wind. Also known by its slang term: topper. Occasionally referred to as an uphaul. Most race boats with a solid boom vang do not need a topping lift to hold up their boom, so the only topping lift is the one connected to the spinnaker pole. A topping lift is part of the running rigging.

topsides — the sides of the hull above the waterline and below the deck. On old wooden ships, these are called the gunwales—pronounced "gunnels" to rhyme with "tunnels." See also: freeboard.

torch — slang for flashlight; used by sailors from Britain and the Commonwealth.

touch and go — 1) When a boat's keel lightly rubs the ground, without damage and without the boat getting stuck. 2) To finish a race and immediately continue on to another location without docking at race headquarters or joining in post-race activities.

towering cumulus — another name for cumulus congestus, a rapidly growing cumulus or an individual dome-shaped cloud whose height exceeds its width. Its distinctive cauliflower top often means showers below, but lacking a cumulonimbus's characteristic anvil, it is not a thunderstorm cloud.

TPYC — Transpacific Yacht Club. The organizing authority for the biennial 2,225-nautical-mile race from Los Angeles to Honolulu and the sporadically held 3,500-nautical-mile race from Los Angeles to Tahiti. For more information, browse to http://www.transpacificyc.org.

tractor — jargon for pulling an overlapping genoa's clew around the mast and past the shrouds, and then holding it down (to keep the clew inside the lifelines), while a jib trimmer or grinder tails the jib sheet. Tractor also describes grabbing an asymmetrical spinnaker's clew at the headstay during a jibe and running it aft. The mast crew is often who tractors the clew. Also known as diving the clew.

Transderm-Scop — an antiemetic medication used to treat and prevent motion sickness, nausea, and vomiting. Transderm-Scop is a registered trademark of Novartis Consumer Health and is administered as a patch applied to the skin. Its generic name is scopolamine topical. Transderm-Scop is available by prescription in the United States or over the counter in Canada and Bermuda. See also: Bonine and Dramamine.

Trans-Erie — an annual 140-mile race on Lake Erie between Grosse Ile, Michigan, and Erie, Pennsylvania. The race direction switches from year to year. For more information, browse to http://www.erieyachtclub.org.

transit — to align two or more objects, such as a mark and an object on shore, and observe whether the relationship between the objects remains constant. A transit is used to judge your position. Also called establishing a range, a line sight or ranging.

transom — a stern's aft face. Modern race boats are designed with an open or scoop transom, which allows any water taken in over the stern or sides to drain away.

transom ballast — slang for a helmsman. Stern ballast is another term used.

transom stern — a flat surface that is either oriented vertically or raked aft (i.e., an outward rake) across the aft end of a boat. Compare to reverse transom and sugar scoop stern.

Transpac — the 2,225-nautical-mile transpacific yacht race from Los Angeles to Honolulu. Held in odd-numbered years since 1939 and sporadically prior to then. Conducted as a pursuit race. Promoted as the oldest and longest-enduring ocean race in the world. As one of the longest Corinthian yacht races, the Transpac tests a crew's mental and physical endurance as much as it tests their racing ability. For more information, browse to http://www.transpacrace.com. See also: North Pacific High and slot cars.

Trans-Superior — a biennial 338-mile race from Sault Ste. Marie, Ontario to Duluth, Minnesota, across Lake Superior. For more information, browse to http://www.transsuperior.com.

trap — to position a line in such a way that it prevents another line or object from moving in its intended fashion. Examples are running a jib sheet over the top of an afterguy during rigging, which prevents the afterguy from flying freely when the spinnaker is raised; and running a spinnaker halyard around a jib sheet when clipping the halyard to the mast base, which traps the jib sheet and prevents its jib from tacking.

traveler — a device used to adjust a mainsail's sheeting angle. Consists of a block attached to a car that slides on a track oriented perpendicular to the boat's centerline; i.e., athwartships. The mainsheet is led through the block and to its attachment point on the boom. The car may be adjusted from side-to-side so that the sheeting angle to the mainsail can be changed to suit conditions. Old Salts may refer to this as a horse.

trick — time spent on duty at the helm.

trigger cleat — a pair of lockable spring-loaded cams that come together to clamp their teeth on a line rove between them. A trigger mechanism releases the lock.

trigger-release snap shackle — a metal U-shaped connector that attaches to other fittings by means of a closeable latch. Operating a trigger mechanism with your finger or a fid opens the latch. Used on the end of a sheet, guy, or halyard that is frequently removed. Various companies, including Gibb, Tylaska, and Wichard, make trigger-release snap shackles. See also: plug fid.

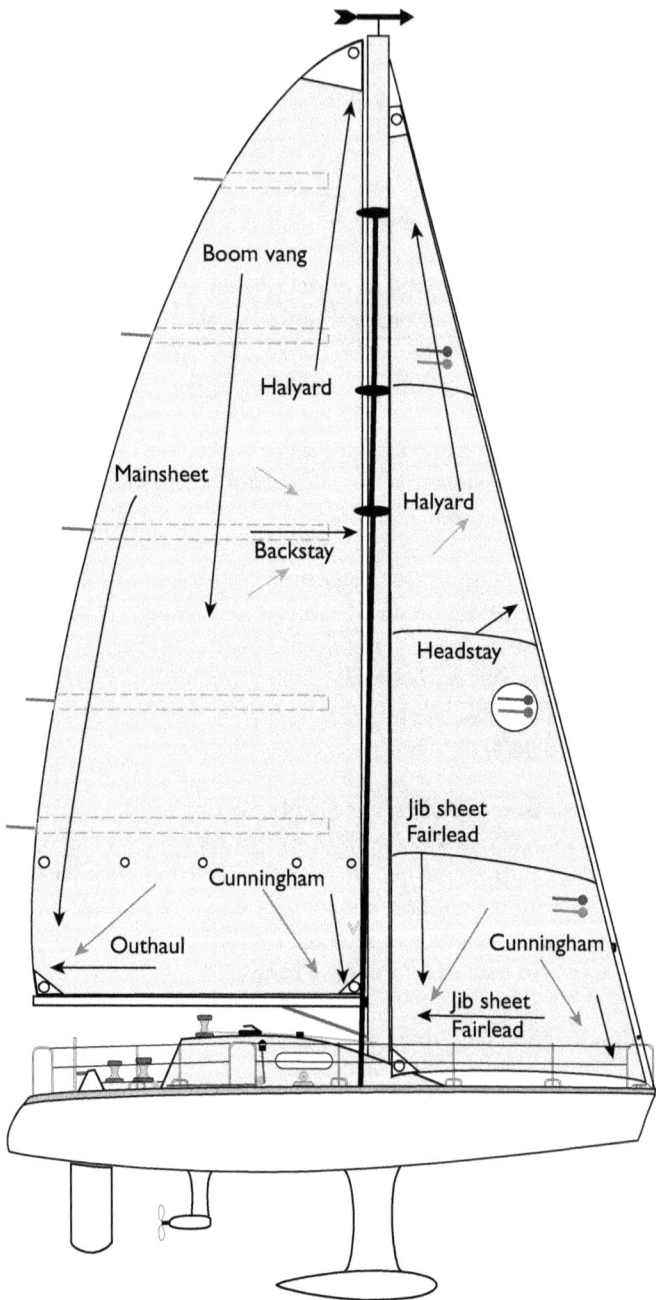

Boom vang

Halyard

Mainsheet

Halyard

Backstay

Headstay

Cunningham

Jib sheet
Fairlead

Outhaul

Cunningham

Jib sheet
Fairlead

Trim Forces

trim — to adjust a sail's shape and angle to the wind for optimum performance. Or to adjust another control line for optimum performance. To pull in on a sheet—the opposite of ease. To sheet a sail home is to trim it until the sail is set properly.

trimmer — a crew member whose core responsibilities include controlling a sail's shape and position. Examples are the jib or headsail trimmer, mainsail trimmer, and spinnaker trimmer. See also: tweaker.

trip! / trip it! — a command to pull on a spinnaker pole's trip line, to open its jaw, and to free it from the working guy, so the spinnaker can be jibed and its pole reset on the opposite side.

trip line — 1) A line used to remotely open the jaw on a spinnaker pole's outboard end, such as during a jibe. 2) The line attached to an anchor's crown to help free it from the bottom, or the line that is attached to a sea anchor and used to collapse it for retrieval. Anchor trip lines are also called retrieval lines.

trough — 1) The lowest point in the depression between two waves. Compare to: crest. 2) An elongated region of relatively low atmospheric pressure; often associated with a front.

true wind angle (TWA) — the wind angle relative to a boat's centerline, if the boat were motionless in the water. The angle between the true wind direction and a boat's heading.

true wind direction (TWD) — the compass direction from which the wind blows over a boat that is motionless in the water.

true wind speed (TWS) — the speed of the wind that blows across a boat that is motionless in the water.

TSA — Texas Sailing Association. For more information, browse to http://www.txsail.org.

TTSA — Trinidad & Tobago Sailing Association. For more information, browse to http://www.ttsailing.org.

Tuff Luff — Schaefer Marine's brand name for its dual-groove head foil. A device that is fitted over the headstay or forestay and that contains one or more luff grooves to accommodate and provide continuous support for headsails that use boltrope. The device is usually made from aerodynamically shaped extruded aluminum or plastic. A headsail is secured at the luff by sliding its luff tape/boltrope through a pre-feeder and then into the head foil's feeder and up its luff groove. A dual-groove head foil allows for hoisting a second headsail in the second groove before dousing the first, so a boat can avoid running bare headed and losing performance. Harken's brand is called Carbo Racing Foil. Also known as forestay track.

tune the rig — the process of adjusting mast pre-bend and mast rake in order to best accommodate the expected wind and wave conditions—to extract the best performance from a boat. Mast pre-bend is adjusted by altering the tension on the wire rope or solid rod used as standing rigging, or by adjusting a mast jack. Mast rake is adjusted by altering mast heel position. Class rules may prohibit altering a rig's tuning during a race. See also: partners.

turbo'd / turbo-ing — collective terms for improving an older boat's performance through hull, keel, and rig modifications, such as adding a taller mast, using carbon fiber components, or adding a plumb bow.

turbosled — an ultra-light displacement boat (ULDB) modified with such upgrades as a taller, carbon mast and larger sails. See also: sled.

turnbuckle — a threaded, adjustable fitting that is used for shrouds, stays, lifelines, and sometimes other rigging. It is used to maintain correct tension. Also called a bottle screw or rigging screw. See also: anti-seize and mast jack.

turning mark — a buoy that denotes a leg's end, and that the applicable *Sailing Instructions* require a boat to leave on a specified side as she passes onto the next leg. Also known as a rounding mark. See also: mark. Compare to: scoring gate.

turn turtle — slang for a capsized boat that is completely inverted in the water and helpless to right herself. Named for the appearance of the upside-down hull in water.

turtle — a spinnaker or headsail storage bag that allows the appropriate running rigging to be quickly and easily connected without having to open the bag. This allows the sail to be ready for rapid deployment without being exposed to wind and weather. This also allows for the sail to quickly be disconnected and removed from the deck, if a last-minute sail change is called for. Just before the sail is hoisted, the Velcro, zipper, or drawstring that holds the bag closed is opened, and the sail is hoisted without fouling or wrapping. The nicer style of spinnaker turtle is a cube that has Velcro straps to secure the clews at opposite ends of the side that opens, with the head secured between the two clews. The other style is a stuff sack with one end held closed by a drawstring. Also called a sausage, sausage bag, or spinnaker pouch. See also: flake, pack, run the tapes, and z-fold.

tweaker — 1) Another name for a twinger, the device used to adjust a spinnaker's sheeting angle. 2) A term of endearment for a trimmer who constantly adjusts a sail to the point of obsession. 3) A backup chute trimmer who stands by at the lazy spinnaker guy, behind the guy block, and who uses it to trim the chute if the chute gets away from the primary trimmer and collapses. The sheeting angle from the lazy guy chokes the chute down and gets it to fill more easily compared to how much the primary trimmer would have to trim.

twilight racing — the semi-organized, informal type of boat racing that is typically held in the evening after work. Also known as beer can racing.

twinger — a snatch block placed on a spinnaker sheet between a spinnaker clew and an aft sheet block. The snatch block is a flying block that is manually adjusted by means of a control line led through a turning block or D ring at the rail. Used in a manner similar to a jib lead car to adjust a spinnaker's sheeting angle. On a small boat that controls a chute with just two sheets, a twinger is trimmed in all the way on the line that is acting as a guy, to maintain a better working angle. Also referred to as a down-puller or, sometimes, a barber hauler.

twisted — describes a sail's shape by the amount the sail's leech curves leeward near its head compared to its clew. If the leech is curved farther to leeward near its head than its clew, the sail is said to be open or twisted. See also: closed, jib lead car, and sheeting angle.

twisted line — rope composed of three or more strands that are twisted tightly—usually clockwise. Used for dock and anchor lines. Is less expensive than braided rope and is easier to splice, but stretches more and is harder on the hand. Also called laid line or laid rope.

two-boat-length circle — old terminology for the area that is around a mark or obstruction and where certain rules are turned on or off. *RRS-2009* changed the definition of the zone at a mark to be a distance of three hull lengths (for fleet races) and removed from the zone's definition any area that surrounds obstructions. See also: three-hull-length zone.

two-pole jibe — running almost dead downwind, setting a second spinnaker pole on the mast and lazy guy, jibing the main, heading up, and then disconnecting the leeward pole.

Two-Turns Penalty — a self-imposed penalty for violating any rule from *RRS-2009* Part 2—When Boats Meet. A competitor performs a Two-Turns Penalty, by promptly making two turns in the same direction, including two tacks and two jibes, in exoneration for the rule violation instead of retiring from a race. Often referred to as "doing turns" or a "720." Failure to do turns may result in a witness lodging a protest and the infringing competitor being disqualified. Ring around the rosie is slang for doing penalty turns. See also: *RRS-2009* rule 44.2.

U / V

ULDB — an initialism for "ultra-light displacement boat." A boat with a hull shape designed to develop positive dynamic pressure, so that its draft decreases with increasing speed. Given enough driving force, a ULDB can achieve higher speeds than a similarly sized conventional displacement hull boat, as it is less limited by waterline length. Typically referred to as a sled.

under-square — as it relates to a spinnaker pole, means that the pole is set at an angle greater than perpendicular to the wind; the outboard end is pointed somewhat away from the wind. Also known as under-trimming the pole.

universal rule — an antiquated rating and measurement rule. See also: ORR and PHRF.

unobtainium — a colloquialism that refers to any extremely rare, costly, or special material needed to create whatever sail, line, or device that would certainly allow a competitor to win all races, if only it could be obtained.

unstable — as it relates to air, describes air that is warmer than the surrounding air and that is rising.

up — towards the direction from which the wind blows. To head up is to turn the bow more towards the wind.

updraft — a small-scale rising air current, usually generated by convection, and that is near or within a developing cumuliform cloud—the first step towards thunderstorm development. Updraft is also generated by turbulence within an air layer. See also: downdraft.

upslope fog — the fog that forms when wind forces warm, moist surface air up a slope. It is adiabatically cooled to below its initial dew point; i.e., the air cools by expansion as it rises and not from a heat exchange with its environment. Upslope fog forms best on a gradual slope, and it can become quite deep and require considerable time to dissipate.

upwind — towards the direction from which the wind blows. The opposite of downwind.

US Sailing — the national governing body for the sport of sailing in the United States. US Sailing is also the national authority for the *Racing Rules of Sailing* in the United States. For more information, browse to http://www.ussailing.org.

UTC — Universal Time, Coordinated. The standard time reference used internationally for navigational information since 1972. UTC was chosen as a compromise between what the United States wanted to call Coordinated Universal Time (CUT) and what the French wanted to call Temps Universel Coordonné (TUC). What is now UTC used to be referred to as Greenwich Mean Time.

valid time — the timeframe during which a forecast or warning is in effect, unless a new forecast issuance updates or supersedes it.

valise — an inflatable life raft packed into a heavy-duty soft container.

Vanderbilt rules – a set of yacht racing rules developed by Harold Stirling Vanderbilt and others during the period of 1930 to 1960 until they were formally adopted by the International Yacht Racing Union (predecessor to the International Sailing Federation or ISAF).

Vanderbilt start — a starting maneuver where a boat heads away from her intended starting point on a broad reach for a pre-determined time, tacks, sails close-hauled, and then arrives at the start line at full speed just as the starting gun is fired. Named for Harold Stirling Vanderbilt, a three-time defender of the America's Cup. Also known as a timed run.

vang sheeting — a mainsail trimming technique that uses the boom vang to control leech tension and the mainsheet to control angle of attack.

v-berth — a boat's forward berth. Is located in the bow and is shaped like the letter V lying on its back.

VC-17 — Interlux's brand of anti-fouling paint that is applied to a boat's underwater surfaces to repel undesirable marine growth.

veer — wind is said to veer when it shifts in a clockwise direction, as from north to northeast—the true wind compass direction numbers increase. Some use clock interchangeably with veer. Wind is said to back when it shifts counterclockwise. See also: righty.

Velcro clew strap — a device used to secure a main or storm trysail's clew to a boom and to allow it to slide fore and aft when adjusted by the outhaul. A Velcro clew strap also keeps the clew from flying free if the outhaul is released or fails. Also known as a clew safety strap.

velocity header — a sudden drop in wind speed (i.e., a lull) mistaken for a change in true wind direction more forward on a boat's sail plan; i.e., a header. It is the change in vector between boat speed and true wind speed, not a change in true wind direction, that moves the apparent wind forward. A fast bear away also creates a velocity header.

velocity lift — a sudden increase in wind speed (i.e., a puff) mistaken for a change in true wind direction more aft on a boat's sail plan; i.e., a lift. It is the change in vector between boat speed and true wind speed, not a change in true wind direction, that moves the apparent wind aft.

velocity prediction program — a complex computer program that estimates a specific boat's performance over a range of wind speeds and sailing angles. The results are normally presented in a series of polar graphs, which plot target performance data. The VPP results also list theoretical boat speed and heeling angle, for every true wind speed and true wind angle combination, along with the associated upwind and downwind VMGs (velocity made good against the wind direction).

ventilating the rudder — to rapidly turn a helm from one side to the other and return it to its starting position. This movement is done to rid the rudder of a bubble that has formed on one or both of its vertical control surfaces, and that has degraded the rudder's performance. See also: cavitation.

Verve Cup — a three-day offshore regatta conducted by the Chicago Yacht Club. One of the premier yachting events for racing sailors in Chicago and from around the Great Lakes. The Verve Cup trophy dates from 1893. For more information, browse to http://www.chicagoyachtclub.org.

Vic-Maui — the Victoria to Maui International Yacht Race, which has run in even-numbered years since 1968. The race starts at Victoria, British Columbia, in mid-summer and finishes near Lahaina, Maui, approximately 2,308 nautical miles away. For more information, browse to http://www.vicmaui.org. See also: North Pacific High.

virga — the precipitation that falls from a cloud but that evaporates in dry air beneath the cloud before it reaches the ground. Virga resembles streaks of water that extend downward from a cloud. Typically, virga falls from altocumulus, altostratus, or high-based cumulonimbus.

VMC — an initialism for "velocity made good (toward a course or mark)." Applicable to offshore race strategy, where a priority is to maximize boat speed to the next mark. Another reference to this same speed is WCV or waypoint closure velocity.

VMG — an initialism for "velocity made good (toward the wind)." The upwind component of boat speed. Considered an information resource more for the trimmers than for the helm because changes in wind angle will immediately affect VMG, but boat speed lags in response to helm changes.

Volvo Open 70 — the current class of racing boats designed to the Volvo Ocean Race Box Rule. Anything is permitted in an open class unless the rules specifically prohibit it. Scored using a High Point System. For each leg, each boat receives points equal to the number of entries at the start of the leg less the number of boats that placed above her on that leg. Each boat can also earn points for passing through any defined scoring gates. The best cumulative score at the race's end determines the winner. See also: box-rule and *Equipment Rules of Sailing 2009-2012* rule C.2.3.

VPIRB — an acronym for "VHF Position-Indicating Radio Beacon." An emergency signal beacon that can be triggered when a rescue is needed; sending GPS coordinates and a distress signal over VHF channels 16 and 70. See also: EPIRB, GPIRB and PLB.

VPP — an initialism for "velocity prediction program." A complex computer program that estimates a specific boat's performance over a range of wind speeds and sailing angles.

W

wake — the waves caused by a boat as it moves through the water.

wally — to sail above target boat speed when lifted, and below target when headed. A tactical method reportedly developed by the 1987 America's Cup team Stars & Stripes. See also: scallop. Compare to: feather.

wardrobe — the sails that are onboard at any one time. The number of sails carried aboard may be limited by class rules, *Sailing Instructions* or rating rules, All the sails aboard a boat are also called its suit of sails.

warm eddie - a whirlpool of water that has broken off from the main body of the Gulf Stream and that is warmer than the surrounding water. Warm eddies circulate in a clockwise direction and can be up to 180 miles (300 km) in diameter. Warm eddies form off a northward bending lobe (meander) and are found north of the Gulf Stream. Also known as a warm core eddie or warm core ring. Compare to cold eddie.

warm front — the leading edge of an advancing synoptic-scale warm-air boundary that is replacing a retreating, relatively colder air mass. Generally, with a warm-front passage, the temperature and humidity increase, and the barometric pressure rises. Although there is a wind shift—usually from the southwest to the northwest in the Northern Hemisphere—it is less pronounced than with a cold-front passage. Precipitation, such as rain, snow, or drizzle, as well as convective showers and thunderstorms are generally found ahead of the surface front. Fog is common in the cold air ahead of the front. Although clearing usually occurs after a warm front passes, some conditions may produce fog in the warm air.

warning flag — a flag hoisted on a committee boat to indicate the beginning of the five-minute start sequence for a particular class or section. The warning flag is taken down simultaneously with the race start. Sometimes, the code flag for the number that corresponds to the starting order of the class is used as the warning flag. At other times, solid-color flags in differing colors are used. Whatever flag is used, it has the same design and color scheme as the class or section's class flag. The applicable *Sailing Instructions* indicate the starting order for multi-class races and may modify the sequence timing.

warp — a long bight of sturdy line streamed behind a boat from strong attachment points on each quarter, such as the mainsheet or primary winches. Its primary purpose is to keep a boat's stern pointed into oncoming waves to resist broaching. Used when running downwind under bare poles in extremely heavy weather. See also: drogue, pooped, and sea room.

washboards — the removable wooden or plastic boards that slide vertically into grooves on either side of a companionway—one above the other—and that prevent water from getting below. Also used to secure a boat when she is unattended.

watch — the group of crew members who operate a boat and perform other duties while the other crew members are resting; i.e., off watch. Also known as a sched. Compare to: trick.

watch captain — the crew member in charge of a watch. Typically someone who has a lot of experience or is familiar with the particular race or passage. Also referred to as the watch leader.

watch system — a method of assigning or scheduling regular work periods when crew members stand watch. An example of a two-watch system is: 6 hours on/6 hours off between 6:00 am and 6:00 pm, and 4 hours on/4 hours off between 6:00 pm and 6:00 am. See also: dog watch.

water ballast — rigid internal water tanks that are strategically placed within a boat and are filled or drained as needed. Used to help control the heeling a boat experiences when under sail, or to adjust fore and aft trim. The windward tank is filled to reduce heel when sailing upwind, and is emptied to reduce weight when sailing downwind. A centerline-mounted tank is filled or emptied to adjust fore-aft trim. See also: stack.

waterworld — a jocular term for the bow because it is always wet.

wave — the rise and fall of the water's surface caused by local winds that blow over the water and by the transfer of wind energy to the water through friction. The transferred energy, not the particular water particles first affected, continues to move horizontally. The water particles move in a circular motion within the wave. Swell refers to wind-generated waves produced some distance away, perhaps hundreds or thousands of miles away, or at an earlier time. Swell are waves that have lasted longer or have traveled farther than the winds that produced them. As these waves approach areas of weaker winds, their crest-heights diminish and their wave periods elongate.

wavelength — the horizontal distance between two wave crests.

wave period — the number of seconds it takes for two consecutive crests to pass a given, fixed point.

weather — towards where the wind comes from. Also known as windward; to weather is to windward.

weather end — a start line's end that is biased to weather. The starboard end of a start line is not necessarily the weather end, especially if the line is set square to the wind, though people refer to it as such. It is more precisely known as the starboard end.

weather helm — a boat's tendency to steer herself to weather when her rudder is in a neutral position. This tendency increases as a sailboat becomes overpowered or as the Center of Effort moves farther aft in relation to the Center of Lateral Resistance—the sail plan becomes out of balance. An example is when you use a #4 jib without reefing the main. The water that passes the lee side of a hull heeled over also tends to push the bow to weather. A slight weather helm is desirable, as it offers increased steering feel and responsiveness. The slight angle applied to the rudder to counteract weather helm generates lift that allows the boat to sail faster and point higher, and provides a safety mechanism: if you let go of the helm, the boat turns into the wind, slows down, and stands upright. A helmsman holds a wheel to leeward or a tiller to windward to counteract weather helm. The opposite of lee helm. See also: king spoke.

weather mark — a mark at the end of a racecourse's upwind leg. Synonymous with top mark or windward mark.

weather rail — the rail on a boat's upwind side. The higher rail, or the high side.

weather sheet — a non-loaded sheet on a boat's upwind side. See also: lazy sheet.

weather shore — the coast that lies in the direction from which the wind is blowing. Compare to: lee shore.

weed stick — a long, flexible rod that has a plastic hook on one end and that is used to clean weeds, lobster pots, or other flotsam from a keel or rudder's leading edge. Optionally, the rod is wrapped with cloth to prevent it from scratching the hull. A crew member secured to the boat pushes the hooked end into the water forward of where he or she thinks the weed or other item is lodged, directs the rod towards the boat's centerline, sweeps the rod aft to dislodge the trash, and then directs the rod back to the surface. To reduce drag, the sweeping is coordinated with the water that flows along the hull. An alternative design adds a short length of knotted line to the stick's working end. Also known as a kelp stick. See also: flossing.

wetted surface — a boat's external surface that is in contact with the water in which she is floating.

wharf — a man-made structure over water, parallel to shore, with piles or pillars for support. Designed to allow for boats to moor alongside. Compare to: dock, marina, and pier.

whip — 1) To bind together the strands at the end of a line. 2) A bent fiberglass arm that is connected to a masthead crane and hooked onto a permanent backstay. Used to lift the backstay out of the way of an over-sized roach on a mainsail during a tack or jibe, when tension on the backstay is eased. May be prohibited under some class or box rules.

whisker pole — a short spar used to hold a headsail's clew outboard when reaching or running. It is attached to the mast and set perpendicular and abeam just above the lifelines. Also called a jib-stick by sailors from Britain and the Commonwealth.

Whitbread douse — a spinnaker takedown used during heavy weather or when you are sailing hot angles with a large asymmetrical kite. The spinnaker is hidden behind the main. The lazy guy on a symmetrical kite or the lazy sheet on an a-sail is run over the boom from the leeward side, under the main's loose foot, and down the companionway. The trimmer trims hard to get the spinnaker's foot closer to the boom. When the douse is called, the pit blows the halyard halfway down and a floater hauls in on the line down the companionway. The trimmer eases the sheet as the kite is pulled in, and when the kite is under control, the pit blows the halyard and the foredeck spikes off the tack shackle with a fid. Also known as a letterbox douse.

whitecaps — the white foamy tops on waves. Are caused by winds in excess of 11 knots (12 miles per hour or force 4 on the Beaufort wind scale). Ancient mariners referred to these as white horses.

white sails — slang for the jib and mainsail, because of their bland or monochromatic color versus brightly colored spinnakers.

whomper — a monstrous masthead spinnaker made famous by the movie, *Wind*. A film starring Jennifer Grey and Matthew Modine about a fictitious America's Cup challenge.

Wichard — a snap hook design that can be opened only by pressing the rear release lever and the gate simultaneously. Mostly used on safety tethers.

wicking layer — a base clothing layer that is worn next to the skin, moves moisture away, and allows it to pass through the fabric and evaporate. Also known as a base layer or as a rash guard (because it provides chafe protection).

winch — a geared drum that provides mechanical advantage for applying tension to a line, sheet, or halyard. The drum is turned with a winch handle, or by a grinding pedestal or electric motor. A ratchet stops the drum from turning back under load. Some winches are equipped with a self-tailer, a clamping device that grips the tail and prevents it from accidentally loosening. Some winches offer varying ratios of mechanical advantage and rotational speed that are selected by reversing winch handle rotation, or by moving a switch or lever. Also referred to as a coffee grinder.

winch feeder — a horizontally oriented sheave, mounted aft of the clutch bank on each side of a coachroof, used to route a line to a winch on the opposite side. Also called a crossover block, halyard turning block, or winch turning block.

winch pedestal — an alternative term for a grinding pedestal with mechanically operated, dual-opposing hand cranks. Either a single crew member or two crew members who work in tandem operate the handles to provide turning power to one or more deck-mounted winch drums. See also: grinding pedestal.

wind bend — wind direction affected by local terrain. The more tactically advantaged course, whether sailing upwind or down, is to sail to the inside of a wind bend.

Windex — the brand name of a wind vane or masthead fly from Davis Instruments. Mounted on the masthead. A Windex shows apparent wind angle by the relationship of the wind vane's head or tail to stationary tabs placed aft of its pivot point and at an approximately 30-degree angle to either side of the boat's centerline.

wind gradient — the effect of moving air that comes into contact with the ground, slowing, changing direction, and creating wind shear. Wind gradient is the reason the wind direction at the masthead and the wind direction on deck appear to be from different directions.

windseeker — 1) A small, light sail used for very light winds or in drifting or zephyr conditions. Used when the little wind energy available is used to move a boat forward, instead of expending it on filling a heavy sail. A windseeker is used to help get a boat moving, to create apparent wind, and to add to the small amount of true wind available. 2) A crew member who watches the water and other boats, looks for signs of wind puffs and lulls, and ascertains whether they are headers or lifts.

wind shadow — an area within which the wind is being blocked or disturbed by a land mass, an obstruction, or—most useful or damaging to racers—sails. A wind shadow's length, shape, and density will depend on several factors, including wind velocity, sea state, sailing angle, shape of a boat's sail plan, and a boat's speed. For example, in heavy air, a boat's wind shadow might extend four mast-heights to leeward. In light air, that same boat might cast a wind shadow for eight or more mast-heights. The wind shadow also extends to windward, though to a lesser degree. This area of disturbed airflow can be used to your advantage to slow down or control opponents that are downwind, or to your detriment by an opponent that is upwind. Sometimes referred to as backwind. See also: blanket, disturbed air and lee bow.

wind shear — refers to the frequent change in wind speed within a short distance. The typically experienced wind shear on a boat is the increase in the wind's velocity at increasing heights, due to the friction of the water. There can be 15-25% more wind at the masthead than at deck level.

windward — a boat's windward side is the side that is, or was (when she is head-to-wind), toward the direction from which the wind blows. However, when you are sailing by the lee or directly downwind, her windward side is the side opposite of where her mainsail lies. When two boats on the same tack overlap, the one on the windward side of the other is the windward boat. The other is the leeward boat. Synonymous with weather. Old Salts will pronounce this "win-erd."

windward boat — a boat that is overlapped with and upwind of another boat. The other boat is the leeward boat and may have rights.

windward douse / windward drop / windward takedown — a spinnaker douse where the sail is brought down on a boat's windward side. The pole gets tripped and put on deck. Optionally, someone pushes the afterguy out abeam (i.e., a human guy) to keep the spinnaker clews as wide apart as possible, to present more surface area to the wind, and to keep the spinnaker drawing as much as possible until it is doused. If the kite is to leeward and needs to be on the windward side so it is in position for the next hoist, consider a Mexican douse, a windward drop after a jibe. Also called a weather strip.

windward-leeward course — a racecourse configuration with a minimum of two marks: one placed directly upwind from the start line's center (the windward mark or weather mark), and the other placed directly downwind from the first (the leeward mark). There may be an offset mark set perpendicular to the windward mark. A gate may be set at the course's leeward end. You must first tack upwind to round the windward mark, and then sail downwind to round the leeward mark. Also known as a windward return course. See also: gate and offset mark.

windward leg — a racecourse leg where you must sail close-hauled and tack to reach the windward or weather mark.

windward mark — a mark at the end of a racecourse's windward leg. Synonymous with weather mark.

Wind

Weather Mark

Rhumb Line

Leeward Mark

Windward-leeward Course

windward sheeting (traveler) — a self-tacking traveler. The windward sheeting traveler car has control cleats built into a special mechanism that automatically opens and closes the cleat opposite the one whose control line is being trimmed.

wing and wing — to sail downwind with a mainsail out to one side and a headsail out to the other. Often, the headsail's clew is held out abeam with a spar, such as a whisker pole. Also known as goosewinged. See also: poor man's twin.

wing block — a block mounted on a swivel at or near a masthead at its outward lateral edge, or optionally from a crane or spinnaker bail. Often used to allow a full range of horizontal rotation for a spinnaker halyard, so it does not jump out of or bind on its sheave.

wing mast — a teardrop-shaped airfoil/spar that rotates to match the optimum angle of attack for the mainsail. Offers improved boat speed and pointing ability over a conventional, fixed mast.

wipe off — to use boats on the opposite tack or obstructions to break free from a covering boat. Compare to: shut the door.

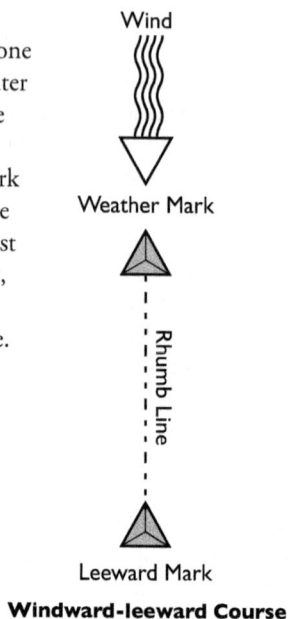

wipeout — slang for broaching. See also: jibe broach, leeward broach, and round down.

woolies — slang used for either woolen undergarments or telltales. Wool is also a term for the string or yarn used to stop or band a spinnaker. See also: insulating layer, spinnaker bands / spinnaker stops.

wooling — to tie a spinnaker's cloth in such a way that enables fully hoisting it and pre-feeding its tack to the pole end in strong winds without the spinnaker filling prematurely. See also: spinnaker bands / spinnaker stops.

working deck — the permanent horizontal structure that forms the cover over a hull, inside of the lifelines and pulpits. The crew remains on it or moves around on it during the normal course of their duties.

working end — the fastened or manipulated end of a line, as opposed to the standing part or bitter end.

working guy / working sheet — a line that actively controls a sail. Examples are a working spinnaker afterguy, which is rigged and connected to a spinnaker's tack and carries a lazy spinnaker sheet; a working spinnaker sheet, which is connected to a spinnaker's clew and carries a lazy spinnaker guy; and a working jib sheet, which is a jib sheet that is on a boat's leeward side, is connected to a jib's clew, and carries a lazy jib sheet. Compare to: lazy guy / lazy sheet.

WORSA — Women's Ocean Racing Sailing Association. For more information, browse to http://www.worsa.org.

wrap up — sailing legend Terry Hutchinson's term for the final approach to a start line, just prior to a starting gun, when the boat is brought up hard on the wind.

X / Y / Z

yacht — an expensive sailboat or motorboat used for cruising or racing, as opposed to a working boat.

yours! — an indication from a tailer or grinder who has temporarily taken control of a sheet or other control line (such as to add wraps to or to take wraps off a winch) that control of the line is being returned to the trimmer. Compare to: mine!

you tack! — a response to a boat sailing close-hauled or above on the same tack that has requested room to tack at an obstruction (under *RRS-2009* rule 20.1). This response acknowledges that the responding boat will give the requesting boat room to tack and will keep clear.

YRALIS — Yacht Racing Association of Long Island Sound. For more information, browse to http://www.yralis.org.

YRASFB — Yacht Racing Association of San Francisco Bay. For more information, browse to http://www.yra.org.

YRAT — Yacht Racing Association of Thailand. For more information, browse to http://www.yrat.or.th.

YRUGL — Yacht Racing Union of the Great Lakes. For more information, browse to http://www.lmsrf.org/yrugl.

YRUSC — Yacht Racing Union of Southern California. For more information, browse to http://www.yrusc.org.

zephyr — any soft, gentle breeze. The name derives from the ancient Greek name for the west wind, Zephyrus, a light and beneficial wind in Greece. On the Tower of the Winds in Athens, a lightly clad youth whose skirt is filled with flowers represents Zephyrus.

Z flag rule — *RRS-2009* 30.2 states, "If flag Z has been displayed, no part of a boat's hull, crew or equipment shall be in the triangle formed by the ends of the start line and the first mark during the last minute before her starting signal. If a boat breaks this rule and is identified, she shall receive, without a hearing, a 20% Scoring Penalty calculated as stated in rule 44.3(c)." The Z flag rule imposes a severe penalty on any boat that crosses the start line before her starting gun.

z-fold — a method for folding an overlapping genoa to fit in a turtle that is shorter than the sail's foot length while also keeping the sail's tack and clew accessible. With the sail flaked over the bag and with the tack within the turtle's tack end, grab the entire flake at the turtle's clew end and fold it forward until the sail's clew is over the turtle. From the side, the flaked sail will look like a Z with a long foot.

ZFP — an initialism for "Z flag penalty." The scoring abbreviation used to indicate that a boat violated *RRS-2009* rule 30.2 and has been assessed a 20% scoring penalty. The adjustment may be different for an individual race than for a race that is part of a series longer than a regatta. See *RRS-2009* Appendix A. The applicable *Notice of Race* or *Sailing Instructions* may also modify the number of points assessed. See also: Z flag rule.

zincs — a less noble metal used to protect structural metals (such as through-hull fittings, propellers, and shafts) from the electrochemical degradation of galvanic corrosion. Though commonly known as zincs, magnesium is often used in freshwater, while zinc is used in saltwater. See also: sacrificial anode.

zone — for fleet racing, the zone is an area around a mark within a distance of three hull lengths of the boat nearest to it. For match racing and team racing, the zone is the area around a mark within a distance of two hull lengths of the boat nearest to it. A boat is considered to be in the zone when any part of her hull is in the zone. Applicable *Sailing Instructions* can modify the definition of the zone under *RRS-2009* rule 86.1(b). With the publication of *RRS-2009*, there is no longer a zone surrounding an obstruction. The zones around a gate may or may not overlap. See also: three-hull-length zone and two-boat-length circle.

Weather

Fronts and Radar		Selected Weather Symbols	
cold front	▲▲	•	Rain
warm front	●●●	• ▽	Rain Shower
stationary front	▲●▲●	↰	Thunderstorm
occluded front	▲●▲	↱	Severe Thunderstorm
trough	— — —	△ ↰	Thunderstorm & Hail
squall line	—✴✴—	✳ ↰	Thunderstorm & Snow
ridge line	⋀⋀⋀⋀	△	Hail or Ice Pellets
frontal change	‖	'	Drizzle
High Pressure System	**H**	✳	Snow
Low Pressure System	**L**	✳ ▽	Snow Shower

Wind Shaft is direction wind is coming from		(•)	Freezing Rain
◎	Calm	(')	Freezing Drizzle
—	1-2 knots (1-2 mph)	)(	Tornado/Funnel Cloud
⌐	3-7 knots (3-8 mph)	⭘	Hurricane
⟍	8-12 knots (9-14 mph)	6	Tropical Storm
⟍	13-17 knots (15-20mph)	☰	Fog
⟍	18-22 knots (21-25 mph)	∞	Haze
⟍	23-27 knots (26-31 mph)	⌐∿	Smoke
▼	48-52 knots (55-60mph)	$	Dust or Sand
▼	73-77 knots (84-89 mph)	↑→	Blowing Snow
▼▼	103-107 knots (119-123 mph)